D0408627

Coyote Nowhere

Also by John Holt

❧

JOHN HOLT

❧

PHOTOGRAPHS BY GINNY DIERS

Coyote Nowhere

In Search of America's

Last Frontier

Thomas Dunne Books

St. Martin's Press New York

For Bob Jones,
who helped make CN happen and who was with us in spirit
all the way down the line . . .

Contents

❧

Acknowledgments

❧

T HANKS GO TO, first of all, our mothers, Jo Welles and Cyrilla Diers. And to Tom Rosenbauer of Orvis for the usual over-the-top assistance, Rick Harrison of Rikshots Photography for in-spired darkroom work, Jim and Jerry Liska, Dr. Erich Pessl (it's hard to write a book when you're dead), Louise Jones for a number of great ideas, Diana Finch of the Ellen Levine Agency for doing the deal and for all her support, and to Pete Wolverton at Thomas Dunne Books for editorial expertise and support. Thanks to three fine musicians—Danny O'Keefe, Amos Garrett, Ian Tyson—not only for their help with the book but for some great road music. And finally, our love and thanks go to Jack and Rachel.

Coyote Nowhere

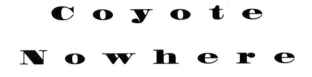

The road rolls east from the Rocky Mountains Front out onto the northern high plains in central Montana.

THE NORTHERN HIGH PLAINS
FROM LIVINGSTON

T HE LAND HOLDS FORTH OUT HERE alone beneath skies filled with so many stars, planets, moons, and fizzling meteors that to look up at all of it is to knock out your head. The brain can't take in all of the information, all the truth that shines away up in the eternal dark. One look at this sky slams the message home. We aren't much of anything in the scheme of things. Eyes roll back into the head and thought processes short-circuit. That's what the northern high plains are. What they do to a person. Look above or let the eye wander along the incomprehensible vastness of this wide-open country, and you drift swiftly away into a world of history, myth, and legend. Forget about the one-dimensional world of television and other objects electric. None of that applies in the untamed emptiness of this country. If you want to feel what flows out here, hell, if you just want to survive way back in the middle of nowhere, you have to open way up, suspend your beliefs, and submit to the land. Harsh, bone dry, freezing, unforgiving. And magic.

The northern high plains roll east from the base of the Rocky

Mountains like still-life waves for hundreds of miles. From Canada's Northwest Territories down through Montana and into Wyoming, the sparsely populated country drifts off eternally. Isolated pockets of mountains rise thousands of feet above what was once an ancient seabed and home to dinosaurs. Millions of acres of native grass buffet back and forth in the wind, always the wind or bake under a wicked sun. Yet despite all this space, threats to the country rain down in the form of strip mining, oil exploration, and logging, to name a few. Where is this place headed? Where has it been through time?

This is a land where millions of bison roamed a little over a century ago. Two-hundred-pound buffalo wolves dogged the animals, dragging down one of the half-ton or larger animals when the killing time was right. Huge grizzlies wandered the sage and cactus doing pretty much the same thing. The bison herds were so large, they took days to pass through a single spot, peacefully grazing on the protein-rich grasses or running through the draws and over the hills with a sound so deafening it shook the ground for miles. Today, antelope, mule and white-tailed deer, coyotes, eagles, vultures, badgers, brown recluse spiders, and rattlesnakes wander the big open country. Remnant herds of bison still fatten up on blue grama and buffalo grass growing on windblown benches at the base of the mountains. Grizzlies careen down out of the high country and knock out a cow or two or gorge on a rancher's honey.

Coyote Nowhere—a phrase taken from Jack Kerouac's *On the Road*—will explore and examine the northern high plains, the true West, not the shortsighted vision myopically viewed by most, as they whiz here and there along the interstate, rarely seeing anything. The mountain West—what we see in the Coors commercials and SUV ads on television—has been pretty much spoiled for us by too many drive-in espresso kiosks, glitzy ski lodges, swank dude ranches, and fly-fishing guides in pastel waders who

serve champagne and caviar in their drift boats. In a word "Cal-
ifornicated." This book will look at what's left, the generally perceived unglamorous part. It will reflect the damage laid on the
land by two centuries of European greed and mismanagement, yet
show that enough still remains of the "Old West" to make it
worth saving. What's real, what never was, all the while conveying
the wonder and awe of this wild, elegant land. Country so powerful that a Blackfeet Indian friend of ours says his people do not
see our one-dimensional world, but rather one filled with layers
of life, beings, and mystery.

And there are the people who live here. The ranchers whose lives
revolve around their cattle, their land, the merciless weather—
blizzards, drought, wind, lightning that blasts down on a soul with
such unrelenting force. The ranch wives, capable, no-nonsense
women who can cook up a feast for a dozen cowhands during
roundup, then hop on a D8 Cat and grade a gravel road or butcher
a steer for the next meal. The solitary hard-rock miners lost in
dreams of sudden wealth locked in stone. Crow, Cheyenne, Blackfeet, Assiniboine Indians, clinging to tradition and natural wis-
dom. The roaming loners such as ourselves who will travel and
die nowhere else. All of us are not merely drawn to this country.
We're dragged into the ragged coulees, eroding bluffs, parched
alkali flats, and streams by an overwhelming need to confront the
American Real. Artists, such as C. M. Russell, Frederic Reming-
ton, and Russell Chatham, and writers, such as A. B. Guthrie,
Wallace Stegner, and more recently Annie Proulx, capture the
intensity that comes from giving in to the power of the northern
high plains. (Each chapter will explore a certain area of the region
and while the sections will not be aligned seasonally or necessarily
in the order we explored and reexplored them, the individual
chapters will progress in a time orderly fashion.) That is what will
show through the words and photographs in *Coyote Nowhere*—the
absolute power that comes from the recognition of an individual's

relative insignificance standing far out in the middle of all this—
unprotected, often terrified, truly alive.

All of this begins and ends in Livingston, Montana, because that's
home these days. A good place to be after too many years watching
Whitefish, a used-to-be-small mountain town in the northwest
corner of the state, get steamrolled by the developer-ski industry-
golf crazies-tourista juggernaut. Around here the high plains roll
off to the north and east. Rugged mountain ranges dominate most
of the horizon. Beautiful, world-class trout streams are everywhere.
The dusty wind blows like hell, close to one hundred mph sometimes. The summers are hot, the winters cold. The autumns surreal in the unearthly golden light. The blooming springs of green
grass and wildflowers are heaven. The people who stay here are
friendly, with a live-and-let-live attitude.

Sure, Livingston has changed some over the years, but not as
much as places west of the Continental Divide, towns fast-
changed, or perhaps short-changed, into mini-cities with strip de-
velopments, malls, ski resorts, and all the horrible nonsense those
atrocities entail, with part-time out-of-staters who treat those who
call those besieged places home like hicks or wildlife—places like
Jackson, Missoula, and Hamilton. But Livingston, unlike Bozeman (a wanna-be Aspen) just to the west, isn't like that. Neither
are most of the other towns riding the prairies.

Sixty years ago Livingston was a bustling railroad town and a
trade center in cattle and farming. Cattlemen, cowboys, railroad
workers, and merchants did their business here. The Indian Wars
had ended less than fifty years back. The Crows no longer wintered
along the Yellowstone, a location of mild winters, light snowpack,
and some grass even in February. The Blackfeet were no longer
the feared raiders of the high plains. Things had settled down on
this front.

Even back in the 1930s hunters and some fishermen descended on the place. Big game was plentiful and the rivers were filled with trout and whitefish. Like most western towns that sprang up in a hurry the architecture was chaotic, a mixture of Gothic, Romanesque, company homes, log cabins, stone block mansions, and whatnot.

Probably the first whites to come here were Lieutenant Clark of the Lewis and Clark Expedition and his men when they slogged down nearby Billman Creek and arrived at the Yellowstone River just south of town on July 15, 1806. The first settlement in the area was made around 1873 when Benson's Landing came into being at a ferry crossing four miles south of the present-day townsite. The Yellowstone is wide, deep, and fast, not readily fordable in all but a few places. Livingston proper came into being on July 14, 1882, when railroad surveyors camped on its site and called it Clark City for the now-late Lieutenant Clark. Late in the same year Northern Pacific Rails reached the town, opening the country to readily accessible trade with the East. Throughout its history Livingston has depended greatly on the railroad. Even its name was changed to honor the director of the Northern Pacific, Crawford Livingston of St. Paul, Minnesota.

Mountain men such as Jim Bridger and John Bozeman spent a good deal of time in the region. Calamity Jane lived here in her later years. Drifters, outlaws, gamblers, and roustabouts passed through town in a steady stream that swirled with drunkenness, gambling, and some violence. During the railroad strike in the summer of 1894, when service was interrupted for two weeks, federal troops were brought in to protect railroad property. A drunken army captain stabbed a townsman with a sword, and President Cleveland declared martial law to maintain order. Guns kept the peace one hundred years ago far more than they do today.

Mountain lions, black and grizzly bears, elk, and whitetail deer would come down from the high country and wander through town on a regular basis, that is until a barrage of gunfire by eager residents either killed them or drove them fleeing back into the hills. Framed newspaper accounts of such activities adorn the walls of one restaurant-bar.

So how has the place changed at the end of the millennium? Well, the railroad isn't as big here as it used to be, though the Burlington Northern Santa Fe still rumbles through town, whistles calling in the night. The burgeoning sport of fly-fishing brings thousands of anglers through here to fish the holy waters, such as the Yellowstone, those in Yellowstone Park fifty miles to the south, the Madison and the Gallatin, and the many lakes and streams in the surrounding Absaroka, Bridger, and Crazy mountain ranges. Motels are filled with cars, trucks, and SUVs bearing out-of-state plates. There are several fly shops including Dan Baileys, which was once the Montana gathering place for serious fly fishers from everywhere in the world; the Federation of Flyfisher's International Flyfishing Center and museum is located a block or two from the cop shop; and guides and outfitters are all over the place. There are times when the Yellowstone River looks as if it has been invaded by an armada of McKenzie River drift boats filled with clients frantically casting flies over trout who have seen it all before hundreds of times, often in the same day. At times, restaurants and bars are filled with enough neoprene and garishly colored angling attire to scare away even the most hardened whiskey drinker.

And Livingston and the surrounding valleys are now home to many top writers—Tom McGuane, Tim Cahill, William Hjortsberg, Richard Wheeler, Walter Kirn, Jamie Harrison, Scott McMillion, and on and on. Artist Russell Chatham has lived here for years and owns one of the finest restaurants anywhere, The Livingston Bar and Grill. Photographers Paul Dix and Tom Murphy, along with fly-fishing artists Michael Simon and Rod Walinchus, also call this place home, as does painter Parks Reece.

Hollywood notables such as Peter Fonda, Margot Kidder, and Jeff Bridges live here, too. As former resident David McCumber, author of *The Cowboy Way*, said last winter, "John, there are so many of us here that it would be just too damn much trouble to run us all out of town." That about says it.

So, there are fancy restaurants, art galleries, fly shops, and derelict writers rubbing day-to-day elbows with ranchers, railroad workers, and merchants at down-to-earth basic food diners such as Martins on Park Street or The Paradise Cafe, or the Coast to Coast Hardware Store, or at the Stockman's or Mint bars. Or the retrograde sixties Beartooth Bakery and Cafe where a friend of mine once walked into the comfortable, wooden-floored establishment for breakfast to find a man in his mid-seventies singing along to arias playing on the jukebox all the while dancing among the tables with graceful wavings of his arms. Mildly eccentric customers and hearty breakfasts are part of the routine in the place. Bears and mountain lions still sneak into town on occasion as do the deer. Canada geese and wood ducks paddle about the lagoon at Sacajawea Park. The architecture is still the distinctly Montana "Whatever I damn well please to build," along with many homes one hundred years old or close to it thrown in the mix. Gated communities and pretension are virtually nonexistent. The big money and its ostentation keeps pretty much to itself. The local golf course wasn't designed by Jack Nicklaus and doesn't cost an arm and a leg to play. People smile, nod, and say hello to each other. Pedestrians still have the right of way, and of course, as is true of the rest of the high plains, unemployment is high. Many of us have few skills and little inclination to get a real job, but we get by.

The West has always been a swirling amalgam of contrasts. Present-day Livingston is no exception as was its 1880s counterpart. Everyone largely gets along, tolerates each other to the point of appreciating most eccentricities partially through the big-time trivial pursuit of gossip that plays as well here as anywhere. And except for youthful hormones behind the wheel of high-rise pick-ups sporting forty thousand dollars' worth of tires, the streets are pretty easy to negotiate, even on foot. Tahoes, Land Rovers, and Expeditions share the road with beat-up 1965 Chevy pickups, battered Oldsmobile Cutlasses, and rusted-out 1964 Dodge Power Wagons. In the 1930s the population was about 6,400. Today it's around 7,000. And the elevation is holding at 4,490 feet above sea level. The chance of a massive earthquake or an explosive erup-tion of the nearby Yellowstone caldera or even a rip-roaring spring runoff flood that would soak the downtown exists, but no one worries about these natural possibilities. People still drink too much. Do drugs. Have affairs with others' husbands and/or wives, shoot guns occasionally at each other, hold up stores on rare oc-casions, and have serious differences of opinion about politics, re-ligion, and the economy. There are big plans to add six more stoplights and maybe build another motel, but the boys drinking down at the Murray Hotel or Owl bars don't give a damn. Not too much pretension here, just a regular east of the divide Mon-tana town in most respects.

The planet's a too-fast place with way too many people these days, but Livingston, like most high plains communities, is laid-back in its own crazy way and is taking the punches dolled out by a self-absorbed outside world in its stride.

As we walked into the Bar and Grill one cool September evening, Michael Simon was there to greet us as he always seems to be. Nattily dressed as ever, this time wearing brown corduroys, vest, plaid wool shirt, and brown waxed cotton jacket, Michael cut a dapper figure highlighted by his warm smile.

Michael is Livingston's ubiquitous, sometimes gadabout, man about town. Fishing friends of mine from around the country have bumped into Michael before they've tracked me down and I only live one block off Main Street. Michael seems to be everywhere all at once, all of the time. He's also a talented artist. He recently completed a mural at the Flyfishing Center that surrounds an aquarium filled with various species of game fish. His work hangs from walls in fly shops, restaurants, coffee houses, and galleries throughout the area. A drawing of his of a bull trout, my favorite salmonid species, dominates one wall in our living room. He graciously colored in the work with the characteristic olives, oranges, whites, and yellows of the species for Ginny and I in exchange for a few inscribed copies of some of my books. A more than fair trade to my way of thinking, but Michael apparently felt otherwise, calling me on the phone one day soon after he'd received the books and inviting me to his studio located in space provided by Russell Chatham above his gallery. At the top of the stairs Michael greeted me with a smile and a hand-colored print of a cutthroat trout, saying, "I thought you might like to have this." I did. Looking over to the other half of the lofty space I noticed an abundance of amplifiers, guitars, a drum kit, and a replica (I hoped) of a human skull nailed to a wall. "Russell offered the space to a local band," Michael offered. When I asked what kind of music they played, he said, "I'm not sure," and laughed.

Michael is also a fine photographer. Dozens of his "bar fly" portraits hang from the walls of the Murray Bar just down the street from the Bar and Grill. Photos of notable fly fishers (and not so notable), writers, agents, painters, actors, the whole sick crew. My photograph is strung next to novelist Peter Bowen's picture. That pretty much says it all. Someday in the distant future anthropologists will examine all of Michael's work in the Murray and realize just how confused Livingston really was way back when. Like the outlaws, gamblers, and cowboys of the Old West, these individuals may be remembered as the characters, the curiosities, of the 1990s.

This night Michael greeted everyone as they passed through the restaurant's entrance and I was beginning to think that he'd forgone his normal evening cocktail routine with friends at the Bar and Grill in exchange for more legitimate employment, that as host for the restaurant, but my fears that he'd gone over to the other side known as gainful employment were allayed when a charming hostess appeared and showed us to our table where we were to have dinner with musician Danny O'Keefe and his companion Laurie Hare. The pair were frequent visitors to town and over the course of several years we'd all become good friends to the extent that Danny, Ginny, and I, with Laurie's invaluable enthusiasm, were about to embark on a book-CD project combining music, words, photos, and recorded natural sounds of Montana. Quite the adventure in the offing. While we waited, Michael and I made plans to fish one of my favorite stretches of the Shields River for brown trout when I returned to town in a few days. We shook hands on the proposed outing just as Danny and Laurie arrived. Dinner was excellent and three hours or so later we left, much to the relief of the patient staff that always tolerates long conversations after late meals.

And the Bar and Grill is what Livingston and the true West are about. Admittedly it's a bit more upscale than most places and the menu ain't fried calf brains and scrambled eggs, though you never know. With Chatham's supervision and occasional forays into the kitchen, the restaurant's cuisine is several levels above that normally found on the plains. But the atmosphere, and again the lack of pretension, are what draws and finally keeps so many of us here. Dress well as Michael does or come in wearing jeans, Converse All-Stars, and an untucked cotton shirt as I often do, or even roll in wearing still-damp waders, it makes no difference. You're welcome here as in most of eastern Montana and the rest of the open country east of the divide. And it really doesn't matter if you're famous or borderline broke and largely (and fortunately) unrecognizable as Ginny and I are. The Bar and Grill, Martins, Stockman's, The Paradise, and the rest of town and this country could care less. Play things reasonably straight, somewhat behave yourself, and don't write too many bad checks. You'll get by and that's what *Coyote Nowhere* is about, too. The genuineness and no bullshit approach to life out here. Just be yourself and let the power of this country bring it to you.

My companion on this book is the woman I live with, photographer Ginny Diers. She's Irish with the red hair and an occasionally fiery temper to prove it. Filled with boundless enthusiasm for wild country, she has the ability to strike up a conversation with strangers and within five minutes they're talking and laughing like long-lost friends. Life stories, personal tragedies, triumphs, and curious experiences are exchanged with total candor. I've never seen anything like it. One time out of the blue in a Wal-Mart a woman came up to her and started offering advice about which daypack to purchase. When I came back to the luggage aisle thirty minutes later they were talking about their mothers. This stuff happens every day with Ginny. We met five years ago over dinner at a mutual friend's house. The first two years of our acquaintance were anything but smooth sailing—off again, on again. She went back to the place of her birth, Belle Plaine, Minnesota, and I wandered Montana somewhat lonely and pathetically morose. Eventually she called one spring day three years ago and asked if I'd like her to come out for a visit. Admittedly a tough decision, but after a second or two of deliberation I casually asked, "How soon can you get here?" By the following November we were living together in Livingston. We get along well, despite the usual bickerings and vehement discussions, tolerate each other's madnesses and shortcomings. We are also in love with the road, driving down back roads and turning off on smaller roads or no roads, pushing on and on to see what's up ahead. Ginny has the ability to see things that I miss and she is able to translate these images through her cameras onto film with powerful, surreal accuracy. I'll look at a sheet of her black-and-white contact prints of someplace we've just returned from and wonder to myself, *Where the hell is this?* Fresh eyes for the West, enthusiasm, and a unique vision account for these photographs. We've done a number of stories for magazines such as *Big Sky Journal, Crossroads, American Cowboy,* and *Men's Journal.* Readers like what we do, so we decided to do this book. We put the proposal together, with a good deal of help from our friend Vermont writer Bob Jones, and sent it to our agent in New York, Diana Finch. She sold it to Thomas Dunne Books, and that's how we got to here.

"The sharp and rugged Crazy Mountains glittering in the clear air are an isolated, geologically young range: they form an almost incredibly jagged upthrust of rock more than 11,000 feet high. Before white men ever saw them, Indians knew them as the Mad Mountains, and feared and avoided them. Their terrifying steepness, their awe-inspiring structure, and the demonic winds that blow continually out of their strange canyons impressed white men as much as it had their coppery brethren, though with less superstitious awe. The epithet 'Mad' became the more familiar 'Crazy.' The weird range is rarely visited," said *The WPA Guide to 1930s Montana.*

The Crazies looked anything but weird as Michael and I drove north up Highway 89 to a little place I know on the Shields. Hunters, fishermen, hikers, and campers trudge up and down the steep, vertiginous trails that give way to the heart of the mountains. The Crazies are far from being overrun with people, but they're not all alone anymore, either. The mountains shone softly, purple-pink in the clear light of noon on this barely hazy mid-

September day. A recent dusting of snow lightly covered the upper thousand feet of the range in pure white. Fall colors were just beginning to show. The cottonwoods that lined the aquamarine river sparkling beneath the sun showed the merest hint of yellow beneath the green. Bankside willows and alders were turning orange, cranberry, and violet. The grass in the area had gone yellow-brown weeks ago in the hundred-degree heat of July. Driving east from Bozeman on I-90 the Crazies are clearly visible as they blast into the sky. From the moment you top the rise that separates Livingston from its frantic urban neighbor the peaks appear as first a vague hint of sheer walls to your right, then more and more of the range as you swing down the interstate at eighty mph. Coming in from the east the mountains play hide-and-seek behind the hills until you approach Big Timber and then the range blasts you between the eyes with its glacier-scoured peaks and sheer-walled valleys, ribs of mountain running for miles to the north. The Yellowstone River flows with stately calm, bending and turning beneath huge cottonwoods and rugged cliffs as the emerald-sapphire water pours over a clean, rocky streambed or glides along in a series of deep, mysterious pools and runs. The Crazies are always stunning, as they should be. Every morning during my walk along the Yellowstone I look to the east and see those mountains standing alone under a clear sky or some days I see only their stern bases as the tops are covered with dark, boiling, surly-looking clouds.

The Crazies are not only unique visually, they are a curious trip geologically, according to the book *Roadside Geology of Montana* by David Alt and David W. Hyndman.

"The Crazy Mountains are so different and so peculiar that a frustrated geologist might have named them . . . There are no volcanic rocks . . . Furthermore, the Crazy Mountains stand in the middle of the Crazy Mountains basin, a part of the crust that was folded down instead of up, as with most of the other igneous centers . . . A lone road on the east side of the range reaches the much higher and more rugged southern end of the Crazy Mountains where the angular peaks and sharp ridges tell of enormous ice age glaciers in the big valleys . . . Spectacular dikes [a body of igneous rock that formed as magma and filled an open fracture in the earth's surface] that radiate north and south from that intrusion follow the axis of the anticline [an arch folded in layered rock], and swarms of sills follow the sedimentary layers on the east and west flanks of the fold."

All well and good and what both books seem to be saying is that the Crazies are a mountain range unto themselves. They've played a part in countless novels and are featured on one paperback version's cover of *Zen and the Art of Motorcycle Maintenance*. I've used them for a backdrop in a murder mystery I wrote, so has Ms. Harrison in *Going Local*. Again, all well and good, but Michael and I are cruising up the highway through the small ranching towns of Clyde Park and Wilsall to work a wonderful stretch of small water that holds browns, Yellowstone cutts, brook trout, and whitefish. The day is glorious—clear, mid-seventies, light breeze—one of those autumn Montana days that blow so far past words that I say to myself while thinking how to describe such an event as this afternoon, "Why bother?"

An hour later we are about two miles downstream from the old bridge that spans the river near where we parked. The river is more a fair-sized creek up here at the edge of the Crazies. Walking through stands of three-to-four-foot-diameter cottonwoods, our footsteps crunching on some already-fallen leaves and across open grazing land, maneuvering among random groups of somnolent cattle, we jump a number of white-tailed deer, roust a kingfisher from his angling perch, and watch as a trio of croaking ravens circle directly above us before heading off in the direction of the Bridger Mountains, a sheer rock wall rising far above the Shields Valley to the west. The land rolls away from us both east and west in a series of gentle, grass-covered steppes. The Shields slides beneath the cottonwoods and runs noisily against ragged cliffs of broken stone. Earlier this summer while standing in water up to my waist I was attempting to retrieve a hopper pattern that had become wedged in a slice in the rocks. A whirring, sizzling buzz a few feet above me snagged my attention. A rattlesnake lay coiled on a ledge, eyes flashing reptilian yellow, its tongue tasting the air with rapid flicks. I staggered and lurched across the river and crash-landed in the shallow water of the far shore, frightened and hopeful that I'd had my snake fix for the year. I've had a nightmare several times that involves me falling face first in a swarming ball of rattlesnakes, being bitten countless times before dying a horribly painful death from circulatory and respiratory complications, my horrible discolored and bloated corpse eventually discovered splayed next to my fly rod alongside some bucolic trout stream. Dream on as they say.

We cross a field of tall, dry grass growing in the deposited silt of many years of spring runoff. At the edge of the water we sit down on a bar of rounded stone. Normally I'm already casting away at the run that cuts along and beneath the rock above us, but Michael and I take out time rigging up. He with a dry for an indicator and a nymph as a dropper, and I with a woolly bugger, my pattern of choice in most places. Michael is a leisurely, sedate fly fisher who loves to make artful casts with one of his bamboo rods. I, on the other hand, work rapidly from holding spot to holding spot hammering away with my graphite rod of choice for that day. In deference to my friend I am trying to slow down, to hold myself back. My friend, being a gentleman at heart, quickens his pace for my benefit, but he keeps looking at me all the while laughing his good laugh and shaking his head. He realizes that my impatience is terminal.

This is some of my favorite trout water anywhere—a series of rocky runs, riffles, deep glides beneath undercut banks, crystalline pools, and tangles of logjams. Brown trout to twenty inches hold beneath the banks and the intensely colored cutthroats lodge back in the jams. The brook trout seem to congregate in herds wherever they damn please and the mountain whitefish, some to three pounds, prefer the sedate atmosphere they find at the tails of the pools.

Michael delicately roll casts his rig just above a seam of current that moves close to the far bank and squeezes between a midstream chunk of rock. Several feet into the drift a brown takes his nymph, the trout running downstream deep or head shaking at the surface. In a couple of minutes the spent fish is at Michael's feet, the browns, reds, blacks, softest of silvers, rich yellows, and off-whites shining like precious metals and gemstones in the light. Sixteen inches and heavy, the trout races for cover at its release.

"Truly gorgeous water, John," says Michael. "I see there appears to be more of it up ahead." I nod, light a cigarette, and watch as he misses two more browns, fools a whitefish with an incredible display of nymphing artifice, and takes another brown of slightly smaller dimensions than the first. All of this in perhaps one hundred yards of water. I cross the stream at a shallow riffle and move well ahead of him through the trees, coming out just below a deep pool that flows deep blue with good current along a downed cottonwood. Several large cutthroats are making spectacles of themselves as they loudly snap at caddis flies. The trout make large widening rings on the surface as they feed with a steady, undisciplined rhythm. The beauty of this species is not only in its flaming colors, the intense orange-red slashes along its lower jaw (hence its name), but its willingness to take a dry fly, even when it's presented with a good deal less than gentleness.

The elk-hair caddis drops on the river drifts along with the flow and a fat cutthroat gulps it down, then races and circles about in total confusion and anger at being caught. The fish plays out quickly, as the cutts normally do, and I bring it to my feet in the shallow water. Perhaps sixteen, seventeen inches with colors on full bore. The reds, oranges, golds, whites, and blacks are spectacular. That's the only word for the fish. Spectacular. I release him, make another short cast, and catch another of the same size, then another. By this time Michael has worked his way up to me, so I step back from the water and let him try his hand, with no success. Three good trout from this one small pool is more than I expected, so we push our way upstream drenched in the liquid orange-gold light of the late-afternoon sun. We take a number of other trout, including one brown hiding beneath a jumble of over-hanging willow limbs, the fish settled into a subtle depression in the streambed. Michael executes a tricky cast beneath the tangle, his line rolling and unfurling in seeming slow motion across the broken face of the water. The fish takes immediately with a ve-hement slashing motion involving its entire body, which crashes and rolls in the shadows beneath the willow. Another brown. Can never have too many of these secretive, voracious predators.

We fish on and I keep thinking what a splendid day. Michael mirrors my sentiments when he turns from working a narrow run and says, "Simply splendid, John," and he looks way off back down the river bubbling away behind me and adds, "Beautiful. Just beautiful."

We drive back down 89 with the Bridgers, Absaroka, and Crazies radiating so many variations of red, orange, yellow, blue, and purple that the entire valley is alive with the radiance, a radiance that continues to grow in intensity as we drive along Old Clyde Park Road back into Livingston. We talk about this and that some, but are too far gone on the day to say much of interest. Rolling down Park past the grain elevators, the idling trains, the Main Hotel, the gas stations, and the old houses, it is easy to realize that living here in this town with the mountains and the high plains soaring off in all directions is not a bad way to spend one's life.

I hang a left on Main and park the Suburban in front of the Bar and Grill, beneath the colorful light of the restaurant's glow-ing neon signs.

Crow chief Plenty Coup's home just north of the Pryor Mountains.

2

THE FIRST ONES—
WILD HORSES OF THE PRYORS

High in the Pryor Mountains
First light of dawn
Coyote Dun walks beneath
the morning star
he became an outlaw . . . his blood
watered some, but the flame still burns
into the new millennium

"LA PRIMERA,"
FROM LOST HERD BY IAN TYSON

DRIVING ALONG THE DUSTY ROAD it was mid-July hot. Nineties around noon with 110 on the near horizon. The sun blasted down directly overhead with no clouds to pass by and create transient shade, marginal relief from the heat and burning rays. Ginny, my daughter, Rachel, and I drove past the turn-in to Chief Plenty Coups State Park. Up the road a few hundred yards was the small town of Pryor (population about fifty) located on the western edge of the Crow Indian Reservation in south-central Montana. We needed some more ice for our coolers so we pulled into the gravel parking lot of a small wooden structure painted white but the boards were faded and peeling. No signs advertised anything for sale, but we took a chance since there was an ice machine out front labeled in large blue letters "ICE." The machine was sitting a few feet from the weathered store out in the sun. Maybe the word should have been "MELTED ICE." Not far away a couple of gas pumps—metal bases dented and rusting, glass faces cracked—offered regular and plus grades of fuel. Through a barred and screened window we could see, barely in the dimness, that the store also sold candy, cigarettes, and other small items that were purchased through a window protected by more iron bars. You slid your money in and the goods were pushed back out to you. To get the ice we had to pay first. Then a man unlocked a door from the inside, stepped outside locking the door behind him, walked over and unlocked the ice machine, and handed us our bags of ice. Then he reversed the process and was soon back inside his place of business taking money from a hard, shifty-looking guy in jeans and beat-up cowboy hat who was paying for gas he'd pumped into an early seventies Dodge flatbed, the red body banged up like the gas pumps. The guy behind the bars also took in handfuls of change from eager, bright-eyed Crow children in exchange for candy and dollar bills for cigarettes from a teenage Crow, his long jet-black hair hanging in tight braids to his waist. The youth unwrapped the pack of Kools and fired one up with a Zippo lighter before lazily walking down the road and out into the country, the road lined with old cottonwoods that gave way to barbed-wire fences protecting large fields of emerald-green hay and alfalfa. Sprinklers sprayed water in long arcs over the acres of grass. Sunlight flashed through the water in a constantly changing prismatic display. Except for the happy Indian children, the place gave us the creeps, though I'm sure all the bad vibes amounted to nothing more than our latent paranoia kicked into high gear by the iron bars, the rough cowhand, and the heat. Sure, Indian reservations have a sometimes deserved reputation of being tough places. Formerly free-roaming people on the high plains now confined to a small fraction of their former territory tend to suffer greatly and become angry at the drastic change in their lifestyle. Add to this monthly checks from the government used primarily by some of them for booze and so forth, and of course alcoholism and drug abuse are often as high as in an inner big city. Violent crimes and deadly eccentric driving are also part of the mix. But this downscale Fort Knox, sort of gas station-convenience store, seemed a bit excessive. What do I know? I don't live here in the dead of a brutally cold January, government-checks-just-in Friday night and really drunk-out. Maybe things really do get ugly around here. All the same, we hurriedly spread the ice over our food and drinks in the two coolers and quietly drove out of there aiming for Plenty Coups's home.

After pulling into the parking lot at the Plenty Coups State Park, I made a brief tour of the modern, natural stone-sided museum. Two cars were parked nearby. One from Alabama and the other from Wisconsin. Inside, an older couple, and also a young family, were quietly touring the various exhibits of arrowheads, ornate Crow beadwork, archival black-and-white photographs depicting the place as it was years ago, dioramas showing Indian life, and displays of leather work. The place was softly lit and cool, a pleasant change from the blistering day outside. All of us in the museum were quiet, as much from the tranquil nature of the building as out of respect for Chief Plenty Coups, whose grave was located in a copse of trees near the entrance. The Crows were a true high plains warrior society who jealously guarded their prime bison hunting lands that extended over millions of acres. Their chief foes were the equally warlike Blackfeet, whose homelands were more to the north and west of this south-central Montana location. Both tribes along with the Northern Cheyenne and others depended upon the vast herds of millions of the huge, massive-headed, black-furred beasts for clothing, shelter, food, and perhaps most importantly, spiritual sustenance. With the extermination of the bison by white hunters for hides and some meat, and then the confinement of these nomadic people within the artificial environment of reservations, people who roamed where the buffalo roamed, a number of wild and free societies—groups of individuals who had lived in this country for thousands of years—came to an end. Plenty Coups was the last Crow chief and perhaps their most revered leader. There has been no Crow chief since his death decades ago. In 1928 he donated his home and land for a "Nation's Park," saying when he did so, "This park is not to be a memorial to me, but to the Crow Nation. It is given as a token of my friendship for all people red and white."

Recognizing the impossibility of holding off the onslaught of white settlers and the U.S. Army, Plenty Coups was a constant voice for peace and compromise among his people. In his youth he was a fierce and respected warrior, so his words carried a good deal of weight. An old photograph of him shows a stern, wise, and weathered face that has seen its share of violence, death, sorrow, and joy. He was clearly a true leader of not only his people but, indirectly through his actions, all native people.

Stepping outside I was momentarily blinded by the sun and the heat hit me like a red-hot wall. By the time I found the gravel path that led to Plenty Coups's home I was drenched in sweat, even though the way wound through the shade of huge, ancient cottonwoods. A soft breeze worked its way across the hills and green fields and rustled the trees' leaves. The log home was a large, somewhat rambling, two-story structure with many windows and was located in the shade of still more massive cottonwoods. A sign informed me that the home was only sparsely furnished when the chief and his wife lived here. A white-man-style home outfitted as a plains Indian would his lodge, with buffalo robes, blankets, and only a few pieces of furniture. Walking about the home alone

I was overwhelmed with the peace and the power of the place. It was easy to imagine the presence of Plenty Coups at my shoulder. From a downstairs window I could see Castle Rock shimmering in the haze several miles to the south. This was a place of power and spirituality for the Crows and the chief in particular. Ponderosa pines climbed gentle hills, then clung to steep slopes that gave way to the base of the rock structures that were located on the northern side of the Pryor Mountains.

After walking around the home one more time I went out a back door that led to a small, cool spring, again situated beneath old, huge cottonwoods. Plenty Coups also saw this as a place of power, spirituality, and a place to gain visions. The sense of strength and peace as in the home was overwhelming and I sat down in the green-turning-brown summer grass and scanned the horizons. The Pryors rose in the south, and rolling hills, fields, and bluffs drifted off for miles in the other directions. I could see why he chose this land to live out his years and wondered at the generosity of the man to donate all of this to all people. Had I been treated the way he and his people had been, I probably would have burned the place down and gone out with all guns blazing.

The gravel road that leads through a gap in the northern beginnings of the Pryor Mountains bends and twists like a rattlesnake with a badly broken back. The way grows steadily narrower, rockier, and climbs gradually upward between immense, cracked walls and sheets of Madison limestone that are 650 million years old and rest upon partially exposed thrusts of basement rock of at least 1.5 billion years. Castle Rock towers above and behind us now and as we drive across a wide-open grassy plain, the prominent geological feature eventually fades in the heat haze and the distance. We are headed to Sage Creek Campground located on the northern flank of West Pryor Mountain. With the exception of residents of Billings a couple hours north, the mountains receive little visitation, except for those who come to see the wild horses of this country. Perhaps 150 of them roam free in several bands way out here on the sage and cactus flats, or out on the south end of the range in the desolate desert of southern Montana and northern Wyoming. Or they could be hunkered down in one of the rugged canyons that tear through the mountains that reach almost 9,000 feet, or they could even be grazing on the alpine grasses that far above sea level. The Pryors are actually an extension of Wyoming's Big Horn Mountains that climb to more than 13,000 feet. The Bighorn (one word for the river, two for the mountains) flows between a ten-mile-wide rift that now separates the two ranges. This is harsh, surprisingly rough country. From I-90 to the east the Pryors look like long, gentle mounds, more like foothills than mountains, but as we drive farther in and eventually turn east on a dirt road that is baked dry but filled with deep ruts that indicate impassability during wet times, I realize that the seemingly innocuous and enticing side roads and two-tracks that wander off into the hills and through narrow canyons are more than likely potential death trips for us in our Suburban. West Pryor towers above us. Ponderosa pines give way to fir, and through my binoculars I can see wind-beat clumps of subalpine fir thousands of feet above. The meadows are rich green that far up, and patches of bright yellows, blues, whites, and reds catch my eye. Wildflowers are still blooming up that way. Large patches of melting snow cling to feminine creases and dips in the steep upper slopes. The creek bubbles and sparkles as it pours through a steep-sided stream course choked with alder, willow, dense brush, cactus, and sage. This will be a tough little bugger to fish, but the water looks too trouty, even out here in all this dryness, to pass up. Maybe some rainbows of four or five inches. All my addictions are hopeless.

After seven or eight miles that seem like fifty, we turn off on an even smaller road and lurch into camp. About a dozen picnic tables with wooden shade shelters, a couple of outhouses, plenty of wood around, and no other people. Ideal. We choose a site that scans the heights of West Pryor, provides a serious view up the creek's valley, and overlooks a couple of bends in the creek. While setting up camp my attention is drawn by lots of silvery trout— rainbows and brookies—that are leaping and splashing as they madly chase emerging caddis flies and breeze-borne grasshoppers. A few of the trout look immense. Seven, possibly eight inches. I rig a one-ounce two-weight and a #16 gray elk hair. Camp's done. Dinner can wait until the late-afternoon heat dissipates. I smile at Ginny and wander off. She prepares for a dip in an emerald pool that has a large plank across it.

Looking down into deep green water I can see dozens of trout holding throughout the water column, keeping their various feeding positions with gentle flickerings of their fins. The fish cast dark, wavering shadows on the sandy bottom or upon the chocolate-colored mud deposited on the inside bends of the creek. The casting is tight with straight-up above me back casts and swift twenty-to-thirty-foot shoots between the brush. I mend and curve the line just before it hits the water. The first cast is greeted by a show-off rainbow that clears the surface of the water with the fly stuck in a corner of its jaws. The trout continues leaping until it crashes into some overhanging brush where it winds up dangling suspended from the branch-entangled tippet. The rainbow quivers and shakes until the line breaks and then it plops back into the water. I am crestfallen. This is an enormous fish. Perhaps nine inches. I cast again and hook a fish that sails over my head and lands on the grassy bank behind. I quickly retrieve it. A three-inch brook trout. Intensely colored with blues, oranges, golds, reds, emeralds, blacks, whites, purples. It dashes off when I release it. I take another dozen trout from this run and then another dozen at the next pool and on and on it goes. One rainbow reached ten inches. One brookie seven. Who cares. The sun is setting. The light growing dim, but I could have fished this delightful brook all night. No pretense. No unctuous, gaudily catalogued outfitted anglers with misguided intentions. No territorial guides with all the social sophistications of Mike Tyson. Just perfect small-stream fishing. The land glows orange as the day nears its end. Purple shadows edging darker drift across the top of West Pryor. Nighthawks, always nighthawks out west, swoop and dive like fighter pilots along the stream. A coyote or two barks for a while. An eagle soars a thousand feet or more above. The day is cooling. Down to eighty and a slightly warmer breeze brings the aroma of ribs grilling on a fire. I return to camp. Relaxed. Hug Ginny and accept a plate of the meat, baked potatoes, and salad and devour it.

As we finish eating, a car with Oregon plates filled with people pulls into a campsite a quarter mile away. After about four thousand trips unloading gear, food, and God-only-knows-what-else, they retire silently out of sight to their evening's nest. The doors of the compact Detroit beater are left open and we watch as the interior light grows dimmer and dimmer. Periodically one of their party returns to retrieve some other article of outdoor paraphernalia, but the doors are always left open.

A half moon rises just to the north of the Pryors and it casts black shadows across the dry grass. As usual, countless stars eventually come out. The Oregon car's light eventually dies out. And Ginny, Rachel, and I finally pass out.

We wake to another hot rising sun already hammering the day with intense, burning gold and yellow sheets of light that turn the landscape into something resembling an old, overexposed, fading Instamatic snapshot. The Oregon crew is loaded up and now pushing the red car down the road. The driver pops the clutch when the thing reaches three or four miles an hour. The engine catches, roughly at first, belching blue fumes. The remainder of the gang piles in and off they go down the road, soon lost from view. We break camp after I catch a few more of the carefree trout and go our own way, on up the wide gravel road, clearly a Forest Service–maintained item, that winds higher and higher up West Pryor. We have no idea where to begin looking for the wild horses, so when we come to a fork in the road instead of proceeding on up to the top of East Pryor Mountain, we turn right and slant downhill on something called Crooked Creek, which is fine for a couple of miles.

Things go to hell in a hurry.

As soon as the path drops into the pine forest it narrows to one rutted, potholed, boulder-studded red dirt miasmic nightmare. There is nowhere to turn around and the outside edge of the Suburban's tires barely have enough room to keep from slipping over the edge and down several hundred feet of rock ledges, cliffs, and boulder fields. I'm a world-class acrophobic and am coming reasonably close to having a complete and massive nervous breakdown. Rachel is on the far side of the car clutching the door handle in case a quick exit is required. Even Ginny, who is not afraid of heights, is edgy. The road gets tighter and bumpier and I hug the inside of the Crooked Creek byway, limbs and rocks scraping the sides of the rig. The country is growing more severe—the canyon wicked, mangled, deadly. A quick, horrifying look down offers a free-fall glimpse into the next time zone and I think we've had it. Where would we turn around. Could we make it back in reverse. I doubt this. Then at the point of no sane return we cross a cattle guard, the road widens for an easy turnaround. I stop the car, stagger out, and go into the woods to take a shaky leak. Saved. For now at least. If the horses are down this way, they aren't going to be looking at my frightened image. I walk on down the winding road for about a mile. The edge drops into space. The sounds of rushing water barely reach my ears. I bet the fish in this one don't see much attention and I almost begin to consider scrambling down with a fly rod to see what is in the stream before I catch myself. No way will I go down there. A sick man with a bad disease when it comes to fish. I glimpse the road far ahead where it appears even skinnier and is nothing more than a narrow cut along a sheer rock wall. The canyon tumbles away for hundreds of feet.

"We're going back and you'd better drive," I say. "I've had it for this piece of shit road."

Ginny agrees, hops in, and deftly and quickly has us turned around and going in, if not the right direction, at least a safer one. Canyon roads, whether in the Santa Rita Mountains of Arizona or in the Missouri Breaks or here, are almost always dead-end trips for me.

When we reach the fork again we look at the map, talk some, then decide to head back the way we came and then another sixty or so miles on through Lovell, Wyoming, and on up to the Pryor Mountain National Wild Horse Range headquarters at Britton Springs.

Dropping back down the way we rode up, we break out onto a vast, arid sage flat. Barely midmorning and already a hundred out here. No clouds. Even the cactus looks withered, dead, as the stuff tries to eke out an existence in the rock-hard, cracked ground.

Long, sweeping hills cling low to the horizon in the west. The western flank of the Pryors is slab stacked upon slab of more ancient gray and rust-brown rock. Clumps of juniper grow in eroded slashes. We are miles from these and they look like relatively smooth gullies, but so did Crooked Creek from a distance. We turn onto a state highway near a concrete plant. Large trucks hauling boulders the size of the Suburban roar past us until I notice a gap in the chain of semis and speed out onto the pavement. Racing through the heat headed for Lovell we cross into Wyoming and drive into Cowley, one of several small towns between us and Britton Springs. The place is a typical small western town with mainly residential neighborhoods—well-kept houses, lawns, and gardens. That is until we come to a house hiding beneath another huge cottonwood back off the main drag. No one is in sight. The place appears at least temporarily empty, with thousands of knickknacks—wooden and plastic elves, ducks, songbirds, sheep, strange-looking people, wishing wells—and countless bunches of plastic flowers and even bushes. Nothing seems real about this place. I wonder if the house is nothing more than a Hollywood facade. A block farther down the street a brick home gives way to a well-tended backyard full of picnic tables covered with brightly colored tablecloths, plates, dishes, cups, and pitchers of beverages. A couple of small tents shelter two more tables piled high with turkeys, roast beef, salads, potatoes, sweet corn, and so on. Dozens of people dressed in summer wear are milling around eating from plates piled with the food or they are sitting at the tables eating. They are all laughing and chattering away, we can hear the noise through the open windows as we cruise by. A midweek, afternoon blowout in Cowley, Wyoming. As we drift by the front of the house, I notice a long, black hearse parked in front of the festivities. If this is a wake, I hope they've already planted the stiff as the heat now stands at 107 according to the downtown bank thermometer. We cruise on, not quite sure about this town. We pass through Lovell, stopping, as always, for more ice at a grocery store, and then glide along a two-lane highway that leads both to the Big Horn (two words this time) Canyon Recreation Area and Britton Springs. Bighorn Lake is a large impoundment holding behind Yellowtail Dam. Speed boats, water-skiers, jet skis, well-organized mayhem at well-organized campgrounds—the usual silliness. Below the dam the river in Montana is considered one of the world's finest tailwater trophy trout fisheries. "The First Thirteen" miles of this wide, clear, ice-cold water is filled with aquatic plants that grow thickly in the nutrient-rich water. This spawns enormous hatches of countless species of mayflies, caddis flies, scuds, stone flies, which in turn feed a large number of very big trout—rainbows and browns. This in turn has spawned an insanely greedy hatch of guides, outfitters, and aggressive fly fishers that are well known for throwing rocks into each other's fishing water, having fistfights over prime trout holding areas, or featuring heartless guides floating over wading anglers (this happened to a friend of mine), swearing, obscene gestures, and the like. I haven't fished here for years and have no intention of doing so ever again.

As we drive into progressively drier, harsher, and more unfor-giving country we pass a long, high sandstone wall filled with dark faces that resemble Egyptian pharaohs. The faces clearly ex-hibit expressions and they do not appear happy. Hundred-foot-high, naturally eroded, and obviously angry entities embedded in stone. Maybe they are from Cowley. Another ten miles of desert driving, a large round Pepsi thermometer hanging on a ranch gate, sort of in the shade, registers 122. All of us are sweating, guzzling warm water, and are wiped out from the heat when we pull up to the wild horse headquarters. A suntanned older woman and her young apprentice appear on the front steps and greet us. They seem genuinely thrilled when we tell them we've driven all the way from Livingston to see their horses. Corrals fill the distance behind the office. A couple of newer pickups are parked in front.

"Well in this heat they [the horses] are probably hiding out in a shady canyon or up at the top of East Pryor grazing and trying to beat the heat," she says and favors us with a sunbeam smile. "I'd go up high to find them. They'll be there."

When I tell her we almost had been there today but took the Crooked Creek Road, her jaw drops and she says, "You went down *that* road?" and gives us a look that says nobody in their right mind does such a thing. Ginny and the two horsewomen talk about the wild horses, how best to photograph them, and then we begin to leave.

"Please come back anytime and I hope you find them."

We say "We will" to both.

By the time we reach the Sage Creek turnoff it must be two hundred degrees out. The sun has baked the landscape to a seared yellow-white. The sky is a washed-out blue. We pull over by a large culvert where the creek flows clear and cool. I take off everything but my cutoffs and go for a dip among the tiny trout that dart up and nip at the hairs on my legs. I just sit down in the water and melt.

"Do you think anyone will come by, John," asks Ginny.

"Hell, there's no one around for miles," I answer. Rachel is already hopping up and down in a pool below me. We all drop into the cool water of this magic little stream flowing all by itself in the middle of some of the hottest, driest country I've ever been in.

We spend most of an hour swimming, soaking, sunning in the creek, watching the trout leap for small bugs or just appreciate the water as it races over copper-colored shallows or swirls perfectly clear as it rushes out of the culvert. There are only the three of us enjoying the cool water on a scorching day out in a desert. Ignore the road and the culvert and this place could be two hundred years ago. A moist, cool time trip. Reluctantly we dress and head for the top of East Pryor.

From the Crooked Creek fork in the road the top of East Pryor Mountain is about ten miles of rocky switchbacks that throw us back and forth and up and down as we careen through stands of mature ponderosa or across expanses of tall, native grasses that grow in gentle, open meadows or on severe slopes. Looking south we can see far down the Crooked Creek drainage out onto the dry broken dunes, bluffs, and flats that lead to Britton Springs. We jump numerous whitetail deer that bound away into the trees at our approach. We don't see any other cars or trucks. Coming around a looping bend we spot a sign indicating an ice cave. We take the turnoff, park, and head down an asphalt walkway that declines quickly to a long series of stairs that lead to a rectangular hole in a rock wall. As we approach the cave entrance we can feel the frigid air. A wooden platform leads out over a vast sheet of pockmarked ice that disappears into blackness. Our voices and footfalls echo bleakly in the cold darkness. Apparently this cave stretches on for thousands of feet and opens into vast vaults and chambers filled with towering, many-hued stalactites and stalag-mites formed by the relentless dripping of mineral-laden water. You need permission to go beyond the wooden deck. Too many visitors far inside would bring not only warm outside air in, but their body heat would eventually melt the ice that forms in these north-facing caves from wind-packed snow driven into the cham-ber by winter onslaughts. We have no desire to explore this eerie place so we puff back up to the parking lot. It is now around six-thirty but the sun has several hours to go until setting. A couple miles more to the top.

Then as we climb up on a broad grassy plateau that is con-toured with soft eroded creases filled with ponderosa, the drainages breaking open into rugged canyons, we see the heads and flicking tails of the horses. As we top a rise the land falls away abruptly to the north and east and the horses are everywhere. Groups of four, five, or more lazily grazing on the rich native grains, colts rolling in patches of dirt, the stallions slightly distant from them and the mares. The males are alert, ears twitching, and they keep a sharp eye on us. I stop the Suburban and turn off the engine. Ginny grabs her camera gear and stalks off carefully down the two-track and works her way gradually to within thirty feet of one group—a black stallion, a roan mare, a buckskin mare and colt, and off to one side a younger stallion with a dorsal stripe down his charcoal back and the vestiges of zebra stripes on his legs. The wild horses of the Pryor Mountains. These are the distant genetic relations to the European Spanish horse brought over on galleons centuries before. Horses pirated away by plains Indians. Horses that changed these Indians' way of hunting and living. Horses that eventually escaped from their Crow, Blackfeet, and Cheyenne masters and now in a long-distance way carry on the heritage. Blood typing by the Genetics Department of the University of Kentucky has confirmed that these animals are closely related to their Spanish ancestors. There may be as many as twenty-five family groups along with "bachelor" stallions. Most families or "harems" average five to six animals with a dominate stallion, a lead mare, a variety of other mares and young animals.

The group Ginny is photographing allows her to approach even closer, though the lead stallion snorts and occasionally pounds his hooves to let her know who is in charge. Rachel and I walk about a mile to another group grazing in a miniature valley below us. We stand next to a lone fir tree and watch. The horses notice us and move to within twenty feet of our vantage point, again snorting and giving us a strong once-over. Then they resume their grazing. One of the stallions in this group has striped markings along his flanks. We watch this family unit for over an hour as it slowly moves off out of sight down the beginnings of a canyon, then we return to the car and Ginny. Several other groups of horses are feeding nearby and one bunch walks past us on the road. From what the woman at Britton Springs had told us, the wild horses are skittish and will usually move off at the sight of humans, often at a gallop. None of the horses we observed seem concerned in the least. Cautious to be sure, but not frightened.

"Do you believe this, you guys?" Ginny exclaims.

We didn't. I really didn't expect to find the animals, let alone watch them at arm's length for so long.

"Amazing. Fabulous. I can't believe it," she says.

I can't either. Rachel merely smiles.

By now the sun is only an hour above the horizon so we rattle our way to the rolling crest of the mountain and set up camp in the lee of an island of subalpine fir. The air is cool up here. Sixties. And the wind is kicking up to a gale. Large clouds approach from the south only to be torn into shreds by the wind and vanish into nothingness. We look out over the Bighorn Valley in Montana, beyond the rugged salmon and orange walls of Bighorn Canyon far to the north and east, past the winking lights of Hardin and Crow Agency, on to the subtle rises of the plateau of Tongue River country. To the northwest our own Crazy Mountains glow bloodred in the setting sun. Far to the south we can see the lights of Lovell and Cowley. We grill some game hens, sweet corn, and potatoes, boil tea, and eat chocolate-chip cookies. We sit around a small fire until well after dark as the moon rises over the Tongue River plateau and the stars come out. We even see a few nighthawks and bats swooping as they feed on insects. Then we turn in.

The sound of whining engines wakes us at dawn. I sit up and see a half-dozen all-terrain vehicles roaring up the road to the loop turnaround that offers a 360-degree view of the horizon. The noise of the machines is raucous, out of place, obscene. The drivers circle and roar across the grass meadows in a spray of dirt and grass. More ATVs arrive, speed around, and zip back down the way the came. As the sun begins to rise above the horizon a series of late-model pickups and SUVs—all driven by men, all the rigs have the number "3" on their license plates, indicating that they are from the Billings area (ours are number "49" saying we are from Park County, the numbers based on an out-of-date county census in Montana)—rumble past the two-track not far from our camp. They proceed on to the middle of a large grove of fir. I can hear the sounds of engines being shut down, doors opening and slamming shut. Then silence. Then high-pitched wailing and the discordant, nonrhythmic beating of drums and more wailings. This continues for a long time as still more ATVs zoom up and roar around. The three of us are stunned, silent as we eat breakfast. As all this uproar continues, the sound of gunfire echoing off the canyon walls where Rachel and I had watched the horses disappear last evening reverberates. This wild, beautiful place is being overrun by subnormal, brain-dead, self-absorbed lunatics. More sickly Iron John pseudo-masculine chanting and pathetic drumming issues from the trees. More exhaust-belching ATVs. More gunfire. We take a long walk and look for the horses. We walk for miles. Through the pines. Across the meadows. Down to the canyon's edge. All the while the sounds of the chanting-drums foolishness, the ratcheting whine of the ATVs, and the sporadic gunfire rips apart the fragile, peaceful fabric of this beautiful scenic place. All I can think is, *Fucking people*. We keep looking.

But the horses are gone. Vanished.

Soon we do the same.

*The Middle Fork of the Powder River flowing through the canyon near Butch
and Sundance's Outlaw Cave in Wyoming.*

3

WYOMING'S POWDER
RIVER COUNTRY

THE CANYON IS SPECTACULAR, from another time, perhaps another world. Stumbling upon (or sometimes staggering
upon) good country is one of the true pleasures of doing the road,
one of the benefits of working at an occupation that everyone else
considers play. Telling people that I write and Ginny photographs, that we do books and magazine articles based on our experiences, mishaps, and, infrequently, uncommon revelations
traveling around the West, leaves most people including many of
our friends and family asking, "Yes, and what do you do to make
money?" And I'll reply without a trace of sarcasm, "Well, you see
I bang out about seventy thousand words or so in a few days,
maybe as much as a week if I want the stuff to be real good, and
we throw a few of Ginny's photos in for kicks, ship the whole
mess back East, and then we wait a week or so for a check that
usually runs to the tune of one hundred grand," and the subject
dies an uncomfortable death around the dinner table. We look at
each other and laugh while the rest of the diners play slow-motion
games with their forks and bits of food. So what does this have

to do with the two of us standing at the edge of a thousand feet of space that plummets down upon the Middle Fork of the Powder River as it cuts between sheer rock walls marked by isolated bands of ponderosa pine clinging for their lives in sparse soil along narrow ledges holding just enough dirt to allow the trees' roots adequate purchase to withstand wind, rain, snow, and gravity, the sound of the rushing, falling water audible as a distant roar that blends well with the breeze sighing through the trees? Not much actually, except that it's the only dependable form of remuneration we ever get in this carefree, lackadaisical existence. We've heard tales of $100,000 or more for books, but we've never seen it. Maybe someday. And as for magazine work, well, the checks are always in the mail, sometimes for months, and they're never more than enough to buy us a couple of weeks of freedom. So what? Living on the financial edge makes us a bit arrogant, if only with each other, and what price can you put on this place?

The drive into here bumps and grinds over exposed seams of rock and red dirt along a course that tilts and twists the Suburban to its own edge, then the path plows through a thick sand washout along the gash of the canyon. Native grass meadows turned gold in the heat and drought of August and covered with spacious expanses of the large pines along with some bushlike juniper surround us. A blue sky holding a blaze-yellow sun supports a few puffy white cumulus clouds and all of it wails toward infinity while overhead hawks and eagles cruise the thermal highways on the rim of the canyon. Red walls of rock hundreds of feet high run from north to south for miles, the still snowcapped Big Horn Mountains loom far in the distance, the Middle Fork of the Powder lazily pours out onto open range, huge cottonwoods glow bright green in the midafternoon summer light, layers of rocks and foothills shove and slip at a downward slope toward the south to such an extent that the entire landscape appears to be sinking back into the earth, and the tendency is to stand at an angle to offset the perceived distortion in commonly accepted levels. The river below cascades over falls formed by huge boulders before the clear water gathers in deep sapphire pools no doubt filled with rainbow and brown trout. Our campsite lies beneath the shade provided by an ancient ponderosa that is over one hundred feet tall, our sleeping bags pitched on the thick grass near the edge (as usual) of this precipice, and no other people to destroy our illusion of being a pair of intrepid, throw-all-caution-to-the-wind road bums.

We've done pretty good for ourselves here in Wyoming at a little over 7,000 feet above sea level, or rather this incredible country has done very well by us. Looking west the land keeps rising to over 8,500 feet in gentle sweeps of sloping plateau and hill, all of it covered in grass, pine, and juniper; enormous rock outcroppings explode still-life throughout the country and mark the edge of the diminishing road as it winds farther back into the high country; and again there is the immense drop of the ocher, salmon, rust-brown, and gray cliffs down to the Middle Fork. Near camp, mountain lion tracks—the paw prints five inches wide, at least—pad away in the soft tan sand toward the edge of the canyon. Pinyon jays inform us that they know we have food and lots of it. The gray birds yell and screech at us from the safety of fifty feet of altitude. A raven cruises by much higher in the deepening blue sky. Not indigo and not cerulean. Plain, damn, beautiful blue. Deer browse on a sandstone shelf behind our camp and another golden eagle soars by. We can hear the wind whooshing over its wings, a wind that is hot, dry, and smells faintly of pine, and more than anything, it smells clean. Finding a place like this is our currency, one of the reasons we do what we do.

To reach where we're standing takes about ninety minutes driving west-southwest from the small town of Kaycee, first on a two-lane highway that runs into the Middle Fork through country that grows progressively drier and marked by sage- and cactus-covered hills and bluffs. Eventually the road turns to gravel and within a few miles winds between the buttes of the red wall, a burnt sienna geologic structure that rolls down south toward Casper. Several miles of this and you turn due west on the road in, three miles of five-mph crawling that climbs hundreds of feet above the valley floor.

Kaycee is a typical high plains community with less than three hundred residents, a grocery store-mercantile, several gas stations, a museum, post office, hardware store, motels, and a couple of bars including the Hole-in-the-Wall. Lying out on the high plains as Kaycee does, the wind blows. It's very hot and fly-blown in the summer and very cold with gale-force, sideways snowstorms in the winter. The river flows nearby and where there's water (the true gold of the West) there are cottonwoods. Even in the dryness they smell of damp, slightly rotting wood mixed with a richness of fallen leaves and fertile earth . . . of life. The townsite is dominated by the trees and their shade. The town is located on the southern edge of the old KC cattle ranch, which figured prominently in the Johnson County cattle wars of a century before. The town shows little sign of being ravaged by tourism. No fast-food atrocities, chain motels advertising free continental breakfasts featuring warm milk and orange juice, insipid coffee, dead donuts, and little boxes of brand-name cereals, nor are there any phony replica forts trying to rip off a fast buck on some long-ago Indian War battle site. The majority of travelers pull in off I-25 for fuel or to stretch their legs at the new rest area. Before heading to the canyon we stock up with groceries, gas, and ice along with a few books purchased at the museum. The surest tip-off that tourism isn't full tilt here is the fact that everyone we encounter is friendly, helpful, and eager to talk about directions, the weather, and Butch Cassidy and the Sundance Kid, though the latter subject produces a trace of disgruntlement from a few people, most notably the gray-haired woman running the museum.

These two outlaws of recent overblown reputation—sure they robbed people and more than likely killed their share, but then way back when, who didn't?—are the main reason people stop here to visit. My God, you certainly wouldn't expect someone to drive all the way from Rhode Island for the country or the people. The Wyoming state highway map clearly marks where the infamous Hole-in-the-Wall hideout was and directions guide one somewhat directly to the notorious pair's Outlaw Cave. Two problems present themselves to the superficial visiting historian. One, the road into Hole-in-the-Wall crosses private land and is closed to all but hearty pedestrian traffic and offers a long, strenuous hike through arid snake country. The Outlaw Cave Trail is reached by very tough road, the type that eats two-wheel-drive vehicles and motor homes for brunch. And the trail to the bottom of the canyon and to the cave is a mile-and-one-half scramble straight down over loose rock and cliff. Only one out of a hundred people ever reaches even one of these places, the rest careen madly past the end of the road looking for the cave and are only saved from a Thelma and Louise-esque conclusion to their motorized lives when the bottoms of their cars begin scraping boulders or run into trees just short of a free fall into the abyss. They only get this far after being thoroughly outraged by the fact that they must walk a half-dozen miles or more to see where Butch and Sundance supposedly hid out, and so they press on firmly convinced that the state of Wyoming would not dare make them get out of their cars twice on the same excursion. If they actually reach the cave, the outlaws' names that were carved in the soft rock decades ago are obliterated by graffiti along the lines of Tammy loves Juanita or Bill gives his heart to Bob. Love in the nineties. If Redford and Newman had never been in the fantastical movie that bears the outlaws' names, no one would give a damn about their hideouts in this harsh country, let alone bother to try to track down either location. The few tourists we see far up the canyon road want nothing better than to regain the perceived security of the interstate system, and they all look like they have martinis and Holiday Inns on their minds. Nothing like a summer two-track sojourn in 110-degree heat in the family Plymouth to bring one to his or her senses.

"Honey, I've had enough. I went along with you on your little fiasco down in Cheyenne with that cowgirl, and now this horrible drive to find a couple of damn outlaws that have been dead for years, but enough is enough," the wife says with a mad look promising that the poor guy will never be allowed to forget his brief flirtation with a lithesome ranching lass in the Stockman's bar the other evening. Damn bourbon does it every time. "Get me out of here and to our room in Sheridan before they cancel the reservation. I need a bath, a drink, and a good night's sleep."

And the old boy shrugs and says, "Sure, honey," and wheels the Lincoln Town Car with the Texas plates around in the dust for the long grind back to I-25, but he can't erase the recent vision of that young woman in the Stockman's wearing the skin-tight Levi's, the tight silk blouse, and the worn Stetson. *Whatever hell Martha puts me through, it was worth it,* he thinks as the Lincoln lurches and grinds over the hard rocky road.

Powder River country has long been considered everything some people could ever desire. The Sioux were no exception. What today's ranchers like about this land, the Indians venerated for centuries. As the late T. J. Gatchell of Buffalo, a small town forty miles north of Kaycee, put it, "From the Indians' standpoint, the country was all that could be desired—plenty of shelter, mild winters, sufficient food for their ponies, and an abundance of game in the broken country surrounding them for their own subsistence. It was an Indian paradise." The idea of sharing this land with other tribes, let alone with invading hordes of white men, didn't sit well with the Sioux.

In 1863 John Bozeman had forged a cutoff route to the Montana gold fields. A path that went through the heart of the Indians' paradise. There was a good deal of fighting and mayhem between the miners, settlers, and soldiers and the Sioux, Arapaho, and Cheyenne. Attacks, skirmishes, deaths, tortures. The Bozeman Trail became known as The Bloody Bozeman. Mountain man Jim Bridger's trail was longer but skirted most of the Indians' turf. Eventually a treaty was hammered out among everyone concerned. Unfortunately, while all of this peacemaking was in progress at Fort Laramie, Colonel Henry B. Carrington with seven hundred infantrymen marched past the fort bound for Powder River country. Red Cloud, a Sioux chief, considered this action hypocritical and withheld his signature from the treaty. Little Wolf and Man-Afraid-Of-His-Horse weren't too high on the idea, either. While the Interior Department was negotiating peace, the War Department was organizing what was, in the eyes of many Sioux, aggressive behavior. Government agencies at cross-purposes. Unheard of.

During the Indian Wars of this time a favorite battle tactic of the Sioux was to have a small decoy party lead troops into an ambush where they could be surrounded and wiped out by an overwhelming number of concealed warriors. On December 21, 1866, a detachment was sent out from Fort Phil Kearny to relieve a wood train under attack. Enormous quantities of wood were burned to keep the garrisons of high plains forts warm during the brutal winters that saw temperatures drop to fifty below zero or more. The soldiers toiled constantly at felling, bucking, and hauling the wood to the fort. Captain (brevet Lieutenant Colonel) W. J. Fetterman along with eighty-one officers and men, including two civilians, were slain. Red Cloud, the recognized war chief of the Oglala Sioux; Crazy Horse, who was at that time gaining stature as an Oglala war leader; and High-Back-Bone, Miniconjou war leader, participated in the massacre. Crazy Horse led the decoy party in what may have been the most successful trap in Sioux history, one where perhaps between one hundred to three hundred

Indians were killed, but in the eyes of the warriors, a great defeat had been inflicted on the white man.

Although Carrington still had more than three hundred men at his disposal, the colonel was afraid that the Indians might storm the fort and overwhelm them. John "Portugee" Phillips and Daniel Dixon were sent to Fort Laramie, a distance of 235 miles. They made the trip under extremely cold weather conditions and a pervading fear of being killed by the Indians in four days and nights of hard riding. Some consider this the most remarkable horseback ride in Wyoming history. Reinforcements reached Fort Phil Kearny by mid-January.

The Fetterman Massacre, as it quickly became known back East, caused the Congress to pass an act authorizing the president to appoint a commission to make a general settlement with the Indians of the plains. Fighting, most notably the battle at Little Bighorn that finished off General George Armstrong Custer and his men, continued for years. But the Fetterman Massacre directly and indirectly led to sweeping policy changes that gradually increased the government's military presence in the West, as well as the drafting of numerous treaties that were either revised, and not in the Indians' favor, or never kept, the formation of Indian reservations, and the influx of large numbers of settlers as the century wound to a close. The fort was abandoned in 1882.

Well, hell, that's about as much history as I can usually take in one dose. What I see on this hot, sky-blue, early September day as I walk the land where the Fetterman Massacre occurred, the ground where Fort Phil Kearny stood, are a few remnants of the place as it was decades ago and the locations of facilities like the troop quarters, a hospital, parade grounds, stables, and so on. There is a paved parking lot and a nice air-conditioned museum to my right as I gaze up and down the Piney Fork of the Clear Fork of the Powder River. Succinctly worded signs with detailed maps and layouts tell me where I am standing and where I shouldn't stand. Thick green and brown grasses wave gently in a hot breeze. Trees and bushes line the creek as it flows down out of the Big Horn Mountains towering far beyond the museum in the west. The valley opens onto a framed view of the prairie rolling off toward South Dakota. A few tourists quickly walk the site, then either head into the museum, determinedly to the rest rooms, or back to their cars, bound for someplace more exciting.

Old battlegrounds don't do much for me. I can never really get a sense of what it was like—all of the killing, the dismemberment, the confusion, the gore, the terror, the wild killing rush. None of it. Not at Bull Run or Gettysburg. Not even on the ridge where Custer died. That place reminds me of a theme park now. Another nice museum. A cemetery. Paved walkways and ample signage explaining things. Like the one telling me that men died here. I always wondered what all of those stone markers were about. Thanks to the signs, now I know. Occasionally a rattlesnake suns itself on the baking asphalt. More than twenty years ago I pulled up to the gate at Little Bighorn in the dead of night. The sky was packed with stars and an icy wind was blowing as I struggled over the fence with a bottle of Jim Beam clutched firmly in one hand. I remember wandering the grounds, working my way up to the obelisk that marks the battle site. The feeling was eerie, frightening, and sorrowful. The whiskey didn't help cut the emotions and what initially seemed like a bold, to-hell-with-it lark now felt wrong. I rushed back downhill to my VW Squareback, the hair rising on my neck with the feeling that I was being watched. Now when I pull in here I expect to find cotton-candy booths and carnival rides. That's history in the West. It all gets washed away or blurred until it means nothing. Like here at this now-peaceful, pretty place, a piece of land where so many died so horribly one winter over a century ago does not communicate any of the violence of the Fetterman Massacre, an admittedly key moment in western history. Perhaps I lack the imagination to pick up on any of this. Damn, sometimes I believe in ghosts, like the youthful night at the Little Bighorn. And the tales of early explorers looking for the Northwest Passage intrigue me, their struggles with extreme cold, being terminally lost, or poisoned by the lead sealing containers of their food. All of the weirdness that surrounds that powerful arctic madness. But for some reason the history of the high plains, land I love more than anything, does not have a hold on me. Most likely, I don't care all that much. Obviously what happened in the past dictates to at least a small degree what I'm doing right now, but I still don't really care. I guess I'm doomed to repeat the past in some curiously bizarre way over and over. Maybe I'm doing so right now and am not aware of it. Who the hell knows? What I do know is that I'd rather be standing in a cold, clear trout stream harassing some fat rainbows or waking up some sharp-tailed grouse along the sere hills beyond Piney Creek. I turn and walk back to the parking lot, climb in the Suburban, and head for water, any water.

Before heading back up to the Middle Fork of the Powder and a touch of fishing and imagined solitude, we decide to head out to the Pumpkin Buttes, a series of striking geologic structures rising more than a thousand feet above the surrounding plains. From camp on the rim of the Middle Fork the buttes are visible at fifty miles, shimmering lavender and soft brown like ghosts who have paired things down to basic landscape shapes on an immense scale. The formations are located not far to the west of one of the units of the Thunder Basin National Grasslands. Millions and millions of acres of native grasses, cactus, alkali flats, muddy streams with no hopes of ever becoming rivers, dry creekbeds, bluffs, coulees, buttes, cattle ranches, antelope, jackrabbits, raptors—this is the grasslands. This, like most of the high plains, is a land of little or no water, few people, pump jacks pulling crude oil up from thousands of feet below the sun-baked, cracked dry surface, small towns subsisting mainly on the crapshoot cattle game, and in the fall, big-game hunters looking to pop a big buck mule deer, an antelope, or even an elk wandering among the scattered ponderosa stands of forest. Looking at maps of the country reveals few roads, most of them vastly unimproved dirt, rock, or dust, and most of these petering out at the base of a geologic structure such as the Pumpkin Buttes or at the abrupt edge of a dry wash or just out on some windswept, barren flat.

Prior to entering what appears to be harsh country in the 110-degree plus heat we head back up to Buffalo, a small town of a little more than three thousand people, for supplies. Before visiting the Fetterman Massacre site, we'd loaded up on food and Mounds bars in Sheridan, a bustling town of almost fourteen thousand. Sheridan is slowly undergoing the changes that much of the West is experiencing. Invasions of well-monied out-of-staters leading inevitably to an onslaught of money-crazed developers and their rapacious plans for gated golf course communities, condo-clogged ski resorts, along with highway-straddling strip development featuring the usual fast-food and chain-store suspects. But the downtown is still intact. Main street boasts a western goods store that has a museum filled with Sharps buffalo guns, leather chaps, Winchester rifles, six-shooters, boots, old photos, saddles, and more. Downstairs they use a strong, simple machine that twists hemp fibers into the ropes that world-famous cowboys and plain old working stiffs use throughout the West. I bought a pair of thick calfskin work gloves that went through the mill over these past months with little sign of wear, except for a few bloodstains and singed spots from late-night campfire confusion. There's a fine bookstore, several great bars including the obligatory one called The Mint, cafes, and coffee shops. The people here are laidback and friendly.

Such is not the case in Buffalo, which is undergoing the same growing pains, but not with the same patience and grace. Everyone here is in a hurry, mostly grumpy bordering on rude. The main drag dips and curves narrowly through town. Finding a place to park is troublesome. Asking for directions becomes either an act of courage or foolishness. One gentleman, when asked if there was a bakery in town, said, "Who the hell cares?" We did without donuts. Before the situation turned truly ugly—I was growing restless, angry, and, worst of all, bored with the boorish behavior—we quickly and with stunning élan grab several bags of ice, gas up, and fill our water jugs. When we jump back on the interstate after two hours that lasted too long we are relieved to see Buffalo fade from view in our rearview mirrors.

Why one town, Sheridan, can face adversity with calm, smiling panache and another, in this case Buffalo, can turn into a disgruntled, frantic mess is something of a mystery. They both lie at the base of the Big Horn Mountains. They both have charming creeks flowing through them. Clear Creek at Buffalo. Goose at Sheridan. The weather seems pretty much the same. Hot, cold, windy, snowy, thunderstorms, hailstorms, unreal blue skies. Ranching and recreation are the key businesses in both places. Each time we visit either town over the course of our travels, the personalities of Sheridan and Buffalo hold true to form. Maybe it's the water. Maybe it's the way the wind blows. Beats us. Perhaps some sociologist desperately seeking a grant can do a book on why places like Whitefish and Bozeman have been hell on earth while towns like Broadus and Plentywood feel like home on the road. A couple of clues. Ski areas and yuppies versus hardworking local townspeople with honest values. Don't get me wrong here. I've always dreamed of moving to someplace like Carmel or Newport Beach to while away my life screwing around with stocks and bonds, cell phones, inane cocktail parties, partner swapping, and building a collection of overpriced vintage wines. "I think it has a hint of licorice with a slight taste of pear." Screw that noise. I'd rather work in a hardware store in Kaycee sorting bolts and getting smashed after hours on dago red while comfortably reclined next to the Powder catfishing; or even mend fence out on some godforsaken alkali flat beating off flies and voracious arachnids. But back to the Pumpkin Buttes and their own brand of human-inflicted dysfunction.

To get there you run out Highway 192 that two-lanes it up, down, and around alongside the Powder River. Dry grass hills, sage flats, ranches tucked away beneath tall stands of cottonwoods, bright green irrigated fields of hay, and lots of cattle. Angus. Hereford. A few stray longhorns munching grass next to an irrigation ditch. It's barely noon out and the temperature isn't bothering with hanging around one hundred degrees. One-ten, maybe, as we head north up a relatively level and straight wide dirt road that roughly parallels the Powder along the west side. The country here is open grassland that supports fair numbers of cattle that could be described as a bit thin. The few horses we see look the same as we dip down steeply into a large dry wash and climb back up again rolling along at sixty, dust billowing behind us. The buttes—Table Top Mountain, North, North Middle, South Middle, and South—tower twenty miles to the east with what feels like an ominous disposition. They range in height from 4,825 to 6,049 feet, but seem much higher as they jut straight up from the rolling baseland of the plains. The heat is intense and the air wavers and shimmers causing the buttes to jump in and out of focus. Large lakes appear and vanish with a wild, uncontrollable spontaneity. The water appears to ripple and waves can be seen lapping across the sage desert shoreline. Burned-out summer water, Wyoming mirage style. The only real wet out here is the muddy Powder swooping and bending through the soft variegated claystone, sandstones, and interbedded coals that make up the Wasatch Formation. In some places the coal seams are a couple of miles wide and more than 250 feet deep. Strip mines loom on the baked horizon. Pump jacks work steadily as they pull crude oil from deep beneath the Wasatch and occasionally the rotten egg odor of natural gas fills the air. The land is packed with minerals of all kinds, and of an unexpected nature as we are soon to discover on this bright, sizzling day.

Sixty miles an hour coming up over and around a sweeping bend and the road rolls down past a large ranch yard filled with hard-worked machinery and other cattle business detritus—pickups, tractors, ATVs, flatbeds, semis, haying equipment, a manure spreader, dirt bikes, a couple of snowplows wedged next to a metal Quonset hut, mountains of baled hay, an empty feedlot, riding tractors, an F16, scud missile launcher, stock trucks filled with feed, lawn mowers, a D7, a really banged-up Caterpillar that might be a D9 if size means anything, irrigation pipe, a pair of broken-down pump jacks, a couple of ranch homes in need of paint, repair, and fresh plastic over the cracked storm windows, large cottonwoods hanging on the edge of the Powder, some cows, mangy yard dogs, and yards and yards of gray, collapsing wooden fence. The gravel way narrows and the Suburban lurches across a rusting steel bridge with wooden planking that rattles and buckles as we cross. There are signs all along the way saying we are on a private haul road (running sometimes here and there through Bureau of Land Management land—public turf) and that we must stay on the road or risk running afoul of the law. Or what, man? Lynching? Stoning? Public ridicule? The land looks the same. Wide open. Dry. Rolling hills. Bluffs. Mesas. Sage. Cactus. But what was once fenceless, open range, land free to roam across, is now clearly turning into something contained, controlled, and off-limits, like so much of the good stuff out West. The vibe is taking a dramatic turn for the unpleasantly weird. Feels like mining country to me. Gold. Coal. Copper. Always the ugly sameness to the feel. Like a bad drug or pop-skull whiskey. Rough, "don't fuck with me" overtones fisting their way through a serenely tough landscape. Around the next curve BIG signs warn of radioactive situations in the immediate area. Flaming red letters screaming warnings along the lines of "DANGER," "DON'T EVEN THINK ABOUT GOING

THERE," and "THIS PLACE IS HOT" let us know we aren't chasing petroglyphs and brown trout up in the high Middle Fork country over behind us to the west anymore. There's a plastic-lined pit filled with ugly orange water covered with strange green moss. "Damn, Ginny. Is that stuff glowing?" A few cows are munching on grass growing next to the fence. Got to get my hands on some of that beef. A pound or two a day for a month and who needs a flashlight. Light my way with sizzling beams of uranium-powered juice buzzing from my eyes. An even *bigger* sign says, "VISITORS HANG A RIGHT HERE AND REPORT IN AT THE MINE OFFICES." Not going to fight this one and sneak off to the left and run on down a well-trodden dusty lane to the Pumpkin Buttes and whatever they may be hiding. God only knows what the uranium mine boys got going up here. I know it's uranium because I remember reading a while back in *Roadside Geology of Wyoming* that J. D. Love of the U.S. Geological Survey discovered the powerful stuff in the Pumpkin Buttes in 1951. And that the uranium was originally deposited from ground water seeping into tiny pore spaces between sand grains in the Wasatch and upper Fort Union Formations. The book doesn't say where the ore originally came from. Perhaps the damn Ruskies planted it a long time ago for reasons too labyrinthine for us to comprehend. So we head up a wide, well-maintained gravel road that leads to huge white metal buildings, lots of trucks, and barbed-wire fence. The wind is hot, cooking and blowing grit in spinning clouds across the parking lot. I pull the Suburban up in front of the place labeled "OFFICES"—arrive in a cloud of dust and squeaking brakes as a matter of fact. The red-brown soil washes over a patch of manicured, hot green grass and blows through the open door that leads to a place where visitors, clearly unwanted, I feel, report in. As we pass through a small gate to the grass-way we notice dozens of fat, tame rabbits waddling around. Gray ones. White and black ones. Brown ones. Noses twitching or faces buried in the grass eating away. Our approach and appearance has the remarkable effect of no effect on the animals. It's like we aren't here for the rabbits. They pay no notice of us. Same for the humans, too, apparently. No sign of workers or other human life as we step into a room with dingy white sheet-rock walls, cheap wooden trim, tile floors, dirty windows, sills littered with dead flies. A distorted electronic voice mumbles something about Section 51 over a PA system, but I can't see any speakers. I feel like Ginny and I have just stepped back in time and into a very bad outtake from *The Texas Chainsaw Massacre.* We move timidly down a long paneled hallway that opens into a blazing white lunch-meeting room. Twelve by twelve with enough fluorescent lights to torch the Superdome. A metal table is littered with notepads, pens, crushed Mountain Dew and Coke cans, and stained ceramic coffee cups. An ashtray is full of mangled butts. Marlboro Lights. Newports. Camel straights. Neither one of us wants to be here, but we've both tripped into enough whacko scenes like this one to know that once in, you've got to ride them out. Walking swiftly outside and running like hell back down the way we came won't play well in this venue. The invisible mine employees would soon be rearview-mirror visible riding down on us in big company trucks and more of those same trucks would be pulling across the road in front of us. Some of the men would most likely be armed: .357 Magnums, .44s, 9mms. We'll have to take our medicine and talk to whoever is in charge of this twisted little radioactive show. Then smile a lot. Say thanks a lot, that we're sorry to have been a bother, all the while backing down the hall without discernible motion on our parts, out the door and past the nuclear bunnies, and maybe, with some luck, even all the way back to Kaycee.

Footsteps come jackbooting loudly across the concrete floor of a work bay that I can see a small portion of through a window in a door that leads out of one end of the room we are in. The sound grows in intensity, but keeps on comin' like it is eternal, our latest purgatorial damnation marching forever across an invisible plane.

Two young toughs, muscular in tight white T-shirts, black jeans, and steel-toed boots, burst in from another door behind us. No dirt or mining grime on either one of them. One kid pulls open a small refrigerator located beneath a large bulletin board with nothing on it except a copy of current big-game hunting regs. He pulls a couple of Cokes out and looks at us with questioning eyes.

"Mind if we have these," he asks while handing one to his friend.

"Fine with me," I say as the work-bay door opens revealing a hard-muscled, tan guy of about fifty. Five-nine, 160. White shirt, jeans, boots. He checks me out and I quickly suck my gut in. If there's going to be fisticuffs here I want to look tough, in my dirty jeans, Converse All-Star tennis shoes, Whitefish Brewery T-shirt, and twenty-year-old Cubs hat. He notices the hat with a dismissive slice of a smile. Looks at my forearms, then glances over at Ginny, before shooting a glance beyond my shoulder at the toughs. I catch the merest flicker in his eyes and the two are gone, out the door as if they ain't never been here. *It's the damn Cubs hat*, I think. *Hell, I'm a half foot and forty pounds more than this guy, and he knows he can toss me through the wall.* His look, demeanor, the way he stands ramrod-straight and looks at us, makes me nervous.

"Help you two?"

"Yeah, we saw the sign and are checking in and I wondered if you could show us how to get to the Pumpkin Buttes," and I open a road-weary copy of the *DeLorme Wyoming Atlas & Gazetteer*, our navigational bible of general accuracy. The guy leans over the maps with me, straightens, and says in a voice filled with man-ufactured disappointment for us, "That's all private property over there. I've worked here over twenty years and I still have to ask the rancher for permission to hunt up that way. You won't be able to get up there."

We both can clearly see that the road in question runs through
BLM land, the orange highlighting is unmistakable. His look is
a challenge. One of those "you want to argue with what I'm tellin'
you here, buddy" numbers. I am pissed about the con, the mine,
and the mining industry in general, but keep my cool while
thankfully Ginny diverts the intensity with talk about the Middle
Fork of the Powder, and the guy, figuring he has this one dealt
with and all but over, generously keeps trying to spin us out of
here and on our way by letting us know where some more petroglyphs are and where some more fishing is. He tells us in vague
terms that there are pine trees and antelope up on the buttes, but
very little water, but my mind is focused on the matter that is
being pushed to the side. I want to find out a little more about
the rancher and his BLM buttes.

"You know this guy?" I ask and Ginny flashes me a "be cool"
look. "If you've got his number, maybe I could give him a call."

"There's no one hunting up there now, but I think he's got it
closed off." This comes from a husky bearded guy wearing the
uranium uniform of choice here: T-shirt, jeans, and boots. Where
or when this one appeared beats me. Maybe he was always here
pretending to be the refrigerator. "Number's in the book,
though."

And the first guy, who never did introduce himself but is most
definitely in charge, pulls a phone book from a chipped and
stained walnut desk hiding in another corner. He thumbs through
the pages and says, "Yeah, I think that's his name. This should
be it," and I copy the rancher's name and number down onto the
map near the road in question; and I sure am wondering about
this mine boss who has been here for twenty years and has to ask
for permission and how come he isn't all that sure of the man's
name or number. Strange shit going down here in Wyoming's
uranium fields.

He turns on me and steps a bit closer without moving his feet.

"You know how bachelor ranchers are," he says by way of apologetic explanation, but what he's really saying is, *Don't bother trying to reach the man. He's one of us and I'll tip him before you call.* "In and out of the house. Never home."

And I nod and we both say thanks while backing out of the room. The two men watch us as do the young toughs leaning on the paneling at the far end of the hall, their T-shirts and complexions glowing with a touch of green. Must be the ultraviolet lights. We casually hustle our act out the door, past the insane rabbits, out to the Suburban, and out of there.

"Yeah, John. You know how ranchers are. Never home," Ginny mocks.

"You bet. Okay, asshole, we get the point. You got some real top-secret, sneaky shit taking place up here and if we don't leave, we'll probably never leave. Probably get to take a dip in that toxic leach pad."

Mining. That's the way it goes. Doing stories on the proposed Seven-Up Pete gold operation on the Blackfoot a decade ago, where the mine manager had all of my books, environmental newspaper columns from fifteen years back, a page full of legal-pad notes on me, all of it spread out on his desk for me to see like "Listen, punk, we know who you are and we can handle it. No sweat. Get it." Or trying to get permission to walk the grounds of a gold mine in central Montana with no luck. Slick stonewall and con all the time.

Yeah, I get it. Mining is big money that owns lots of politicians, and public land isn't really public land when it comes to gold, coal, silver, copper, or uranium. Try taking pictures of the coal strip mines down by Decker, Montana, if you want to check out this industrial grade friendliness.

Yeah, I get it. I'm leaving, but I'm going to write about it.

So we head back down the road, roar across the steel and wood bridge, and blast by the ranch and howl at seventy miles an hour, slipping and sliding in the gravel and dust, back down the road to the highway that leads to Kaycee and back up to upper Powder

River country. Past country where much of the Johnson County wars took place in 1889. Where big-time ranchers claimed to be fed up with the lack of justice being meted out to rustlers or, more likely the case, to homesteaders running small herds and probably walking off with a few of the cattle kings' cows, and grazing their own few animals on prime grass in the region. The kings hung James Averell, a homesteader who was vocal in his opposition to the near absolute land and water control of the big ranchers. They also strung up Ella Watson, also known as Cattle Kate, who has been described as a prostitute and Averell's woman. By 1891–92 things had escalated to the point where a force of cattle king–picked men would invade Johnson County and kill designated rustlers, mostly small-scale ranchers and possibly local law enforcement officials; or as Joe DeBarthe, editor of the *Buffalo Bulletin*, said on December 24, 1891:

> The big cattleman . . . own thousands upon thousands of acres of rich Wyoming land that they have deliberately stolen from the government; land they hired on to take up, make proof on, and deed over . . . They . . . gobbled up all the rich creek bottoms they could . . . and the rest of the state was their range . . . When a man who had been working in one of their outfits had the audacity to take up 160 acres of land for himself the big fellas blackballed him.

Everything came to a head outside of Kaycee when twenty-five Texas gunmen arrived in Casper by train. Assisted by Wyoming men they surrounded a cabin, eventually set fire to it by rolling a flaming wagon at the front door, and killed Nate Champion, a suspected rustler who managed to hold off the Invaders, as they were known, most of a day. The standoff took precious time, time the Invaders feared had been used to alert the state militia, so they figured it was a prudent idea to flee the area and head up to

Buffalo where they got wind from a friendly rancher that the acting governor of Wyoming, Amos Barber, had wired the president of the United States saying that "an insurrection exists in Johnson County . . . against the government of the . . . state . . . Open hostilities exist and large bodies of armed men are engaged in battle." President Harrison authorized the use of federal troops. The Invaders were rounded up. Their attorneys cut the appropriate deals and they went back to Texas, with the Wyoming men who'd joined the fracas along the road released on their own recognizance. And in many ways that was the beginning of the end of the range wars so many movies have been made about. Uranium turf wars. Cattle range wars. Indian wars. I guess musician Joe Jackson had a good reason for naming one of his albums years ago *War All the Time*. More violent, dead history that lives on today in mutated form.

So it's back past where a lot of this happened, into town for more ice and gas, and back up the hard-time track that leads to our aerie high above the Middle Fork of the Powder.

The day breaks clear and slightly warm. Several mule deer were browsing in the tall grass a few yards from where we are sleeping on the ground. When I sit up, they bound in stiff-legged leaps up through an opening in the limestone wall behind camp, their hooves clattering on the rock. As the sun rises, the blaze of yellow light works its way steadily down into the canyon. Layers of sedimentary rock are revealed in a slow-paced slide show. Without even a whisper of wind the muted roar of the Middle Fork drifts up from the bottom of the canyon. We pack water, apples, cheese, bread, and Oreos in a daypack along with a box of flies, tippet material, forceps, splitshot, floatant, and Day-Glo yellow strike indicators. I carry the rod, disassembled in two pieces, in my right hand. A trip down to the river earlier in the year had borne out the truth of a friend's long-ago tip that the fishing for rainbows and brown trout was "not all that bad." Now that I know the lay of the river some after that July exploration, I intend to seek the fish in earnest. The trail, a generous term, we will take is called the Outlaw Cave Trail, supposedly because Butch and Sundance had hidden in one of the many large holes eroded in the rock walls not far above the river.

The way drops steeply down through the ponderosa, juniper, and cactus, sheerly along the faces of rock walls, or tumbles down over loose rock and gravel. Perhaps a mile and a half all but straight down through the layers of rock. The air is cool in the morning shade and smells of pine. We place our feet with care, grab on to limbs, or slide on our butts down slick stone surfaces. By the time we reach a small ledge fifty feet above the water our knees are rubbery from the stress of resisting gravity's pull and fighting miniature landslides. Looking far below the water is the clearest sapphire, flowing along slick runs, cascading over jams of large boulders, or breaking and splashing through swift riffles. Fifteen minutes farther along I stare into a pool below and watch as a couple of dozen rainbows up to twenty inches long glide easily to the surface to sip small aquatic insects trapped in the meniscus. The fish are muscular and full-bodied, perhaps averaging two pounds plus each. More than fifty pounds of rainbows almost at my feet. Now I am really shaking and I scramble, leap, and finally crash-land on a small grass and gravel bank that juts out into a tight seam of current at the end of the pool. I can hear Ginny's laughter from above, the pleasing sound echoing among the narrow canyon's walls.

I'd walked down in a pair of bird hunting boots that would double as wading shoes. Jeans for waders. Shirt with big pockets for a vest. Cubs hat. Shades. Rod rigged. As I strip out line for the first cast upstream I spot a half-dozen good-sized trout holding on the edges of the current, beneath the thin white foam of swirling eddies or just suspended in the still middle of the deep pool that was aquamarine when seen up close, like from waist deep in the river. Small gray caddis are whirring above the water and the trout are eating these now in splashing rises. I run a cast at an angle up to the edge of the current and a pair of fat rainbows comes to the surface, mouths open, and almost take the elk-hair caddis imitation simultaneously. I set the rod with a force more befitting a tuna-boat fisherman and the tippet pops, both fish retreating to submarine invisibility. My legs have stopped shaking in the cool water, but my hands take up the beat, so I spend the next ten minutes tying another elk hair on. At forty-eight my close-work vision is about shot and I am fighting a ridiculous battle to avoid wearing glasses. Threading 5X tippet through the eye of a #16 hook is a case study in self-induced humiliation. The sound of laughter washes across the rock again and I look up to see her red hair burning in the glow of the sun now well over the canyon rim.

"Need longer arms, John."

"I've almost got it now, Ginny," and the line goes through. I don't bother to glance back at her. I know I have the situation under control.

The next cast interested a few more large rainbows, but before they take, the current drags the fly away, exposing the hook and its feathers, dubbing, and thread for what it is. A fake. Another cast connects with a smaller fish that leaps several feet above the water a few times before running deep and scattering the rest of the rainbows to the shelter of underwater, drowned logs and shadowy pockets beneath thick tangles of willow and alder. This trout runs close to fourteen inches, dark green back, hundreds of black spots, silver flanks with a taste of gold, bright purple-crimson lateral band and a white belly. When I slip the fly from his mouth he races to cover. The other trout resume their feeding, but will have nothing to do with my elk hair or my hopper pattern or a half-dozen mayfly ties or even a large brown woolly bugger wrapped with cree hackle. Even this far from the hordes of anglers descending upon western streams, the few souls that have made it all the way down to the bottom of the canyon have proven enough to educate these wild trout. They've learned. A couple of opportunities per pool and that was it. The way it should be. Not like some hammered spring creek that the sports pay too much money to fish with excessively long, spiderweb-fine leaders and #26 flies. Those fish have seen it all and are afraid of nothing in the way of artificials.

As Russell Chatham demonstrated one night outside his Livingston restaurant while crouched down to street level and looking up like a gray-haired brown trout, "Oh, God, what the fuck are these idiots throwing at me now? It's bad enough that I'm stuck in this spring creek trout ghetto, but won't they ever stop throwing this shit at me?" And he's right. The fish could be termed wild, but they are also hardened, streetwise salmonids unlike the fish in this river that are relatively easily fooled once or twice before their natural learning curve kicks in and they vanish like hookers during a LA cop street sweep.

As I work my way upstream the canyon walls close in and lean out over me. Red rock arches and holes worn through the rock cut frames for the blue sky and distant upward panoramas of cliffs, pine, and slide slopes covered in sage. Groupings of mud nests cling to sheer faces. Made by the swallows, which I see soaring and curving along the stream course. Game trails wander along the slopes, appear to vanish when they meet the rock, only to appear again traversing the next sage slope. A band of mule deer picks its way across a trail several hundred feet above, the lean, dusty gray animals enter from the right, pick their way through the rock and brush as though they were part of a living painting before disappearing behind the left edge of a twenty-foot oblong hole in the wall of stone behind me. I fish my way up through several miles of stream taking rainbows in the pools, mostly on dead-drifted Hare's ears nymphs. And browns on the flats of white cobble, the fish coming out of nowhere and pouncing on a #10 elk hair that must look like a grasshopper or some other big bug. The browns are all light-colored on their backs closing in on tan, protective coloration matching the streambed. After a bunch of trout caught, released, missed, or broken off, I retrace my steps down the river, clambering down the falls, walking stooped beneath cottonwoods whose bases are choked with dense undergrowth, and finally wading armpit deep through a last deep run before coming upon Ginny swimming in the first pool with the rainbows that seem to have accepted her as one of them. The fish are feeding on caddis and now small mayflies, some of the rainbows rising within ten feet of her.

She gets out. Shakes herself, hair cascading droplets that sparkle prismatically in the light, and walks over to a flat rock warmed by the sun. We drink our water, munch the cheese, bread, apples, and cookies, and then nod off in the afternoon glow. A few thousand years later we come to and walk downriver to where the Outlaw Cave stares down at us darkly from a vantage point of one hundred feet. We've been told in Kaycee that Butch's and Sundance's names carved in the soft rock so long ago are spoiled by more recent graffiti and that the cave is full of bat guano, bird shit, and spiders. We give the place a pass and hold on to preconceived visuals of just the two outlaw names carved in there. What they must have been like, been thinking, what all of this was like a century ago. Maybe much like today.

We head back up in late afternoon. The scramble down took forty minutes. The climb back up is no longer, but harder on the lungs. Along the way we spook a few rattlesnakes that rattle and hiss at our noisy, grumbling approach before the snakes slither off into the dark, scratchy safety of the thick sage plants that grow six to eight feet tall down here. The heat of the day releases the plants' pungent herbal scent. I also see a few spiders that strongly resemble brown recluses, so I make sure that I watch where I place my hands the rest of the way. Once on top at the rim we look back down at the now turquoise-colored water that sparkles and flashes in the dropping orange sun. We head back to camp, grill some game hens, steam some broccoli and carrots, and drink gallons of water before sitting around a fire sipping tea and shooting the breeze with dozens of bats that swoop and dive around our heads.

The stars come out. The moon rises. We go to sleep.

In the morning we rise and begin packing our gear in preparation for a trip far away to an isolated piece of southeastern Montana. While loading the back of the Suburban, a Johnson County deputy sheriff, driving a marked Ford Bronco, lurches up to our camp. He checks us out with a cop gaze, takes off his Johnson County cop ball cap, wipes his forehead on his uniform shirtsleeve (it's already hot), slicks back his hair, and leans out the window.

After a few conversational warm-ups, he tells us he's up here checking on a bunch of out-of-state "folks" that drove up to hike down the trail, saying five are already down at the river and more are on the way. That's all he tells us about why he's up here, but he tells us about the petroglyphs and the other place to fish. Like the uranium mine guy, only this deputy is pleasant. A good guy who wishes he could fish with us instead of attend to a bunch of out-of-state yahoos.

I mention that I used to live in Whitefish, Montana, up in the northwest part of the state and he asks me why I moved. I'm at a loss for words and just look at him.

"Out-of-staters ruined it, didn't they?" he asks and adds immediately, "California skiers. ATVs. Things should be licensed. They play hell with the land. Ski hills aren't worth much either."

We all talk about the land and how it's being bought up, cut up, and overused, before a couple more cars lurch up near us. Virginia and Colorado plates. The cop sighs resignedly. Wipes his forehead again. Slicks back his hair once more. Puts on his ball cap and leans back out the window.

"I'll let you folks git on your way, now," and the message is clear one more time, though this man is warning us that there could be trouble on the way and he doesn't want to see us caught up in it. "Have a nice trip," and he pulls on his shades, checks the pistol in a holster on his right hip, and drives down to what is now a group of thirty people or more. We finish packing and head out past the gathering of people that seem wildly out of place up here. Wearing double-knit pants, brand-new, store-bought, recreational catalogue-ordered hiking outfits, sport coats, polished street shoes. All new vehicles—cars, SUVs, vans—none of them with Wyoming plates. A plastic scene that looks like trouble. On the way back down we pass more of the same. One guy with poofy white hair, nylon black-checked shirt, wrap-around, large-frame shades, and driving a brand-new shiny green sedan bounces blithely up the track past us. A little farther on we come across four hard-looking men, each carrying a large pistol and preparing to head out on dusty ATVs. They are in direct contrast to the people at the trailhead. These men look like hard-core, oil-field types, or ranch hands or plain old roustabouts working on an early day beer drunk and looking for trouble. They stare at us with cold, mean looks and drink their Oly beers in bottles. Maybe this is what the Johnson County deputy is so worried about. A confrontation between these well-armed, well-oiled four and the out-of-state city slickers. What are they? Animal rights ding-a-lings come to protest my harassing the trout. Environmentalists wanting to save some little-known arachnid species. Addled historians without a cause or a clue looking to rewrite the history of Butch and Sundance? Or maybe they are relatives of the Texas couple in the Lincoln Town Car we saw earlier in the week, concerned relations in search of their wandering family members.

The Johnson County wars, present-day style.

We head on down the road and back to Montana.

Rancher-cowboy Bud Blankenship atop his horse, Jack, one October day in Tongue River country, Montana.

4

DOWN BROADUS,
MONTANA WAY

THERE IS NOTHING TO SEE BUT WHITE. An early April blizzard. Yesterday was sunny and in the seventies, but today the wind is howling and a foot of snow blankets the coulees, bluffs, meadows, our campsite, and the slightest of two-tracks leading to an even trickier road out of here. Somehow Ginny managed to build and start a fire in the fire pit I'd built many years ago, the one I stood around alone for countless nights as I watched the flames flickering as sparks spiraled up to the stars while coyotes howled and late-arriving turkeys "putted" and "purted" to roost trees in the dark. The fire is burning nicely in the storm, orange flames licking at the snow. I toss a couple of pinecones in the blaze. They catch immediately and this time send a few sparks weakly toward the dense mass of dark clouds locked above our dry (though snowbound) camp far out in the middle of the plateau country lying between the Tongue and Powder Rivers of southeastern Montana.

We'd come here to begin working on this book and, more importantly, because we couldn't take hanging around the house or Livingston one more day. Winters are on the mild side in town, but being locked in to one place from November through March with my two children is now way too much. Ginny and I had broken up and made up a dozen times or so during the winter, spent a night or two apart in motel rooms or at friends' homes, tried to quit smoking once or twice to see how ugly things could really get, and to make the whole mad deal truly interesting I'd spent the time writing a novel in complete self-absorption and less than delightful humor. So one day last week Mom called and immediately recognized the signs of terminal cabin fever. She volunteered to make the 360-mile run over from Whitefish in the northwest corner of the state and watch the kids for a week or so. We jumped at the chance and even secured a magazine assignment up north in Jordan. That work done, we drove through the early spring countryside that is just starting to green up. Antelope are grazing on the sides of hills—females grouped below stately bucks who watch their harems with casual alertness.

I've taken few people into this country. With the exception of fellow writer Bob Jones, none of my other close friends can figure out what the hell I'm doing here. They look at me and after a few drinks ask, "So this is it?" Then drain their blue enamel coffee cups and ask, "What do you do here?" When I reply, "Enjoy the peace and solitude," they get up, walk over to where a bottle or two of Jim Beam is resting, grab one or both, bring them back to their chair, take a healthy blast from one or both bottles, throw a stick or two on the fire, and say, "You're fucking nuts, Holt. Let's go fish somewhere, anywhere, tomorrow." That's how it goes except for Bob, who, when I first brought him in up a narrow, deeply rutted, and rocky cut that passes for a road, yelled out the window, "What damn good country, John," and smiled and laughed and added, "damn good." But then Bob and I are easily amused and live for damn good country. The kind like this down on the Custer National Forest where hundreds-of-feet-tall sandstone cliffs guard the entrance to the plateau. Land where you drive along roads that have interesting features like a hairpin curve with space falling away on both sides forever and called "The Dip of Death" by local ranchers. A place where stands of ponderosa weave and wrap themselves along the slopes of the bluffs and hills and grow very large, orange-red, scaly-barked trunks several feet thick, down through steep coulees carved out by spring runoff and heavy rains where the water pours down and over yellow-tan slabs of sandstone that look like steps leading to an unknown temple for a very high priest. Drive for hours without seeing another vehicle as you wind through many square miles of deep green, wild fields or through dense stands of pine or alongside small streams shaded by tall cottonwoods and willows and alder. A vastness where coyotes remember my name and Bob's and now Ginny's. Where eagles and hawks glide across the sky looking for rabbits. Black bears and Roosevelt antelope hide out here, as reportedly do some wolves. Every friendly rancher (and all the people we've met down here are open and gracious) says, "Of course there're wolves around," and shrugs because it's no big deal to him. A place where goofy turkeys up to thirty pounds roam alone or during the fall in groups of a hundred or more—a ton and a half of turkeys in one glance, magnificent birds that sometimes fly off with surprising alacrity and grace instead of running off through the forest with the speed of quarter horses. Country where every so often the stars and planets and galaxies come out with such intensity after midnight that their light makes the land glow as all of them descend on me with such intensity that every time I look up I pass out. And where the northern lights flash up above the horizon like soft green theater lights before sending curtains and streamers shooting far over my head and Bob's and now Ginny's, the light shading all the way south somewhere. This long-time waterless camp is the only place in the world where I am always truly at peace with myself in the company of the wild and benign spirit of this far beyond ancient land.

Yeah, only two of my friends get it, but that's plenty. I always wanted to share Tongue River country with Ginny, but when we split apart four years back for an eternal year that seemed aimed for eternity I figured I'd be coming here alone for the duration, until that one spring she called from Minnesota and asked if she could fly out and visit and would I take her to "your camp in the Tongue." I did and she wondered at first what all my fuss was about or as she said to me later, "I thought that sure this is nice land. There are lots of pretty trees and green grass. And it's quiet and the clouds in the sky are pretty, but so what," and she laughed when she told me this because she "gets it" now. "And then after the first night when we were sleeping on the ground and you kept the fire going all night and that huge, bright full moon came up over the bluffs and trees, right over your, our, fire pit, and then the coyotes started to howl and we howled back and they answered and we kept it up most of the night and that one lonely robin kept trying to call in a mate until he gave up exhausted at dawn"—and she pauses briefly in the telling to look at me and then continues—"and I finally gave up, lost my bullshit ego and preconceptions, and submitted to the place and never felt so much strength and power anywhere before. Not Nepal. Not Texas [well, what did you expect, girl?]. Not anywhere. And all the stars. You were right. They drop down and when you look at them, they knock you out. They're too much. This country is a magic, spiritual place."

Like I said, she "gets it."

And so it's April with an out-of-control blizzard raging around us and Ginny's happy as hell with her fire. I turn on the car radio for the weather and learn first that Annie Proulx will be reading from her new collection of short stories *Close Range* tonight at a bookstore in Sheridan, Wyoming, about ninety minutes' drive from here when it's dry out, but we can't make her gig tonight. The storm is supposed to let up this afternoon and then the temperature will drop to near zero according to the radio. That's our chance, I think. Right now the snow next to the warmer ground is melting and turning the so-called roads into impassable gumbo.

We'll drive out when the stuff is frozen, through the thick snow and ice. I tell Ginny our plan and she smiles, throws some more wood on the fire, and gives me a hug. It beats the hell out of standing here in this storm alone. And I've done that a few times in the past, but for some reason I think of a trip to nearby Broadus for catfish last year in May . . .

. . . It's very dark out, even with all the stars and the random driveby, fizzling green meteor. 'Round midnight songbirds are singing and owls are booming as they charge through the sky. A lone cow is bellowing pitifully, the sound cutting bell-clear through the muddy rushings of the Powder River. Wild, intact country. Whatever is at the end of the rod I am holding is doing whatever it damn pleases, runs up the narrow Little Powder River and boiling rolls along the far bank. Can't see a damn thing, but I can feel and hear the fish as it struggles somewhere out there. Flashes of far-off lightning illuminate jagged bluffs and dry hills that drift off in all directions. The thunder sounds much later, muffled by distance. This natural river system is so intact, so healthy, that the place is alive with life. Songbirds by the hundreds sing and chirp throughout the night. Coyotes howl. Owls hoot, and the catfish bite.

Finally the fish slightly reveals itself. An eight-to-ten-pound channel catfish swirling in the pea-soup water and roiling the muddy bottom. Just a touch closer and I'll grab the sucker, but nothing comes easy for some of us. A pair of curious muskrats motor upstream as though on a leisurely cruise. They circle the angry fish cutely avoiding my line. They look at the mayhem in the water thrashing beneath their paws, then up at us with an expression of natural disgust, before moving off into the night. The catfish is dragged up onto the slippery bank. Thick leather gloves are pulled on. This is man's play here. Chasing the noble cat is the sport of addled kings. The fish's whiskers can cause a most painful sting and I've moved beyond digging pain. Slipping and sliding to the river, I grab the creature by its tail and fling it up on the bank, knocking over a container of ripe chicken livers and another one holding treble hooks and lead sinkers.

Ah yes, the sport of kings right here on the Little Powder, in the depths of a late April evening. We are wandering royalty indulging in regal pleasures.

Ginny photographs the cat as it rests on a huge, long-dead cottonwood trunk. The silver grays, whites, and black spots go nicely with the shades of weathered wood. How artistic. We hurry so that we can plop the fish back into the river. I'm not concerned, but my friend is. She worries about such things. Hell, if you're of a cruel mind you can throw a few of them in the bed of a pickup, lurch and weave along dusty back roads swilling warm cans of Schmidt beer for hours as the cats bounce around with empty oil cans, Jim Beam bottles, rusted tow chains, and Slim Jim wrappers, then return to the river and put the cats back in the water. They'll swim away. They're tough. They won't die, but I don't do this at all anymore. I only mentioned the possible diversion to give some idea of how hearty catfish are. I treat all fish, especially the ones I kill to eat, with respect. There are so many gods and esoteric deities chasing my soul now . . . man, I don't want or need any more running down my ragged ass, but I digress from the cat at hand.

Yes, we are using a fly rod and a spinning rod, too (just in case a local catfisher shows up). But delicate insect imitations, not even woolly buggers drenched in essence of chicken liver, are not being skillfully cast to rising *Ictalurus punctatus*. No way. Size 6 treble hooks loaded with gobs of chicken liver and weighted with several sinkers of marble proportions are heaved into the turbid Little Powder. The channel cats are on their spring spawning run and in this small stream that is no more than fifty feet wide at its most robust and the turbid gem is less than fifteen minutes outside of the cow town of Broadus.

Broadus is a small place of, well, less than a thousand cheerful souls who have always been nothing but friendly and helpful to us whenever we wander down this way, which is often. Cattle ranches are everywhere around here, so are pickups, cowboys, and ranch women. The town is the county seat, features several bars, a damn good restaurant called The Judge's Chambers ("FINEST FOOD IN 2,000 MILES" says one sign not far outside of Biddle, population six, near the Wyoming border a few cold drinks south of here), a couple of bars, motels, gas stations, grocery store, hardware store, beauty parlor, and so on. We once did a story on the restaurant for a magazine and the owner, Jean Hough, has always treated us like long-lost friends (even before the article was published). Hough comes from a ranching background and used to tend sheep far out on the prairie when she was eleven, armed with a rifle and sheltered by an old wagon. She did this on her own. It was her chore. That's Broadus. People work. Take care of their own business. Help their neighbors and are kind to strangers like us. We've often thought of moving here and disappearing from all of it, all of the modern crap, but we don't. Broadus is these people's home and we're not ones to drop in permanently and uninvited.

We hook up (tarpon terms seem appropriate here) with fish from six to ten pounds steadily. Probably tons of them swimming past silently out of sight. There is barely time to set the nine-foot, eight-weight rod into the crook of a stout stick before the tip is jerked toward the river. I dive forward out of my chair, grab the rod, and reel backward to set the hook. The catfish goes ballistic and runs upriver. An eight-weight will at least slow any trout I've caught in Montana. Not catfish, and relatively small ones at that. Twenty pounds is not unheard of in this region. These boys power upstream in a wake of foam and indescribable detritus, the English reel screaming as though it were being subjected to some hideously obscene act, the rod's dainty tip pulled beneath the water's brown surface. Twenty minutes or more later the cat finally tires and is brought in. The hapless cat is tossed on the bank, photographed in a coating of dirt and leaves, then either returned to the river or put in the cooler for a deep-fried fillet dinner the next evening. Blood sport. The best of all behavior.

Earlier in the day the drive in on a sandy two-track was lovely. Huge, very old cottonwoods filter the light turning everything a soft blue-green. Last year's cattails stand tall and silver-gold next to the river. Whitetails bound away, tails brightly signaling our intrusion. Domestic sheep plod off into the trees bleating hoarsely. We set up camp and went off to fish in the mid-eighties, a hot, dry wind blowing sand and dirt in our eyes. I've never caught catfish in daylight, but someone in town said anytime is a good time, so I tried, for hours. Ginny sat on a log clutching her camera that was wrapped in a plastic bag to protect it from damage. Finally she said, "Enough!" and went back for a nap. I hung on for a while longer before giving up and deciding that a brief lie-down would be appropriate.

Now in the cooling darkness I am covered with the blood of chickens, bits of the birds' livers, and the slime of the raging cats, and I'm using a fly rod. At least my integrity as a consummate purveyor of marginally esoteric B.S. remains intact. In addition to channel cats there are also black and yellow bullheads and the most fearsome of all, the stonecat. Prior to this spring I'd only heard rumors of this species' voracious appetites and fearsome power. To catch one of these was a dream beyond imagining or comprehension.

The excitement was intense, palpable, as we drove south on a red dirt road that wound through eroded bluffs and coulees worn ragged by wind and water. I'd often doze off only to be awakened as I banged my head on the dash when Ginny braked for open-range cattle. Ponderosa pine clung to the sides of the hills. Antelope grazed on new grass. The Powder River described long,

lazy curves as it flowed north. A shotgun-blasted sign said "WEL-
COME TO WYOMING," so we turned around, dropped down a two-
track that led to the river, opened a gate, drove through, and set
up camp above the water. The river was already rising from runoff
and rain, slurping by more like mud than water. Thick stuff.
Looking across the river I spotted a dead, bloated cow, legs splayed
and pointing to the sky. The sign I'd been looking for. Dead cow.
Raging catfish. I could see the connection. This had to be the
place.

After impatiently waiting for dusk, I rigged the eight-weight,
pulled out an olive woolly bugger that had been soaking for several days in a plastic container of chicken livers, tied it on, and
launched the thing far across the river. As the pattern was slowly
stripped in something jerked the line and I hauled back to set the
hook, totally unprepared for the struggle that followed. A pale
flesh-colored fish that went easily over six inches soared past my
head and landed in last season's tall, dead grass behind me. I knew
this was tough fishing but I was not ready for the battle that ensued.
Nearly thirty minutes were spent trying to find the fish in the grass,
weeds, and wild roses. When I finally found the thing, I lifted that
catfish in both hands, held it high in the sky as an offering to the
angling gods who once again shone down on me.

A stonecat. A lifetime dream realized, and on a fly with only
0X tippet. More skilled anglers than I have spent lifetimes casting
to these elusive fish, never connecting, let alone landing one. And
this cat measured seven inches. A trophy. (There are unconfirmed
reports of foot-long specimens being taken in the 1890s, but I'm
skeptical.) This fish was at least six years old and weighed three
or four ounces. Ginny documented the event on film. I have
friends who don't believe some things I tell them and her pictures
would silence their rude doubts. The stonecat was put back in the
river. The joy we experienced as we watched that catfish struggle
down through the thick water to freedom was like nothing either

of us had ever known. Hitting a steer with our Suburban outside of Roy, surviving the insane onslaught that is archery season in the Missouri Breaks, doubling on western meadowlarks last year up by Plentywood, none of those touched the magic of this stone-cat. A special fish. We could only smile at each other. Beyond words. Then we returned to our fire and grilled a couple of pounds of Montana beef.

Noble catfish. The only true game fish of the northern high plains. We'd finally come home again and it felt right . . .

Nearly three decades ago when I first started exploring this part of Montana I stopped for gas in Lame Deer, a small town on the northern part of the Northern Cheyenne Indian Reservation. I filled up the truck, paid inside, and then I looked around. It was a cool, blustery late April afternoon. Cheyenne were walking along the streets or coming into the station for cigarettes. I had never seen such impressive people before. The men I saw (I noticed no women on this trip) were all around six feet tall, very dark-skinned, and with features that bore a striking resemblance to photographs I'd seen of Mongolians (more than likely their indirect ancestors). Long, jet-black hair. Most of them were dressed in jeans, cotton plaid shirts or T-shirts, and boots. Physically they were the hardest, toughest people I'd ever encountered. Lean and muscular, this strength wasn't so much visual as sensed. They broadcast an aura of power and endurance that seemed to reflect the harsh country I was in, that was their home. None of them spoke English and the sound of their native tongue seemed out of this world, words and phrases that cut the air in unfamiliar rhythms and tones. The entire scene with these impressive Native Americans seemed alien, much as I'm sure they thought of our brutal white culture, if they thought of us at all. The image of these Cheyenne roaming the high plains hunting and warring with the Crow, Sioux, and Blackfeet, and later my race, struck home. I would not want to fight for my life against these men. I'd be dead in an instant.

All tribes of the high plains were warlike in nature and the Northern Cheyenne were no exception. Long ago Sweet Medicine, considered by the tribe to be a prophet and a savior, and who may have been derived from a distant man, created the four military societies of the tribe when he appeared on different ridges in five kinds of dress—that of a chief and the four groups. He left the tribe after doing this and when he returned he organized the societies. They were called the Fox, Elk, Red Shield, and Dog. Eventually a fifth society, the Contrary or Clown Society, was formed. There were two types of Contraries—individual warriors with strict vows of bravery and those whose activities were of a more ceremonial nature. The bravery of Northern Cheyenne warriors was well known among other tribes and Suicide Warriors would rush the enemy exposing themselves to death until they were killed. These warriors were few in number and their exploits are remembered in stories.

Those free, open days in this country have been over for more than a century. The expansion of the white race saw to that, and this was foretold by Sweet Medicine who is said to have had visions that led to these words:

They will be powerful people, strong, tough. They will fly up in the air, into the sky, they will dig into the earth, they will drain the earth and kill it. All over the earth they will kill the trees and the grass, they will put their own grass and their own hay, but the earth will be dead—all the old trees and grass and animals. They are coming closer all the time. Back there, New York, those places, the earth is already dead. Here we are lucky. It is nice here . . . But they are coming all the time, turn the land over and kill it . . .

Clearly Sweet Medicine was a man of vision. All he saw came true or is coming true. Every time I call up the vision of the first time I saw the Northern Cheyenne men in the early 1970s I wonder what all of this country must have been like two hundred years ago.

There's a spring blizzard blowing snow down on us now. The storm came out of nowhere and was only vaguely predicted by area weather forecasters. Yesterday was warm, late-springlike weather. Today is cold, white-out, winter, a not uncommon happening in the West in April. I wish it was that warm right now and that we will be able to sneak out of here tomorrow at dawn under the cover of cold temperatures. The wind picks up. Ginny stokes the fire and we climb into the back of the Suburban to read and rest. While lying down I pause in my reading of *Man with an Axe* by Jon Jackson and think about the threats to this place. Nowhere is safe anymore. Some well-monied West Coast yahoos have already built a gated golfing community down in Wyoming along the Tongue River. Damn straight. That's why I'm out here. To live behind a gate with a rent-a-cop harassing my visiting friends for ID and motive all the while secure in my cookie-cutter condo that looks out over eighteen holes of water-sucking, overfertilized idiocy. If the high plains and Tongue River country mean anything to me, it certainly doesn't have anything to do with golf; or coal and strip mining, either.

Only forty miles from here massive machinery, tons of explosives, and hundreds of men are tearing the land apart at a series of strip mines by the tiny wayside of Decker. Mineral extraction companies have mined billions of tons of low-sulfur, high-energy coal from the Fort Union Formation, formed 55 million years ago, that runs beneath all of this country. Seams of coal are more than thirty feet thick and it is estimated that upward of 50 billion tons of the bituminous coal are contained in the formation that stretches into

Saskatchewan. The massive pits have torn up thousands of acres of land for miles around on the edge of the plateau, the holes hundreds of feet deep. Coal dust frequently darkens the air as trains pulling hundreds of cars line up to be loaded with the black mineral. The noise from haul trucks as big as houses, loaders that can scoop up Buicks by the handful, the blasting, the loading, the chugging trains, all of it, is unbelievable. The coal companies don't care, but they don't want the public taking pictures of their dirty business, either. Try driving in on a mine entrance road sometime, pulling over and stepping out with a camera or two. Five minutes max and then you're discovered and firmly sent on your way by hard-looking, big-bouncer types. And even if all of this nonreclaimable destruction—mining companies claim the land can be recovered, replanted, but that takes constant doses of tons of fertilizer and un-imaginable quantities of water that will swiftly drain the aquifer around here—isn't enough, there are now plans to build a rail line to haul the coal from Decker to Miles City for the sake of expediency—a few miles cut from the current haul line—right next to the Tongue River with all its isolated, quiet beauty and its smallmouth bass, catfish, sauger, walleyes, and even brown trout. If the proposed line is blasted and ripped through the heart of the river corridor some of the most pristine country in North America will be destroyed. The coal lying beneath our camp will be next. But if that push comes to shove, it will be a call to arms from me. Enough greed, rape, and avarice. Oil, gas, coal, gold, timber, gated communities. All of the big-money crap has gone too far.

I swear out loud and Ginny looks over, knowing what I'm thinking about as always, and says softly, "Calm down," but I don't.

I think about another time here when, after setting up camp, Ginny answered the coyotes' calls and they recognized her and sang a familiar riff. And they called again as we began eating a grilled London broil and once again with obvious joy when she and I laughed aloud about the travails of our tough winters. All of it, the animals, land, trees, us, are connected here. Whatever actions we take send ripples across the various planes that are Tongue River country, this camp, the strip mines, the high plains. This is absolutely nothing like plugging into the one-dimensional, electronic, cerebral death trip of the Internet and all its facile jive. When you do something out in good country—eat, mine coal, have sex, even think—the action resonates and comes back. Crazy. Perhaps. Real. For the two of us, definitely.

And I remember back to a summer evening when we watched a tornado form a quarter mile from us over there between the salmon, ocher, and gray outbreaks of rock and dirt and ponderosa forest. The dark boiling, spinning cloud shifting abruptly from a tight, horizontal spinning form to a now-vertical, loose spiral that gradually tightened and increased in intensity. All silent, the wind down, and we heard the embryonic roar of the cyclone as the thing sent a whirling spiral toward the ground and we watched, hypnotized, not even thinking about shelter as the tornado held steady and then began to drift toward us, like it knew we were watching and it came still closer and grew louder, but there was not any wind anywhere else. The trees and grass were dead-still. The air was charged. The hair stood out on our arms. And then, suddenly, the funnel broke apart into black-purple spinning tufts of cloud and anger, the entire, spread-out system spinning very slowly for long minutes until all of it was gone, and robin's egg blue sky and gold sunlight pushed in from the west.

And I remember one Sunday morning as Ginny and I drove up a red dirt road and down the other way a rancher came on his horse followed by his dog. We stopped and chatted for half an hour with Jim atop his horse Bud while his dog Spud lay in the tall grass. He smiled and said to her, "Don't be nervous on my account," as she took his picture and said to me, "I'm 'bout half busy, but I always have time to talk to folks." We marveled at all of the cold springs and little reservoirs, all the water (relatively speaking) in this dry land. He agreed that there were wolves around here and said, "No big deal. They don't take too many of my cows." Then he started to ride off to his ranch, but turned in his saddle and called out, "I mean it when I say, you two be sure and stop by my place next time you're down this way." He smiled and turned back in the direction he was headed, waved over his shoulder. Jim, Bud, and Spud rode off down the stream drainage, then glowing in autumn oranges, crimsons, indigos, flaming yellows, and hangers-on deep greens.

I remember times like that and hope they never end, are never destroyed by heartless greed, but I wonder . . .

We break camp in the very cold and deep dark. The snow crunches beneath our boots and our fingers grow numb. I warm up the Suburban, shift into four-wheel-high, and ease on out on the two-track lane. The ground is hard-frozen and the rig crunches steadily through the crusted snow and seems to have a good bite on the now rock-hard mud. We nudge on down the four miles of wicked path that leads to a somewhat main road and have no trouble. The '83 Suburban is "a good piece of Detroit steel" as our friend McCumber often says of older cars like ours. On the "main" road we are able to accelerate from five miles an hour to twenty-five. We plow through a foot or more of snow and ice. The Suburban chugs away, happy in its work, the V8 growling as we climb steep hills or push through two-foot-plus drifts. The sun clears the horizon and blazes above and through the ponderosa. The land, cloaked in its deep layer of snow glistens with countless crystalline specks of ice that flash and flicker with shafts and sharp points of ruby, sapphire, emerald, and gold that highlights the pure whitewash of snow or illuminates the pink-purple shadows. The land is alive with the light that is the honest treasure of this land.

We drive out in awed silence.

Capitol Rock holds forth over the southeastern Montana landscape not far from South Dakota and Wyoming.

5

CAPITOL COUNTRY

W E'D BEEN TO THIS PLACE BEFORE, but never at night. The early October evening is dark even with all the stars out. I've been driving back and forth along a good gravel road that skirts the southern edge of a unit of the Custer National Forest on the edge of the Montana-South Dakota border for over an hour now looking for the rough little dirt and rock trail that leads up to Capitol Rock. All of the country, what I can see of it in the blackness, looks vaguely familiar but different at this hour, like a long-ago friend who I haven't seen in thirty years. The same face, but changed by the years and experience.

We are back in this country because it's relatively unvisited and the place's almost-abandoned feel is as much a part of the high plains as anything to us. Much of the West is undergoing a rapid, frantic, piecemeal growth. No planning. No respect for the land or the people that have lived here all their lives. On the other side of the equation a good deal of the region is losing population as the always present boom-and-bust cycle plays its up-and-down tune. Towns are withering or vanishing entirely. Spur railroad lines that once serviced thriving communities are now nothing but miles of rusting rails with thistles and tall grass growing between the rotting wooden ties. Towering wooden grain bins stand empty, the painted wood now weathered to an aged gray. Long-ago service stations (remember those places where they would check your oil without asking, wash your windshield, and gas was thirty cents a gallon?) sit empty at formally busy intersections, the buildings' windows long gone, gas reservoirs atop corroded 1950s pumps either cracked or busted to pieces. Indeed, despite the influx of newcomers to Montana, the population of the state has not risen dramatically. In 1980 there were 786,690 of us here. According to the 1994 census that number stood at 856,057. A jump of less than 10 percent in fourteen years. The nearby town of Camp Crook in South Dakota looks and feels as though it were dying, shriveling up and about to be scattered by the ever-present wind. No new convenience stores or motels or liquor stores. Not even any old ones. There are large chunks of country like this all over the plains and within this sense of decay or death there is also the embryonic feel of rebirth, like huge chunks of the West are reevolving into time as it was a century or more back in history. The feeling is slightly spooky and exciting. That's why we've returned.

I keep driving beyond the gravel road and onto a paved highway that ran north and south along the border—State Line Road, only to stop and turn around to retrace my steps fearing I have gone too far or the wrong way and missed the turnoff. Finally Ginny has had enough.

"Turn in here and drive down to that ranch house, the one with the lights," she commands with a trace of anger. I imagine her Irish eyes flashing with emotion. I do as I am told and within a mile we pull up in front of an old wooden house. Ginny steps gingerly out into the yard looking for barking and possibly biting dogs. There are none. She goes up the steps to the door and knocks. A couple in their sixties invites her in. She disappears for a long time, then waves me inside and yells, "Bring the maps." I do as I am told once again.

The home is filled with furniture made from large gnarled pieces of wood, the pieces smoothly sanded and highly polished. Heads of antelope and deer hang from the walls as does a large color photograph of Capitol Rock, a huge, wildly shaped eroding remnant of sandstone and white clay from the Tertiary period millions of years ago. The rock does resemble the nation's capitol when viewed face-on. Gimme ball caps and well-used Carhart coveralls and coats hang from a rack. The couple and Ginny are sitting at the table drinking coffee and the husband is drawing a map on a piece of paper with the stub of a pencil. They both look up, say "Hello" in unison, and the wife pours me a cup of the hot, very strong coffee. Something that I desperately need. We've been on the road all day winding our way up from the Pumpkin Buttes in Wyoming. Much of the drive is on back roads. The Suburban is down to only dim lights. No brights. Dodging and braking for the hundreds of deer and antelope either eating alongside the road or leaping across it has been nerve-wracking.

"Let me see your map," the husband commands. Must be one of Ginny's relatives. He looks Irish. I do as I am told. "You're here and you need to be here which is here on the map from what she told me," and he looks at Ginny. "You got as far as here on State Line. You needed to go around the next curve and then turn at the first road to the left. You almost made it, but came up just short."

"He does that a lot," Ginny offers and the three of them have a good laugh. I am tired and edgy from the dusty miles and the nuance of her humor escapes me.

We thank them for the coffee and guidance and begin to leave.

"Wait. You forgot something," and the guy thrusts the map he has drawn at me with a look that seems to say, "Boy, you look stretched pretty thin. Get some sleep soon." I accept the map (which I still have), nod a thanks, and totter out to the car. Ginny follows, talking with the woman about sunflowers and cats. Looking at the tall stems and autumn-drooping large flowers reminds me of an old Grateful Dead song, "China Cat Sunflower," and the swooping in-and-out rhythms of the music begin kicking around in my head. With luck and the juice from the internal music we have a fighting chance at this rate to make the turnoff by midnight.

Eventually we pull out of there, back down the long entrance road, back down the gravel road, and back down State Line. I swing the Suburban through the described curve and there is the road with the beat-up brown wooden National Forest sign pointing the way to Capitol Rock and our campsite, hopefully. Six more miles of ruts, rocks, sharp turns, and eight-mile-an-hour chugging along in the dead of night, dead-tired.

What the hell, at least a full moon is rising across the Dakota plains behind us. Even in the darkness the road looks familiar now. The old, wind-battered ranch house on the left. The dead, gray hulks of burned ponderosa standing like skeletons in the ghostly light. A large portion of the forest on this unit was razed in the drought years of the late eighties, but the land still retains its wildness and beauty. Lush grass has sprung up in the burned-over areas that surround still sizable stands of healthy pine forest. Small ponderosa, a foot or so tall, are making a new start. And the fire's damage drives away the few tourists that managed to get lost over this way. We had the place to ourselves last June and apparently so now. The tall grass, now a dusky autumn tan-brown, the 180-degree turns, and mid-course boulders are all recognizable. I slip the car into four-wheel and climb ever so cautiously over a sharp-looking shelf of exposed rock. I keep looking at the odometer. We've come 4.2 miles. Capitol Rock should be visible soon. The air is warm for October, in the high fifties. We have the windows down and the breeze that sweeps in smells of pine, dying grass, and clean air. Not much in the way of pollution out here. The nearest town of substance is Gillette, Wyoming, hours to the south. No industry either, unless you count ranching for cattle and a herd of bison we saw earlier in the year at an operation back west and not far from Ekalaka. In a few more minutes I check the odometer again: 5.3 miles.

And suddenly there it is. Glowing silver-white from the moon and rising up several hundred feet above us, the eroded pillars at its base drifting in and out of view like ghosts gliding through the trees. Capitol Rock. Clearly a place of power. The sudden image of this geologic feature hits me in the stomach and drives the Dead tune from my head.

"God, John. This place is strong," whispers Ginny. "Powerful. When I first saw it as we came around that turn back there I got a feeling in my stomach. Not scared, really, but strange."

I nod at her.

Capitol Rock keeps growing in stature as we creep nearer to it. Perhaps over a quarter mile long from north to south and a couple of hundred yards wide. At night in this moonlight the pillars that give way to the main walled formation that in turn support a towering rectangular column glow a nearly fluorescent white. Even from a mile away we can make out all of the subtle ridges, curved ledges, and cavelike swirling depressions in Capitol Rock's eastern face. I am not frightened by the feeling we experienced just now, but I feel the need to be quiet and respectful as we approach the turn to camp that is nothing more than a wide spot in the road where we hang another left and drive up and down a grassy hill, inch our way across a water-eroded, smooth, rounded series of granite shelves, then up again for a hundred yards through more grass to a level spot beneath dozens of live ponderosa. The fires stopped short of this elevated peninsula. Dead trunks line the valley leading up here. I park the Suburban. We step out and turn to look at the rock now almost shining as the moon rises higher. All is silent. No birds. No wind. Not a hint of breeze. Eerie and peaceful and damn powerful all at once. We quietly unload our gear. Ginny makes scrambled eggs and bacon in a cast-iron skillet on our Coleman stove. I arrange our pads and sleeping bags in the back of the car. We are too tired to deal with finding a soft place on the ground. After wolfing down the food and chugging a coffee cup full of orange juice, we each smoke a cigarette and turn in.

Lying down in the Suburban we are facing Capitol Rock that now shines as brightly as though it were first light of day. Nothing stirs around us. We speak briefly about the wonderful drive from a little spot on the road called Biddle to here through a land full of big game, turkeys, pine forest, bluffs, rolling grass meadows—all of it bathed in the changing oranges, reds, purples, yellows, and golds of a full-bore Montana October sunset, the sun finally dropping below the horizon as a large bloodred disk. In over one hundred miles of driving we saw two cars and one pickup truck and very few ranch lights. No towns to speak of. As soon as we climb into our sleeping bags we start to drift off. The place grows quieter still.

In the morning around seven-thirty, the sun, now a bright yellow coin climbing above South Dakota, wakes us to the singing of the birds that haven't already flown south for the winter. Black-capped chickadees. Nuthatches. Brown creepers. Magpies. A pair of red-shafted flickers screeching their lonesome call. A late-migrating flock of robins. The day is cloudless. Capitol Rock is showing shades of white, buckskin, blue-green, and lavender. A slight breeze rustles the long pine needles creating a soft, soothing sound. The feeling that approached the edges of fear last night is gone. In its place is the sense that we are all alone here, that we have this beautiful place to ourselves.

After breakfast we walk up the hill south of camp and take in the view. With my binoculars I can make out the faint outline of the Black Hills of South Dakota, a dark band on the southeast horizon. Trending northeastward the riparian corridor of the Little Missouri River is distinctly defined by the thick stands of cottonwoods that crowd its banks, the leaves going yellow-gold now. The river serpentines its way through the rolling rangeland. East beyond this the land rises in an immense, gentle wave that breaks up onto a badlands shore of the horizon. To the immediate west is Capitol Rock and beyond a narrow, jagged valley that up until a decade ago had been a thick pine forest but is now reduced by the fires to acres of dead standing and fallen tree trunks with more thick grass growing on the slopes. A graveyard. Here and there the soil had slumped away leaving large brown-orange dirt gashes and exposed rock cliffs and boulders. To the north the forest and the low mountains we are in drop away to a flat expanse of fields and grasslands that roll away before disappearing in the haze. I can see herds of black Angus and brown Hereford cattle grazing out in the vast emptiness that way. To the south, east, and north we can gaze for over a hundred miles. No interstate highway systems. No Billings. No Glendive. No Rapid City. No frantic traffic or pollution. No sounds of police sirens or screeching tires or jackhammers. Only the wind blowing up from Wyoming rustling the dry grasses and the pines.

This is the West I say to myself, and Ginny, once again reading my mind, says, "Yes it is," as she scans the panorama through her viewfinder. Imagining that the one hundred-mile gaze goes full circle means we can take in about 7,500 square miles of country that is approximately the size of New Jersey with perhaps less than twenty thousand people living in it. How many hapless souls are crammed into New Jersey? Eight million? That's four hundred times, at least, the population density of where we are. No wonder everyone moves at an insanely rapid pace. Sure there are urban junkyards out on the high plains. Cities are cities wherever they spring up, but the West, not the West of the Rocky Mountains, but the open West, is so vast and still so sparsely populated, definitely not underpopulated, that it is easy to think that this is one hundred years ago or more. Real easy even with the sight of the sun glinting off a pickup raising a cloud of dust as it rolls down the gravel road we got to know so well last night. The nearest town is Camp Crook in South Dakota on the Little Missouri, and if one hundred souls hang out there I'd be surprised. What's the population of Ekalaka? Six-fifty? That's a big town out this way.

This quantity of space and lack of people is probably unimaginable to those living on the East or West Coasts. Here is country where the nearest neighbor may be twenty miles away, not twenty feet. Living out here requires self-reliance and to some extent guts. When the power goes out in a storm or the truck breaks down miles from nowhere, those who live on the Great Plains can't pick up the phone, even the invasive cellular version, and call a cop or tow truck; or the power company, which may be an hour or more away. They have to ride out the trouble, fix it themselves if they can, and if not, take it easy and find a solution themselves. You don't see flashy new black Volvo station wagons out this way. Parts are light-years distant and the utilitarian value of these overpriced foreigners slight. Instead you see lots of McCumber's Detroit steel in the form of Chevys, Fords, Dodges, and GMC pickups.

Self-reliance is one of the main progenitors for the independence of western people, those that have lived here for years and not in glitzy boom towns like Bozeman or Jackson. The vastness of the landscape, the insanely, true madness when the wind blows fifty or sixty miles an hour for weeks on end, open land, and lifestyle breed this independent and to a degree arrogant nature. I feel this way and I've only been here thirty years.

"Screw the East and the West Coasts, especially California. God, especially California. Let's put a fence up and keep everyone

else out. They don't know what this place really is and never will,"
is pretty much the sentiment of those who are seventh generation
or seventh day. This land does that to us. Blows away the dependent, neurotic, frantic madness of cramped living and turns all
of us into our own half-assed versions of pioneers and explorers.

We talk about this as we walk up the final gentle rise before
us as the day grows steadily warmer and more majestic . . .

The first time we came to Capitol Rock was in late June. We
wandered down this intending to explore the Chalk Buttes, a
similar grouping of tall hills or low mountains rising out of the
prairie due south of Ekalaka. The Chalk Buttes are impressive,
seeming much taller than their four thousand feet or so as they
rise up from the plains like clipper ships breaking an ocean horizon, and they are unscarred by fire. A friend of ours gathers
medicinal plants here.

We never made it to the Chalk Buttes.

A few days prior to our aborted sojourn into them we'd been
touring the Theodore Roosevelt National Park in North Dakota.
This is the badlands country of the Little Missouri, similar to the
Missouri Breaks of central Montana but smaller in scale. A land
first popularized, if that is indeed the correct word, by Theodore
Roosevelt.

"I never would have been president if it had not been for my
experiences in North Dakota," Roosevelt said.

He first came to the Badlands in September 1883. Before returning back to New York, he developed an interest in cattle and
with two others formed the Maltese Cross Ranch. The next year
he came back and started up another open-range operation called
the Elkhorn. This became his primary residence, a place where he
could live the "strenuous" life he enjoyed. His place of residence
on the Elkhorn is preserved as a reminder of Roosevelt's life on

the grasslands and in the Breaks. A world-renowned big-game hunter, Roosevelt watched the destruction of big-game species like the grizzly and elk, along with the overgrazing of the grasslands. When he became president in 1901, Roosevelt established the U.S. Forest Service, and by signing the 1906 Antiquities Act he proclaimed eighteen national monuments. He also obtained congressional approval for the establishment of five national parks and fifty-one wildlife refuges and set aside vast tracts of land as national forests. The North Dakota national park is named in his honor.

Nearly 60 million years ago streams carried eroded materials eastward from the newly formed Rocky Mountains and deposited them across a vast lowland that is today's Great Plains. During the warm, moist periods that followed, thick vegetation grew, died, and dropped into swampy areas and was eventually covered by more eroded sediments. Over time the plant material transformed into lignite. Some plants petrified and are exposed throughout the West today as petrified wood. Bentonite, a blue-gray layer of clay, can be traced to ash spewed from ancient volcanoes far to the west. The stuff is used to line reservoirs, irrigation ditches, and anything else that needs to conserve water. While these sediments were being deposited, rivers began slicing through the relatively soft layers or strata of soils cutting rugged canyons and coulees, leaving stark benches and bluffs all of which further eroded into fantastic, surreal shapes.

The land like the Missouri Breaks and much of the West appears barren, but there is sufficient rainfall to grow the lush grasslands. Over eight hundred species of birds live or pass through here. Mule deer and whitetail deer are common as are prairie dogs. Bison were reintroduced in 1956. Elk in 1985.

On our drive through the park we'd planned to spend at least one night but after cruising the "campground" we changed our minds. Two men on exhaust-spewing, loud-riding mowers were trimming the grass around the paved sites that were already filling with campers and motor homes. Music from tape players, CD players, and radios was blaring everywhere. Dogs, most not on leashes, were barking and cavorting in displaced packs that formed before our eyes. Tourists with license plates from Georgia, Mississippi, Alaska, and even Hawaii were shambling about dressed in discordant combinations of L. L. Bean, Patagonia, REI, and Wal-Mart polyester. Cheap wraparound sunglasses appeared to be a way of life. No way. Not our style. We left in a hurry and drove out to an overlook of the Little Missouri where the river snaked its way through pale shades of ocher, charcoal, brown, gray, and salmon. Hot as usual at this time of the season in this country and already dry. The grasses and wildflowers looked beat on the verge of heat prostration. The shattered land rolled off for miles, again much like the Missouri Breaks, but without the overall size or the electric juice that zings through that country. I picked a wild rose bloom from a bush filled with dozens and out of nowhere a park ranger jumped me and said I'd done a horrible, illegal thing and if everyone did what I did there would be no more wild roses. I saw his point and handed him the flower. He let me off with a stern warning and a paternally stern grimace. Bad boy.

I turned to Ginny and said, "Let's get out of here."

The only reason we'd really come anyway was to see and photograph the bison, but they were not to be found. Though as we passed out through the entrance gate a man in a national park uniform asked, "Did you see the bison?"

We said, "No."

"Well they're only forty-five minutes down this road," and he proceeded to give us detailed directions. We'd asked this same guy where the animals were on the way in and he'd said, "They could be anywhere."

He leered at us with a whacko smile and asked if we were going to turn around and find the bison.

We said, "No. Not this time," and headed off for the Chalk Buttes, which we found but never explored. Something in my head said, *Go here* when I looked at the map and saw the words "Capitol Rock." So we went there instead.

. . . As we near the crest of the final hill that October morning I look back to Capitol Rock and recall our June visit and the time we'd spent climbing around the spires, columns, towers, ridges, and cliffs late in the afternoon.

Mid-seventies. Blue sky filled with white clouds riding the wind eastward. Thick hummocks of grass and sage guarded the way up to the base of the rock. Once there the blue-green columns turned out to be an eroded system of pillars with narrow channels leading inside. In some places I could walk behind the pillars and look out over our camp and far off into South Dakota. The setting reminded me of looking out from the capitol in Washington, D.C., though with a dramatically different view. The soft soil at my feet was a mixture of the colorful rock, bird droppings, and most likely bat dung. Back in the narrow caves I could see some bats hanging asleep upside down in miniature chambers. None of them stirred when I ran the beam of my flashlight over them. Back outside I climbed up a steep slope of broken rock and eroded soil that was covered with a thick matting of grass and small cactus. One hundred feet up a few small ponderosa clung to ledges.

The ponderosa were everywhere we traveled doing this book as were the cottonwoods. They are to me the true trees of this country, along with, to a lesser extent, the junipers and pinyons. The pines offer shade and shelter. Many people unfamiliar with the West mistakenly think that ponderosa are mainly a tree of the southern Rockies. Not so. Vast stands of the pines stretch far north into the Canadian provinces of Alberta and British Columbia. As for the stately cottonwoods, a tree that is a sure sign of water, they are common throughout the lower half of the northern high plains. If there are cottonwoods there must be water around nearby—standing, flowing, or pooled beneath the ground.

I walk along the ledge and looked up at the top of Capitol Rock towering many feet above when I see an incongruous sight. Two sharp-tailed grouse are perched on a point of rock jutting out into space. I've seen the birds on tree limbs, but never this far above ground exposed to predators, and there were many in the area including red-tailed hawks and golden eagles. I pick up a couple of rocks and launch them at the grouse. The stones clatter off the wall well below their intended targets, but the noise frightens the sharptails. They burst into flight, fast-beating wings drumming in the air, squawking as they fly down from their perch, over our camp, then swiftly down the small valley. Eventually I come to the side of the formation and look up again. The summit is no more than a dozen feet thick, if that, and looks like a very large, square slab of rock that had been lowered into place by some otherworldly crane. What looked substantial from camp is really in geologic terms ephemeral in nature. Someday, maybe in the next windstorm, the rock will topple and crash down to the eroded, pillared base. When I return to the east side of Capitol Rock I see the land that stretches for many miles turn from deep, rich orange to crimson. Long dark purple shadows drift across the land beginning from the Badlands, covering the trees lining the Little Missouri and working their way toward camp. I climb back down and return to the small fire of twigs and pine cones Ginny has going in our miniature Weber grill, something we use when we want to watch flames at night but are concerned about the fire conditions of a given area and are concerned about torching thousands of acres of land. The grill is one of my few wise and reasonably priced purchases in nearly fifty years of costly mistakes, like cheap tents that collapse in a soft breeze, still cheaper hiking boots that fall apart in a few days, and sheets of plastic for tarps instead of coated nylon ones.

When we top the hill the light even at midday is amber. The October sun is muted, has lost its summer-sharp edge. The sun is now much lower in the sky to the south of us instead of directly overhead or even north of us as in July. We walk along the top of the hill. A neat oblong pile of rock and small chipped ocher and brown stones catches my eye.

An unmarked grave.

Who is buried here? A Northern Cheyenne warrior? A homesteader? A long-ago fur trapper? The grave is old. Lichen is growing on the rocks, connecting with other colonies shaded in delicate patterns of gray-greens, burnt oranges, and dead charcoals. The plants take decades to grow as much as a half inch, so this mound must be a century old or more. Ginny wonders about taking a picture of the grave and I say "No" out of respect for whoever is here. I'm not even sure that this place is meant to be found. A nice place to rest with the hundred-mile views, the solitude, and the peace. We look off in all directions and then down at the grave. Ginny places a small rock at the base of the mound and a hand-shaped sage limb just below the head. We begin walking back to camp.

About fifty yards from the hill and its grave I have the oddest sensation. I can feel and even see a transparent shape move up on me from behind, and then give me the gentlest and most subtle of shoves away from the mound. The feeling is like topping a hill at high speed in a low-slung sports car, only less so and more delicate in nature. And the image is not clearly defined and is not seen by my eyes. The figure shapes itself in my mind and I think I hear the words "You've seen me, now please leave my place alone," and then it is gone. The sense that I can return to this place, but not this particular hill, is clear to me, overpowering in a subliminal way.

Too many drugs too long ago, I think, but as I turn and look back at the hill and the solitary grave site, the image that was in my head, the slightest of diaphanous outlines, merges with the mound of stone.

Capitol Rock.

Quite the place.

A fork of the Poplar River near Peerless in northeastern Montana.

6

EASTERN MONTANA

So far the fines add up to $7,500 and eighteen months in
the slammer. The smart money is saying all of this can go
much higher. I'd forgotten how tough fishing for northern pike
can be. The razor-sharp teeth. The sharklike feeding behavior. The
long casts with large, weighted streamers. Yes, I remembered all
of this, but the expense of going even slightly astray of the law
had slipped my mind. We are 447 miles from Livingston, tossing
large, bright green barracuda flies at the voracious northerns,
swimming, lurking, and skulking in one of the several forks of
the Poplar River as it flows through rolling grassland hill country
south of the not-so-big ranching community of Peerless in the far
northeastern corner of Montana. We'd been camping next to the
little stream for a couple of days now and were packing up to
head off to the Missouri Breaks. That's when the Daniels County
deputy sheriff came lurching down the bumpy two-track in his
older model Ford Bronco and informed us that we've been breaking state law and criminally so.

Pulling abruptly up to us in spacious grazing land, he rolled
down his window and asked, "What're you folks doing here?"

"Fishing for pike and enjoying the country and the quiet," I said.

He didn't believe me and gave me a cop stare, the one that makes you feel like you're doing something wrong even when you're helping a blind person cross a busy street.

"Not hunting or anything like that?"

"No. Just pike fishing. Damn good to. Caught a couple over ten pounds and a lot of smaller ones on this," and I showed him the barracuda streamer. He looked at it and then at me as if I were really odd.

"From Park County I see," as he looked over at the plates on the Suburban. "Came all the way up here to fish pike? Not bird hunting or anything like that?"

"No. We love to fish and this is good water," I said.

"Well, I hate to spoil your Sunday morning, but you're breaking the law having your car down here."

"What? This is state land, isn't it?"

"Yes, but this section is school trust land and you can't access it with a motorized vehicle unless by dedicated public road, and the nearest one of those is over there," and he pointed to a county gravel road running behind a barbed-wire fence about a mile away, and then he showed me a sheet listing all the fines and jail terms Ginny and I had accumulated while illegally fishing for northern pike while camping on public land. I thought back to the wonderful time we'd had here up until now, and the great time we had earlier this year in June, and I began to get angry (pissed off is more accurate) that we couldn't access this public land in our car, land paid for with taxpayer dollars like ours, in our own damn Suburban, and the cop noticed my face getting red and the growing fire of disgust and madness in my eyes, but Ginny once again defused a potentially hot situation.

As the possibility that the fines may go higher, much higher, increases, she notices that the cop possesses an Irish look about him, so she pulls off her hat and unfurls her long red hair and says, "See, I'm Irish, too."

The cop looks surprised, not quite sure what to make of this latest development. Individuals (suspects?) driving nearly five hundred miles to fish pike is suspicious enough. Now this. He looks. She keeps smiling. I keep wondering about how I'll raise the dough for the fines and also I am perversely pleased that at least we'll eat for a few months courtesy of the state penal system. And then the guy breaks into a big smile and tells us all about how he is leaving for Ireland in a few weeks and how he is looking forward to drinking lots of Guinness Stout and the two of them talk Irish on and on and I look back behind me at the marvelous little stream running through this eastern Montana country . . .

. . . Two days ago, around when we crossed the bridge over this nothing fork of the Poplar River, I looked down and was blown away. The water was clear, copper-tinted, running over a bright gravel and stone streambed. I'd expected a warm, turbid sluggish flow more suited to catfish. This looked like a trout stream. We kept on until we came to a wire gate that I opened, and we followed a two-track that led through grazed grass fields filled with huge, platter-shaped, dried cow pies that stretched off to the distant horizons. Long pieces of rusted, twisted barbed wire lay on the ground next to rotted posts. The grass was bright green and went on forever, past the banks of this stream, rolling across vast fields rippled with gentle swales like motionless waves and farther on hills and rounded bluffs rose several hundred feet above the valley and just kept going on to disappear in blue sky. Puffy white clouds drifted by riding a warm northwest wind. Because of the vast scale of this land, the river and hills gently winding out of sight to the north and south, the distant herds of cattle resembling grounded flocks of brown birds, because of all of this, the clouds appeared motionless and if I kept staring at them, they never moved, but if I turned away to work at setting up camp and then turned back some minutes later, it was clear that the cumulus was moving away to the southeast, perhaps bound for Sidney or Glendive, at a good clip.

This place was all but empty of the fast-paced confusion common to humans. No traffic noise, power lines, car alarms going off with machinelike futility, no police sirens, no frantic vibe of too many people doing too much of nothing on a too-tight, can't-make-it-fit, useless schedule. Cows were grazing on the slopes all around us. Large cylindrical bales of hay were stacked neatly here and there. Weathered-gray barns and sheds stood silently in small dips in the land, out of the wind. In the hour we'd been here organizing the cooking area, the coolers, rigging fly rods, only a pair of pickups had rattled by on the gravel county road, the dust the rigs raised disappearing lazily in the breeze. We were less than twenty feet from the stream that was burbling away as it cut into the dirt and gravel banks, squeezed through hard places in the ground or opened wide into mini-lakes. Red-tailed hawks worked in pairs along the crests of the hills. A red fox ran along the road, then darted into the tall grass of the ditch when I looked at it. Nighthawks swooped and boomed in the afternoon light. Coyotes barked off and on from the distance of a couple of cottonwoods a mile or so downstream. A person could live peacefully here and I wondered what it would be like to live on the ranch that I could see clearly in the pure air, the one nestled into a wide groove in a bluff at least three miles away. I could see tall pines planted in neat rows as wind protection, more stacked hay, outbuildings, tractors, and so forth. Did the people that lived there realize the special nature of this place or did they only see a day-to-day never-ending grind involving their cows, cow shit, breaking machinery, heartless banks, constant wind, numbing cold, and blistering heat? Did they fish this stream? Hunt the sharptails and sage grouse and pheasants? Or the deer and antelope? Or was this just home, a place that looked like anywhere else. Like Chicago looks to Chicagoans or the Himalayas look to Tibetans. Pretty. Exciting. The same old, same old. Ugly because of familiarity. Barely noticed most of the time because of this familiarity.

The hell with this introspective jive. I notice the soft power of this country. If the ranchers don't see the place, well, that is their problem. I want to catch the trout this stream surely holds. Maybe browns. Or brookies. I'd know in a few minutes.

I didn't catch anything for a while. Each perfect, artfully presented cast into riffles, small eddies, or beneath slight undercuts in the bank turned nothing. No trout. No bass. Not even a whitefish, though I did see several carp. Ten-pounders sunning themselves in the shallows. I was fishing what looked like ideal holding water for browns or brookies and seeing nothing when it dawned on me with a flash of obviously nascent insight that I was here for northern pike and they, being the insane predators that they are, keep to different water than do trout.

To examine a pike is to experience evolution in the predatory sense at its finest. The fish are designed to kill their prey quickly, efficiently, with little wasted motion. The long, muscular body propels a barracuda-shaped head that is filled with rows of wicked teeth toward unsuspecting prey at astounding velocities, thirty miles an hour or more. I tripped back to the youthful days spent catching the species in the reedy shallows of the North Channel of Lake Huron in Ontario. Back then I used spinning gear to launch Johnson silver minnow spoons, red and white Dardevles, wooden minnows, Lazy Ikes, and anything else that even vaguely resembled food. The lure would arc through the air, plop into the water among the tall reeds, and as soon as I began reeling in, the pike would zoom in out of their nowhere invisibility, making V-shaped wakes and slamming the lures in a voracious splash. I still have several mangled wooden plugs riddled with teeth marks from those days.

With that in mind I began casting to similar water, especially in the slow, wide bends of the stream, in tight to snake grass, grama grass banks, and mossy shallows. Throwing the large, bright green saltwater fly seventy feet (the slow water here grew to widths of well over one hundred feet despite the small volume of flow) in the constant wind with a six-weight fly rod was entertaining and occasionally painful when the weighted pattern would slam into my head or back. The vicissitudes of angling, I guess. The second cast brought a familiar response. A mottled green, cream, and tan shape rocketed from several inches of water and drilled the streamer. The fight wasn't much and the northern was only two pounds, but now I knew the fish were here, and I began casting to all likely looking water with lunatic vigor, laughing and talking to myself.

"Great cast, Holt," as I unhooked the fly from my shirt.

"Son of a bitch" as a six-pound pike boiled and snapped my twenty-pound leader when it pounced from just off a small point in a bay-lake bow in the river. I switched to sixty-pound big-game tippet to try to offset the knifelike effects of the pikes' teeth.

"Damn, this is outrageous," I yelled as a ten-pound pike slammed the chartreuse pattern in the same spot just off the point. The pike ran and churned up the surface as I followed it downstream in knee-deep water. The rod was bent well more than double, and vibrating intensely with the energy from the northern. The fish pulled into the backing, then abruptly gave up. I reeled it in. "Amazing. What a fish in this little thing [the stream]." Close to thirty inches. Deep shades of green. Cream, square spotting. Coppery tints along the back. White belly. Rich brown fins streaked with black. And hundreds of mean, curved teeth in jaws that slowly opened and closed. The pike had crushed the six-inch streamer in its middle to break its back, kill it. As I twisted the hook free of its tough mouth with a pair of pliers the fish shook itself and those teeth raked my thumb and forefinger. Crimson blood dropped onto the fish's flanks and into the water. The price of pike. I continued taking northerns everywhere along the flats and in the wide bends until well into dark. I couldn't stop. The crazed, full-blown nature of these animals hooked me and made me realize what I'd been missing with my obsession for trout at the exclusion of species like this. Straight-ahead, no bullshit killers. No half-assed #22 BWOs on 7X tippets ever-so-lightly cast in fear of spooking neurotic trout that have seen it all too many times from a fly-fishing perspective. Throw the weighted barracuda fly with authority and strip the thing back. The pike aren't scared by the splash and noise. They're attracted to it. I was totally addicted one more time to this passion of hunting, finding fish in out-of-the-way, unexpected locations.

I used to fish to catch fish. That was the only reason. Now I fish to find out what's in a river, stream, lake, pond, reservoir, drainage ditch. Standing in the water and casting and discovering these pike, or ranch pond bluegills, or large brook trout in a high plains lake or diminutive rainbows in a crystalline stream sparking like cut crystal flowing out in the desert of southeastern Montana or catching catfish in a little stream on a late May night in even drier country, all of this connects me to the land and tells me that the natural system is intact.

Of course northern pike are not all what eastern Montana is, at the most only a small part of it. The ranches, the hardworking, tough, generous people that work this spacious, free land, are what this place is. So is the two-million-acre Fort Peck Indian Reservation a few miles south of here and now the confined home of Assiniboine and Sioux Indians, people, along with other tribes, who once roamed this land with fierce abandon.

The main high plains tribes were the Sioux or Dakota, the Minnetaree (Gros Ventres of the River), the Shoshone also living west of the mountains, the Cheyenne in the southeast as did the Crow, the Blackfeet in the northwest to the edge of the Rocky Mountain Front, the Arapaho, or White Claymen or Gros Ventres of the prairie, and the Assiniboine of the northeastern portion of the plains. A third tribe called Gros Ventres of the Mountains (Atsina) spoke the Arapaho dialect.

The Fort Peck Reservation was created in 1872. The Assiniboine, though less than half of the Native American population, were the original controllers of the land. Of Sioux origin long ago, their hunting territory stretched from the Missouri River to the Saskatchewan in the north. The tribe considered the Yankton Sioux, who arrived from South Dakota in 1886, intruders and fought with them for years. Left Hand, an Assiniboine chief, was described as "crafty, cruel, deceitful" and was at war with everyone else in the region back then, though the tribe was often friendly with whites. Left Hand led his people in battles with the Blackfeet in the east and in the process they razed Fort Pigean, but Governor Isaac Stevens, during his railroad survey, said that the Assiniboine "talked straight." The Sioux and the Assiniboine live in separate communities on the reservation and their languages are so different that communication between the two is in English. Under original allotments each tribal member received 320 acres of of grazing land, 40 of land suitable for irrigation, and 20 of timber. One of the major sources of income today is leasing of these lands to nontribal members.

But pike are native to this country and their wild, abundant presence is an indication of how unspoiled this place is. The fact that these fish swim here in these numbers more than likely says that all of the rest of the indigenous species, except bison, are holding their own, too. That the land is still healthy.

This fork of the Poplar River was alive with fish, tons of them lying in wait to eat smaller fish or cruising the shallow eddies at night chasing forage fish in a quicksilver flash and splash of spraying water and terrified leaping minnows. When I'm sunk this deep in one of my true passions I see everything. Nighthawks flitting overhead. Caddis coming off the water. Flickers and bands of crisp orange light tracking the setting sun, slight darkening of clouds indicating night showers, the taste of sweet grass on a cool evening breeze, the long-distant cry of a coyote or out of the corner of my eye a quarter mile away the steep dive of a falcon powering down to hammer some small rodent. The fishing becomes automatic. I know where the pike are and more than this I know I will catch them on nearly every cast. That's the way all of this becomes when I loose the Holt crap and the living-in-town crap and submit to all of this. Chattering away like a truly free madman, casting like a chaotically designed machine with no governor, the streamer landing exactly where I want it to without thinking or calculation, the northern rushing out of skin-thin water, white toothy jaws wide open, the murderous take, and above all this the sharp cry of two red-tailed hawks signaling each other as they stalk jackrabbits over on a low ridge, and the soft sound of this water flowing out of the bend and over a coppery gravel run. Loose the dominate ego and I'm connected in this plane making congruent ripples that echo back and forth from me to the pike to the coyote to the light to the dark to the wind all at once and outside the limitations of linear time. No thought. Just the feel of the cold water, the cut of the pike's teeth as they tear my skin, the predator coldness of the fish's eye as it bores through me, the pull of the line on my backcast, and the rare, insane joy of being alive without thinking about it.

That's what I fish for now. Not numbers. Not species life lists. Not showing off fancy, overpriced equipment. Not geographic checklists.

Only this little river cruising through this wide-open, stoned country and these predacious, wild northerns. I could do this forever and will as long as I can . . .

So I'm back here today with the Daniels County deputy sheriff now and I'm riffing about my feelings about pike fishing and he's beginning to see that I'm not up here with Ginny to poach some rancher's cows or pop an antelope or two on the sly and he says to Ginny for us to call him the next time before we come up here and he'll talk to a rancher friend of his who will let us onto his land to fish where the pike are as big as eighteen pounds and there are some big brook trout, too, and even some walleyes. And he says he hates the state laws we've broken. That they're unenforceable and even the locals can't drive down here for a Sunday picnic. They must walk. He shrugs and looks through his cracked and chipped windshield. He cuts us a break and forgets about the fines and comments on what a great rig our '83 Suburban is and the two of us tell him the story of how we tumbled onto the car . . .

. . . "Store bought. Store thought." Those words keep blasting through my head, the phrase backed up by a discordant melange of violins, trumpets, drums, and a mildly disturbed tenor sax. It is hot and close slouching here in cheap chairs that were made to look expensive. The sun is burning through the lightly tinted windows and our salesman is nowhere to be seen, though the cloying scent of his cologne is everywhere. Breathing is difficult. The place's PA system offers slight clues about the nature of this intense place.

"Bob, see Mark in financing."

"Glenn, customer in Lot B."

"Tattoo, the plane is landing. The plane is landing. The plane."

I look over at Ginny and she shrugs, puts on her sunglasses, and goes invisible. Who can blame her? Three hours of intense negotiations, heated wrangling over sums approaching fourteen dollars, a bunch of cigarettes sucked down—Camels for me. Marlboros for her—and we are faint from hunger. No food since an early breakfast wolfed (an appropriate word considering the situation) down before we made the run over to Billings and this delightful car dealership.

What in the hell are we doing here? And now "Store bought, store thought" seems to be blaring from the joint's PA, vibrating from the showroom cars and up from the tile floor. The Flock was a good band, "Clown" is a delicate, thoughtful piece of music and

I like Jerry Goodman's violin, but I am starting to lose it. All we really want out of life today is to trade our '96 Tahoe in on an '83 Suburban. No big deal. Exchange a classy, yuppie-approved rig for a clean, low-mileage, one-owner (or so we've been told) machine. Cash and a vehicle that runs well; and to escape this place with our lives. We'd decided to get a lower-profile rig in preparation for hitting the road researching this book. We didn't want a scene that might run along the lines of pulling into some rancher's front yard, crazed dogs barking and leaping all over the place, penned cattle endlessly butting their heads against a weathered wood fence, a lanky, wind-cut rancher—faded jeans, scuffed boots, beat cowboy hat, battered work gloves—approaching from the darkness of a barn as we sit sedately in a forty-thousand-buck car, perhaps using a cell phone to talk to our broker.

"Need some help?" he'd ask.

"No. We just wondered if we could talk to you and take your picture for a book we're working on," we'd say.

"From the looks of things," he'd say as he ran an eyeball over our Tahoe, "you don't need me for much of anything," and he'd turn and walk over to his battered, mud- and cow shit–splattered '64 Dodge and that would be all she wrote or didn't write. That was our thinking, anyway.

So all we wanted was an older Suburban. Why all the madness here in Billings?

A couple dressed like Orlando tourists floats by, the woman saying, "We've always wanted to own a new Cadillac." Three salesmen surround the pair like vultures about to pick at a dead steer lying bloated out in the field. A dwarf, nattily dressed in a blue suit coat and school tie, walks past at a sprightly clip. He disappears through a door and I hear one of the salesmen mutter, "Little Hitler."

The Suburban appears to be a great deal. I'd driven it for perhaps a half mile through a garish subdivision near the dealership before turning the wheel over to my friend. She turned and smiled at our salesman, we'll call him Jeff, and asked, "How do I get to the interstate? I want to see how this thing does on the highway?" The Suburban was propelled through frantic intersections, whipped around sharp corners, and then floored as we raced down an on-ramp to I-90. Jeff tried to play it cool, but the scent of his cologne grew in intensity tinged with the acrid smell of fear. His clasped hands were buried in his lap. I looked over at the speedometer and noticed we were doing eighty-five. Ginny was smiling as she skillfully zipped and wove through a high-speed assortment of semis, motor homes, down-sized Detroit atrocities, and a herd of Japanese cars.

"Wha . . . what do you two do for a living?" Jeff gamely asked.

"I'm a writer and Ginny's a photographer. We do stuff about good country and fishing. And I've written a few books."

"What are some of them?" but my reply was drowned out as we roared by a truck hauling huge snowplows.

Now going ninety, Ginny turned to Jeff huddled in the backseat and added, "And we knock off an occasional liquor or convenience store when things are tight. There's a nice one up in White Sulphur Springs we've had our eye on for some time. Care to go with us?"

Jeff laughed weakly, no doubt thinking of the Idaho salesman who was found murdered in Montana up on Skalkaho Pass recently. A grizzly test drive that ended stuck high up in a dying snowbank holding out in the pines. Eventually we rolled back onto the dealer's lot. Jeff escorted us to the cubicle we were in at this moment. The venerable hot box routine, but neither of us is having any of it. Tight places are tight places. You can't change that, so the only way out is to get up and leave, which we do every few minutes, forcing Jeff to run back and forth from our secure position next to an outside ashtray and from his floor manager's (we'll call this one Dwayne) office. During this process other salesmen wander out and ask us about our lives, tell us sordid, predictable tales about theirs, and all of them add, "You're getting a great deal." How do they know? Telepathic flimflam creatures? Secret hand signs? An unspoken communication common to predators everywhere? We started out approximately a couple of grand apart from our bottom figure, what we would take for the Tahoe and that number is our secret. This seemed like weeks ago. A distant time when life was easy and somewhat straightforward. We've had enough humiliation over the years, so the number will never be revealed; and you really can never win with a car salesman, a clown who sells more vehicles in a weekend than you or I will ever own. So, in our own humble way, we are waging a gallant fight against the slimy forces of car dealing. This was about more than our petty transportation needs. Honor for all of us is at stake.

The dwarf reemerges from another door, catches my eye, points a finger at the fast-stepping Jeff who is now flanked by Dwayne. He laughs, shakes his head, and vanishes behind a new pickup.

We are close to home. Only 350 bucks apart.

"Can you do this for me, John? Your windshield's cracked and there are high miles," and Dwayne writes a figure down on paper. Almost there.

"No way. The Tahoe's a damn good car and we've taken good care of it. You know our price." The pair disappears once more. We go out for a smoke and in minutes Jeff returns, face flushed, jumpy, slightly crazed.

"We've got a thousand-dollar spiff on the Suburban, but I fought for you guys. It's a great rig. I'm telling you the truth. There's no more room in the deal for us." He shows me a figure written in blue ink on a legal paid that is fourteen dollars short of our goal.

I look at Ginny and she shrugs once more, so I take Jeff's sweaty hand and say, "What the fuck. Write it up." There is another hour dealing with a numbers-freak insect in finance, and following a lunch break (it was now 4:15 P.M.) we come back to get the papers and our check. As I walk up behind Jeff I hear him say to another salesman, "Four hours to close the deal. If I didn't need the sale for my bonus, I'd have told them to walk," and I say, "I'm here, Jeff, for the check." He jumps, rounds up Tattoo, who then disappears through another door. Jeff sighs. A weary, resigned sound. We have nothing to say to each other anymore. Our little friend returns, making a big show of how hard it is to close this particular door.

"You have no idea what it's like in there. What I had to go through to get your check cut. They're animals in there," and he glances quickly at the thick metal door. He hands me the check. Laughs again. Glances at Jeff, who looks beat and in need of a stiff drink, and then he looks at me, smiles, and says, "This was a lot of fun." He literally disappears behind a high desk.

I walk through a gaggle of salesmen who are shooting the shit about the NBA playoffs. They turn silent at my approach. Ginny is waiting behind the wheel of the Suburban. I'm thinking, *Trenton, New Jersey. Ames, Iowa. The high plains. It's all the same lunatic hustle when it comes to car dealers.* The engine is running . . . smoothly. "We survived, John, and it's a good car. Let's go home."

"See that clown spinning fools around." The Flock playing in my head again. We drive back to Livingston.

It is our first night here and the dusk is a translucent silver cloud that drifts with a peaceful totality all around us. The bluffs, the hills, the darkening sky, the little river, each of us, all is awash in this almost nonlight. We sip our evening tea. I enjoy a Mexican cigar in the stillness. The sound of cows bawling and talking girl talk, mainly about a large bull a rancher dropped in their midst earlier today, is all but gone. The women are grazing on a tabletop grassy bluff. The bull is lying down at the base of the rise. The landscape is quiet now. No coyotes yipping or nighthawks booming or mayflies hatching in a whispering hum. No moving air.

The sound of a truck highballing down the country gravel road that leads to Peerless growls across the fields. The dust the rig raises rests above the road like a red-brown cylindrical cloud. The truck slows down and pulls off at the bridge. The lights go off and the pickup, an old Ford, lurches down to the river, brake lights flashing red in the gathering dark. The driver kills the engine. Everything is still for several minutes, then even over the distance from the bridge to us the sounds of the truck's bench seat creaking drifts to us. Then the moans of a woman grow in passionate intensity and finally a groaning climaxing howl of a man, and then everything is quiet again for a while. Eventually the driver fires the truck's engine, backs up the rise from the river to the road, turns on his headlights, and roars off back to, no doubt, a bar in Peerless. The dust hangs dimly above the road. We look at each other and laugh. Love on the prairie. We turn back to the river and watch as a large northern pike V-wakes back and forth near the surface of a shallow pool. Dozens of small minnows flash blue-silver in the crescent moonlight. The land rolls off in all directions. The cattle turn quiet. Coyotes begin to bark and howl. The remains of the early evening breeze disappear.

During the holiday season of the same year we worked on this book we received a Christmas card from the Daniels County deputy sheriff thanking me for sending a copy of one of my books, *Reel Deep in Montana's Trout Streams*. I'd mailed the book as soon as we'd returned from our October visit to his country. In the card he said that he'd spoken to the rancher who lived near where we'd camped and that the man told him that we were welcome to stay on his land when next we came to the area. The deputy went on to say how he had enjoyed meeting us and that he looked forward to seeing us again. Ginny and I both smiled when we read this. The country up his way is special and we wanted to see it again.

The Musselshell Valley and river with all its glorious brown trout.

The Crazy Mountains as viewed from near Big Timber in southcentral Montana.

Livingston artist poses at his studio above Russell Chatham's gallery, in front of his paintings of bull trout.

A wild mare and her colt on the top of West Pryor Mountain.

A face in the eroded stone along a ridge south of the Pryor Mountains in Northern Wyoming.

ABOVE: A channel catfish taken from the Powder River drainage in May not far from Broadus, Montana.
BELOW: Tazun and Powell Swanser (right) pose in front of their "Cannibal Café" behind their home.

ABOVE: A dirt road leads into the Missouri Breaks on the north side of the river.
LEFT: Missouri Breaks river ferryboat operator Grace Sanford.

A series of waterfalls on the Hay River in Canada's Northwest Territories.

The Sun River, with Castle Reef on the left nestled in the Rockies, just before the river pours out onto the high plains.

ABOVE: Cactus was a constant companion during our wanderings around the northern high plains.

RIGHT: The Murray Bar & Grill on Park Street in Livingston.

THE MUSSELSHELL VALLEY

I AM LYING NAKED on top of my sleeping bag to try to beat the rare humid heat of this August evening. It's after ten and the sky is still tinged with the last glow of the dying day. In the west large thunderstorms roll northeast across the Little Belt Mountains. The thunderheads tower thousands of feet, their boiling tops disappearing in the darkness. Intense series of lightning flashes illuminate the clouds' interiors with blasts of white. Around the fringes of these explosions the clouds are a seething purple. In the light of the strikes I can see sheets of rain falling. Probably hail, as well. And roaring off the north slope of the Crazies is more heavy weather. A series of storms pulse over the peaks all day and into the night. More lightning flashing and booming in the distance, maybe ten miles away. Looking out the front of the tent I can see stars and a meteor or two that fizzle across the sky leaving a sparkling trail in its wake. The weather pattern has held all day, since we pulled into another of my long-time camps, this next to a stretch of the upper Musselshell River in central Montana.

I first found this place in the early seventies while roaring down Highway 12 in my Toyota Land Cruiser bound for Lewistown and

Big Spring Creek. I never made it that far way back then. The Musselshell sparkled and dazzled me in that time-distant sunlight. The small river curved and arced through a corridor of cottonwoods and the water kept calling to me. Loudly. "Brown trout. Brown trout." I couldn't resist and the Toyota pulled automatically to the right, off the highway, down a barely discernible set of tracks, across a deeply rutted wash, and then along a meadow next to the river. Looking at the water I almost had another in an ongoing series of fly fishing–related breakdowns. The Musselshell glided through lush cattle country. I could hear cows bawling not far from me. The sparkling though slightly turbid water bubbled over rocky riffles, swept beneath willow- and alder-covered banks, and poured into deep pools highlighted by foaming eddies. A loud splash pulled my eyes upstream along a three- or four-foot-deep glide. The smooth water mirrored the cottonwoods, the blue sky, and the puffy, white clouds, except near the far shore where large rise forms broke the calm surface in a string of widening concentric circles. A gust of hot wind kicked up, and I watched as two large grasshoppers blew on the water. Instantly several browns, jaws wide open, hammered the insects in boiling rushes. I staggered and crawled back to my car, heart palpitating, mind spinning, chugged a brace of Pabsts, and rigged a four-weight rod in a little less than thirty minutes, hands trembling, body on the verge of convulsions.

Fishing has been a lifelong passion with me that grows in intensity, though it has slightly transmogrified itself into a vaguely more sedate form that is no longer obsessed with catching fish. (I can see friends of mine reading this and saying, "Right, Holt. You bet.") Whatever. Almost all of the good country I have found anywhere, Montana, Wisconsin, Iceland, Alberta, South Dakota, has been a result of seeking out fish in places where there are few if any people. Solitude, a few fish, a nice river or lake, some unspoiled landscape. That's all I need.

So I tied on a battered hopper imitation that fateful July day more than twenty-five years ago and stepped into the river wearing tennis shows, T-shirt, cutoffs, sunglasses, and my Cubs hat. The hat goes where I go. The first cast was a bit long and banged off some exposed dirt and rock on that far bank. Before the fly ever had a chance to ricochet into the water, a brown leaped out and grabbed it. Setting the hook in the trout's jaw provoked a maniac response. The fish raced upstream tearing the surface apart as it thrashed and leaped trying to free itself of the hook, and I thought, *Well, there goes the rest of them over there.* Not likely. The other browns never stopped feeding. Eventually the brown gave up, let go of his hold in the water, leaped once more, and then allowed me to pull him into shallow water. Eighteen inches and heavy. Coppery-red and light black spots. White-tipped fins. A cream belly flecked with charcoal. Deep yellow-gold flanks that shaded to rich brown turning near black on its back. When I released him, he swam back in the direction of where I'd hooked him only a few minutes earlier, and I swear I recognized him resuming feeding. I took a dozen more like this one in the next couple of hours, the first few directly in the first fish's line of fight. When I returned to the Land Cruiser I said, "The hell with Big Spring Creek." Though the fishing has never been that good again in the ensuing years, I've always come back here at least once a year, usually much more often. And not only for the fishing, which can turn so cold in the Musselshell that I wonder if there has been a massive fish kill in the river. Mainly I come here, as I do for most of my favorite places in the West, for the tranquility, the solitude, and the beauty. The Crazies rising to the south, snowcapped into July. The Little Belts doing the same in the northwest. And there is thick grass range rolling off in all directions. Few people come where I come even though it's on the map. And the traffic on the highway that gets me here is marginal.

That's why Ginny and I are here taking a few days break from the road, enjoying the scenery, the fishing, and the quiet.

Looking back west I see a pair of headlights bobbing along the bumpy way that leads to our camp. They grow closer and now I can here the mufflerless roar of a large engine, then make out a pickup coming right for us. I grab the .357 Smith & Wesson Magnum that I keep next to me at night and prepare to defend my lady in full, stark-naked vehemence in the depths of a Musselshell night. The truck stops feet from the tent, engine idling loudly, and a door opens. I see a pair of booted feet and then am blinded by the beam of a flashlight.

"Sorry ta bother you folks this late at night," a cheery, slightly drunk voice yells.

"Think nothing of it," Ginny responds while I pull the sleeping bag over me and the gun.

"We'll be runnin' coons tonight down da river and I didn't want ya all frightened," the bodiless voice says, the beam still in our faces, along with the headlights. "There'll be a bit a shootin' as we run da dogs, but I want ya ta know da dogs're good uns and won't harm ya, so please don't shoot 'em," the headless voice politely requests.

"No problem," I say.

"Have a nice evenin'," and the boots move back out of sight around the raging pickup. A door slams. A transmission clunks as the rig is crammed into gear and off the whole mess goes. I crawl out of the tent, still naked and holding the gun, and watch the red taillights bounce and flicker and sometimes go out (bad wiring?) until they disappear beyond a thatch of willows.

"What was that all about, John?" asks Ginny.

"Damned if I know. Just another weeknight in Montana," and we try to go back to sleep.

About 120 miles downstream from our camp lies the nearly extinct town of Musselshell. In the 1930s the place had a population of 151, but it's nowhere near that now. Thriving communities spring up and then die away out here. Mining booms. Timber booms. Fluctuating beef prices. Bad crop years. New railroad lines or formerly busy ones abandoned as is the case in this valley. The Milwaukee Road pulled out of here years ago taking the rails, most of the electrical gear required to run the trains, and even some ties when they went. Power booster stations decay along the crumbling grade, the abandoned brick buildings sitting out in the weather looking like husks with their windows broken out. Musselshell was named for an old stockman's landmark known as Musselshell Crossing where herds of Texas longhorns driven north in the 1880s were bedded down one last time before being distributed to their new Montana owners. The Crossing was established in 1877, opposite the townsite. The trail between Fort Maginnis and Fort Custer passed through. Three years later a store-post office opened and settlement in the area began in earnest. For nearly three decades stockmen controlled this country with only rustlers to contend with, many of whom were captured and quickly hung, probably from one of the many cottonwoods. All of this ended in 1908 when the railroad arrived bringing with it hordes of sodbusters eager to break up the free range into small tracts of cultivated land. Coal in abundance was discovered and mined. As was true throughout the West, the free-form way of life was rapidly killed by a burgeoning grain industry and miles of barbed wire.

Less than thirty miles downstream is a place known as The Cliff, which was the site of an old piskun or buffalo jump where the Blackfeet herded and drove thousands of buffalo to their deaths. When the highway was first cut through the valley, piles of the animals' bones were exposed.

A touch farther upstream is Harlowton, which used to be a division point for the C. M. St. Paul & Pacific Railroad. This is where the electrified section of the line running west began. There used to be a flour mill here capable of storing over a half million bushels of grain and turning out nearly a thousand bushels of flour per day. Today Harlowton is a quiet place. Stores, shops, and hotels are slowly fading away. Walking through the empty railroad service buildings south of town is a forlorn experience. The immense interiors are gloomy, the air cool. Short stretches of tracks that once held powerful locomotives, while dozens of engineers and mechanics serviced and repaired them, are tarnished and corroded with the passing of years of neglect. The floors of the buildings are covered with large, dark stains of engine oil. There is the faintest smell of this and other lubricants holding in the musty air. Sunlight, dulled by its passage through dingy windows, slowly slips across cracked concrete as the sun moves across the sky. The place is empty. Devoid of energy or even ghosts of times past. I look out the huge doors into the blazing light of day and hear birds singing and see deep green leaves blowing in a hot summer wind. I turn and walk that way.

Highway 12 follows the headwaters of the Musselshell through a canyon between the Little Belts and the Castle Mountains on the south. Large white outcrops in this area are Madison limestone, a sedimentary formation deposited in shallow seawater 300 million years ago. The entire valley was once part of a vast inland sea. Farther downstream older sedimentary formations are primarily shale deposited during the Cretaceous period between 135 and 165 million years ago. Cliffs along the river expose seams of coal that are part of the Fort Union Formation.

Everything is connected on the northern high plains whether it be by weather, economics, or geology such as the Fort Union Formation that ties this land together in a subterranean way from Wyoming north to Saskatchewan.

The Musselshell is a peaceful place. I've been here in the spring when hundreds of sandhill cranes gather in the fields, their prehistoric clacking a prehistoric roar. The three-foot-tall birds are a weird, wonderful sight as they peck at the ground with their elongated beaks while perched on spindly legs. When they lift into flight the huge gray wings flap slowly at first, rapidly gaining speed, and the large birds eventually lift from the ground, describing wide lazy circles as they gain altitude for the next hop north to breeding grounds hundreds of miles away in Canada. By summer only a few nesting pairs remain along the river clacking warnings to stay away at me as I wade after the brown trout.

And there are multitudes of whitetail deer. Working through the tall grass that even grows a couple of feet over my head by late July I've surprised a number of them around as I walk back from an evening's fishing. They are near where they bed down and leap up and often crash right by me as they flee through the grass. At dusk they come out of the cover and graze on the grass near camp, singularly or sometimes in bands of a dozen or more. Black bears are common here and Ginny discovered the nest of one less than thirty feet behind our camp. A large circle of grass was matted down. Large scat was everywhere. I've never seen a bear here, only signs, and blacks don't concern me. They tend to flee humans unless they've been habituated to our food. Grizzlies are another matter, though jumping one this far out on the plains would be highly unlikely.

Owls, eagles, hawks, migrated mallards, wood ducks, western tanagers, western meadowlarks (the Montana state bird), bluebirds, ravens, magpies, and many other species hang around at various times of the year. In autumn flights of Canada geese leave their evening rest areas to fly north from the river at sunrise to gorge on grains growing up that way. As the sun begins to disappear behind the western horizon the same flocks return in large, raggedy V's, the graceful birds honking as they begin to set their wings for a nearby touchdown. These flights often last for an hour or more.

A peaceful place, to be sure, but where my visits to this river are concerned not without some weirdness.

Years ago back in my whiskey drinking and other things days I was sitting on the tailgate of my pickup working on a bottle of Jim Beam and smoking a big, black Honduran cigar. From the corner of my eye I noticed a splash of moving white that turned out to be an older gentleman wearing a white dress shirt, creased black pants, black wingtip shoes, a black beret, and smoking a pipe. He was walking an equally old, fat beagle on a leash. I thought this a bit odd since there was no one camping in the vicinity and the nearest ranches were miles away. In the spirit of the moment I took a healthy blast of whiskey and a big puff on my cigar. Man and dog shuffled through camp.

"Evening," he said, looking briefly my way. "Dog needs to walk. Yes he does. Good night to you," and he disappeared over the next hill. I never saw either of them again.

The next day when I returned from fishing I noticed that my tent was gone, but that all of its contents were folded and neatly stacked on the tailgate. Had the old boy done this? Or was he a spectral omen or warning?

Damned if I knew. I took another slug of Beam (it was near noon back then) and another big puff on another Honduran cigar, loaded my gear, and drove off.

And those coon hunters appeared again later this year. This time in September when musician Danny O'Keefe and his companion, Laurie, joined us for a few days of fishing and general laziness. Danny was sitting in a chair playing a new song for us when the boys, there were three of them, pulled up and ran the same spiel they'd dropped on us earlier in the summer. Laurie and Danny looked at us with curious "what's up?" expressions and Ginny and I shrugged, now inured to the out-of-kilter, mad scene.

The boys returned after dark and stopped again. By this time Danny was working on starting a small, white gas lantern, a spelunker's headlight strapped to his head. The lighting of the device was intriguing, bordering on potentially becoming a conflagration, excessive fumes igniting in a whoosh of flame that leaped above the lantern. He finally persevered, and with the hissing, brightly glowing lantern firmly clutched in one hand, a cup of Irish whiskey in the other, and a Marsh Wheeling stogie smoldering in one corner of his mouth, he approached the raccoon hunters.

Looking down at the three hunters, now sweaty and dirt-covered lads, he said, "I think it's only fair to warn you that you are in the presence of a man with a lit lantern and he knows how to use it."

As he made this pronouncement a flash of lightning issued from a storm building in the Crazies. The strike illuminated the setting with white light. We all looked like escapees from a black-and-white negative. This was followed by a long clap of thunder. I knew O'Keefe was good, but this good? The three stared with open mouths. I could see one of them start to say something, then think better of it. The driver said, "Have a good evenin'," and they drove off in a hurry. Just another weekday night in Montana.

We never did get any sleep that night we first encountered the raccoon hunters. For the next few hours the sounds of a pack of coon hounds baying, yowling, and screeching as they pursued hapless masked mammals down the Musselshell echoed through the night. Then there would be brief moments of quiet followed by intense barking and several shotgun blasts as the clowns finished off their quarry. High sport out here on the Musselshell. Eventually all the racket died down, along with several raccoons, no doubt. We heard truck doors open and close, the engine fire up, then watched as the headlights again bobbed up and down and blinded us once again. The truck passed our camp and lurched back up to the highway and turned right toward Harlowton.

Finally we can get some rest, I thought. I was wrong.

Amid barrages of lightning and thunder from storms that were swarming all around us the sounds of drums, a bass, an organ, and an electric guitar sounded distantly in the direction of Martinsdale, a small town located along the abandoned rail line several miles away. The storms subsided for a while and I could distinctly make out an off-key voice of a woman singing an old Credence Clearwater song, "Tombstone Shadow." Perhaps an appropriate title considering all that had transpired here this evening. The music continued for hours, wavering in and out of my hearing as the storms rose and fell. I could also hear screaming, yelling, and unrestrained applause after each song. Eventually the music and the party in Martinsdale died away. The beer probably ran out. The thunderstorms had moved off to the northeast by now. Flashes of lightning flared on the horizon as if a war were being waged miles away. Everywhere else the sky was clear and packed with stars. Meteors shot overhead again. An owl boomed in the night and the sound of a small animal screaming to its death followed.

I considered the night. This used to be prime hunting grounds for the Blackfeet 150 years ago. Prime trapping terrain for the mountain men seeking beaver pelts. I remembered seeing a picture of Andrew Garcia, a trapper-trader in this area during the 1880s and author of *Tough Trip Through Paradise*, a book that chronicles the man's adventures through Montana back when the place was truly wild. In the photograph Garcia is standing next to his horse in deep snow. The horse's coat is shaggy as a hedge against the cold. Garcia is wearing long, thick fur mitts and chaps and a buckskin shirt. He has long, gray and dark brown hair and an almost equally long beard of similar coloration. Hard, clear eyes bore into the photo's viewer covering the distance of more than a century. I recall some of his words in the book:

Little did I know that day that I was leaving the white man and his ways forever and that I would become innoculated with the wild way of life of the Indian and be one of them, to live and run with them, wild and free like the mustang.

Garcia had traveled this stretch of river I'd camped along and may have even hunted, trapped, and even camped here himself. Water, shelter, and a good view in all directions. Safe and secure. Why not? I chose to believe he'd stood around a fire a century ago where I was now.

The Musselshell was a corridor of travel for Indians and whiskey traders alike. The weather was probably about the same and the land hasn't changed all that much except for the roads, towns, cattle, and barbed wire.

Instead of a hunting party of Blackfeet maybe chanting around a huge blaze and a couple of trappers sitting around another fire some miles away from the Indians and maybe firing guns in the night drunk on trader whiskey, not all that much has changed. The form of activity is altered. Coon hunters chasing raccoons with dogs and shotguns instead of with beaver castor and traps. Or substitute me harassing the brown trout during the day for a group of Blackfeet braves riding down bison bareback atop their ponies, bowstrings taut, arrows aimed. The sound of pounding hooves vibrating the ground for many empty miles. A rock band and its intoxicated minions instead of Blackfeet raiders or mountain men raising hell in a distant night.

All in all things go on over the centuries to approximately the same rhythms.

All of us whether we like it or not dance to the same tune in our own curious, individual ways.

This time around it is to the beat of the Musselshell River, nineties style.

The Hell Creek Bar in Jordan, Montana, on the edge of the Missouri Breaks.

THE MISSOURI BREAKS

W AY OUT IN NOWHERE, I guess that's where this begins and ends, in a place a New York radio station called "the lonesomest town in the world" back in the 1930s. In east-central Montana twenty-five miles south of Fort Peck Reservoir lies Jordan, Montana, with a population of maybe five hundred. In some of the most isolated, powerful country in North America this middle-of-nowhere community stands like an oasis. And if this is a lonesome place, the Hell Creek Bar on the town's main drag is not. All day and well into the night Jordan residents, ranchers, hunters, fishermen, and peripatetic travelers wander in for a cold drink or a cup of coffee or a sandwich and always a little small talk.

For decades Hell Creek has provided a friendly place for people to relax, whoop it up, or just plain regroup from the awesome vastness and relentless loneliness of the miles and miles of open spaces rolling off in every direction. Sage flats, coulees, bluffs, creekbeds that sometimes hold water but usually don't, mule deer, elk, antelope, coyotes, hawks, eagles, and lots of cows and sheep. That's Hell Creek country.

Charlotte and Joe Herbold bought the place four years ago and have done much to renovate and enlarge the operation. When you come in the door dozens of eyes stare down on you—pronghorns, mule deer, northern pike, sauger, walleye. They all glare at the new arrival with unblinking eyes from their mounted positions on the walls. And the patrons will turn ever so slightly from their bar stools, give you a quick appraisal and a smile before turning back to their drinks and conversation.

"What'll you have," asks Charlotte with a smile before we have settled into our places at the bar. We order cold drinks and she fills the order and asks how we're doing. We say, "Just fine," and tell her our business, which is finding out more about her bar, and after a bit of give and take and checking us out to see if our intentions are what we say, Charlotte opens up as if we were old friends.

We remark on the craftsmanship and beauty of the cherry-wood back bar and she tells us that when she and Joe were working on refinishing it she saw a picture of the bar and lighting fixtures at Chatham's Livingston Bar and Grill and away she went with theirs. The bar originally came from France a very long time ago. The racks to hold that country's fine wines are still in place. Once in this country it eventually made its way up the Missouri River from St. Louis to Fort Benton by steamboat, sometime later by ox cart to Hilger, and eventually to Jordan by truck over more than one hundred miles of dusty two-track roads in the 1930s. All of this woodwork is accentuated by a tin ceiling that Char says she could sell for "beaucoup bucks," but she won't.

She leaves us briefly to attend to a customer who just strolled in wearing work boots, dusty jeans, a denim shirt, red suspenders, and a gimme ball cap. She pours him a shot of Jim Beam and opens a can of beer. "I need a puff," he tells Charlotte and she fetches his brand from a cupboard beneath the bar. Camel straights. As it should be. She and the old guy chat for a bit about someone and Charlotte adds, "You don't have to be drunk to deal with him, but it sure helps," and there's a good deal of knowing laughter from the regulars. Another older gentleman, perhaps in his seventies, walks in and says, "Where's my fish?" and Char goes into a room behind the bar and returns with a box of frozen salmon. He says, "Thanks," with a smile and walks back out. That's the way it goes at Hell Creek. Friendly, seemingly happy, and respectful people come and go here as part of their daily routine. And every few months area musicians—fiddlers, guitar players, banjo players—gather at the bar for informal jam sessions that last for hours.

Glancing at the top of the back bar I see a row of hats—New Orleans FBI, Memphis FBI, LA FBI, Kansas City FBI, Denver FBI, Chicago FBI, Atlantic City FBI, and Cincinnati FBI. If a person didn't know the recent history of the town, he might wonder just what in the hell kind of place he staggered into. And if he kept on scanning the hats above him he'd see CBS Sports, Fox News, ABC News, NBC News, and on and on. "What gives here?" he might ask.

Well, back in the spring of 1996 a group of individuals called the Freemen made the national and world news scene when their political views ran so counter to that of the various governmental agencies in the land that things came to a head and the predictable standoff with the Freemen, well armed as is almost everyone in Montana, or at least used to be before things went soft and West Coast, holding up in what the media termed a "compound" not far outside of Jordan. By the time it was all over and settled without bloodshed, unless you count the FBI agent who was killed when he rolled his car over while driving pretty fast on the red-dust roads, literally hundreds of FBI agents, reporters, photographers, and curiosity seekers had dropped in on the town and the Hell Creek Bar. Jordan was on the map thanks to the Freemen and everyone in town still talks about it.

"From March 26 when everything started until April 19 when it was over this place was packed with agents and media people," said Char. "And they were all well behaved and nice. And they left good tips. We made beaucoup bucks then," and she smiled.

"Joe finally started a media sign-up sheet so we could see who was who and who all was here," and Char hands me a sheaf of legal notepad pages filled with names and hometowns of reporters from New York, LA, Chicago, Australia, Japan, and on and on.

It was a warm April day and the town was largely empty because the ranchers were still busy with calving and lambing along with working their fields, but everyone we encountered in Jordan was friendly and helpful, but the great thing about this place is the honest individuality of the people who live here. Like the editor-publisher of the weekly paper, the *Jordan Tribune*. Just before the Freemen story went ballistic she wrote an editorial saying that the *Tribune* would run no more news on the situation and it didn't. When I learned this I smiled, then laughed. Think about it. The biggest story that will probably ever hit Jordan and the editor decides for her own good reasons that she and the town have heard enough already. So, no news on the Freemen in the local paper. Fantastic. Great stuff.

Another story I was told by someone from the area is perhaps apocryphal and perhaps exemplary of the free-form lifestyle swirling around Jordan and the high plains. Purportedly back in "the good old days" there was a guy who passed out in the mud on the street one night after a few drinks. The next morning he woke up to find his hair frozen to the ground. Some helpful souls passing by pooled their resources and pissed on his head until his hair thawed out. Well, tales like that out in the West are sometimes true, partly true, or often weirdly mythical. Take your pick.

A lot of this attitude comes from the sere, wild, rugged landscape that shapes the people who live here and in a large part dictates how they live. And there is the remoteness, a remoteness that makes the Hell Creek Bar not just a great place to go for a drink and catch up on the local news, but an important part of the community. Jordan didn't have phone service until 1935 and back then the editor of the *Tribune* relied on his short-wave radio for world news. The nearest city with more than one thousand people is Miles City and that's eighty-three miles to the south.

And now Char rejoins us and recounts the story of the Fox reporter from Los Angeles who asked her, " 'Can I have deli food shipped here?' and I said, 'Sure. Go right ahead.' But then the Unabomber story broke over in Lincoln and he was sent there a half hour before his food arrived. He called from Lincoln and said to 'spread the food out for everyone,' which we did, except for some deli meats and some kind of soup I can't remember the name of, that we sent to him in Lincoln." Char laughed some and went down to the other end of the bar to pour another round of drinks.

We finished ours and headed out the door saying, "Thanks" and "Good-bye."

"Enjoy the rest of your trip and be sure to stop in the next time you're passing through," Char called out.

We said we would, but for now we were headed for the northwestern end of the Breaks, some lonesome land a couple hours east of the Little Rocky Mountains and a tough walk away to the Missouri River flowing to the south of our planned camp tonight.

Close to sunset and nowhere near camp. Familiar country for us. Earlier in the day, we'd spent several hours climbing some ponderosa-covered hills that gave way to an excellent view of the cyanide heap, leach pit gold-mining operation above the bust-out hamlet of Landusky. Sneaking and skulking among the trees (miners don't like being photographed most times) Ginny took pictures of the huge, football-field-sized-and-shaped, plastic-lined pad that lay at the base of a blasted, scarred mountainside, or rather a nonmountainside. Acres and acres of land lay barren, lev-

eled, and denuded beneath the sun. Large hoses sprayed water on
the diggings to keep the dust down. Though the mine was all
but closed down now, trucks clattered up and down the haul
roads. Men would get out of them and adjust the spray lines. The
men looked like ants against this massive hard-rock operation. A
creek below us at the base of the hill flowed dirty orange with
waste runoff. The mountains themselves, the ones that hadn't been
hacked up for their gold, flashed dark green forest and slate-gray
rock against an intensely blue sky. The entire scene was sad, lifeless. No deer, birds, certainly no fish in the off-color creek. Only
the sounds of flies and dragonflies buzzing in the dryness. Small
devil winds kicked up spirals of dust as they spun themselves out
along the tiered blastings of the mining operation. The Little
Rockies had had their spirit gutted. Unlike the Bears Paw Mountains or the Judiths, hills that were alive and radiant with life,
this country felt dead. Not dead. Murdered. We looked at each
other. I turned to the mine and with a classic gesture of articu-
lation and grace flipped the place off and muttered, "Fuck you."
We trudged back down the hill, climbed into the Suburban, drove
out of the hills, onto the plains, and up the highway to the turnoff
into the Breaks at DY Junction. We were bound for a coulee a
friend of mine had showed me years ago. A small island of pines
out of the wind. His hunting camp in the fall. A quiet place that
looked out over the eroded smooth flats of the land and down
into the pine-filled gullies and washes. His place was nestled inside the Charles M. Russell Wildlife Preserve, a vast area made
up of hundreds of thousands of acres of land like this, solitude,
countless species of migratory and nonmigratory birds, billions of
croaking, screaming striped chorus frogs, and a lot more.

This was not a place to be wandering around in at night. The
ancient seabed of Cretaceous limestone has eroded into fantastic
shapes—raw, ripped draws and coulees, bluffs standing out in the
midst of nothing. Dirt roads wound easily up and down past

stands of ponderosa and juniper, or across sage flats only to dip down sharply and run across a narrow, loose-rocked saddle before ending abruptly at the edge of a several-hundred-foot drop down into some seldom-visited canyon. Backing the mile or so up to level ground and a turnaround was often nightmarish. Doing so in the dark was suicide. I knew we'd never make camp before dark. Bunches of sage grouse busted up into the sky in groups of two, three, a dozen, as we drifted along a smooth, dusty two-track in the fading glow of the sun that was passing from deep yellow into orange with pink and then dusk not far removed. We drove onto the edge of a bluff, stopped the rig, got out, and made camp on the boundary of a large prickly pear cactus garden. The light was now an intense orange, everything, the car, the trees, the sage, Ginny's face, even the air glowed. We made a hasty dinner of hamburgers and salad before sitting back and taking in the blood-red death throes of the day. At the edges of the horizon, for all 360 degrees, huge cumulus clouds boiled many thousands of feet above us. The clouds exploded and expanded rapidly. We could see them grow from second to second. Bolts and jagged rips of lightning arced between ground and storm. Larger strikes illuminated the insides of the clouds as darkness dropped down all at once.

"John, the storms are getting closer and bigger," Ginny said matter-of-factly. "We need to do something." She set about gathering water, a tarp, flashlight, and jackets. I sat in my chair and watched as the weather tightened its huge noose. I was sure we were going to die tonight. Jigs up. Time sometimes well spent. We were the highest objects for miles. Why fight it. Why run. In a day or two someone would find the blasted and burned hulk of our Suburban along with our charred remains. Tremendous claps of thunder boomed across the uninhabited miles, the roaring only slightly muffled by distance. Lightning was hammering the earth with hundreds of strikes per minute and the weather was still thirty, forty miles off. I got up to look for a pack of smokes and get a mug of coffee. I flicked on the car's CD to something called "Crown of Creation" by Jefferson Airplane. *Hell of a time to have quit the booze,* I thought as I returned to my doomed seat. By now Ginny had everything stowed in the tent or the car. She sat down next to me. We smoked in silence.

"When it comes, John," she said with a calm smile, perhaps recognizing that this was the way to deal with my fatalism, "we'll move down into the coulee over there and wait out the storm under the tarp. Okay?"

"Why bother? We're dead."

She ignored me and lit another smoke. The storms were closer now. The thunder was strong enough to compress and expand the air in whooshes that made my ears pop. The electrical aspects of the situation lit up the skyline in a continual barrage of white-silver-gold light, like a natural siege along all fronts.

Looking to the east we noticed a bright set of headlights run around and across the jumbled landscape. The lights would rise up and illuminate the darkness above or flash across the land. Then they'd seem to travel rapidly around in widening circles before disappearing down into some unknown coulee. This went on for many minutes, then the lights remained fixed like a landing beacon at a small airstrip. They'd spin round and round shining brightly in our direction and then vanish as they flashed the opposite way.

"What the hell, Ginny. Some crazy out driving around in the dark and out in this shit. Damn idiots," and she laughed nervously as the lights now resumed their hill-and-dale traverse of the Breaks. Then they started spinning around again. We looked away to the south and watched as lightning illuminated the course of that weather, now only ten miles or so from us. We turned back and the lights were shooting up and down from a ridge revealed by the constant lightning strokes hammering away up there. White, then soft green, then bluish, then white, and up and down.

"Saint Elmo's fire. That's all I can think of unless it's some whacko, dipshit aliens running loose," and the weather was almost upon us. The Breaks are a large, flat heat sink that bakes all day. Toward night this radiant energy rises back into the sky creating an updraft that draws the day's accumulated moisture and attendant thunderstorms to it. We were hopelessly stuck in the middle of all this.

Ginny was up carrying the gear to the coulee, leading our way with the flashlight. I got up and followed her.

"I guess down here is as good a place to die as any," I said. She ignored me and spread the tarp. We crawled beneath the nylon, clutching the edges to hold it from the wind, and we looked up as all of the storms bore down on us from all over hell. The land shook with the ferocity of the strikes. Blasts of wind knocked into swirling gusts and wind shear downdrafts. The outraged air wailed and screamed. Dark masses of thick rain clouds blew through the anvil bases of the thunderheads and exploded in barrages of rain, hail, and lightning. The air reeked of ozone. The wind would blow across our faces hot, like eighties or nineties, then whip around and chill us with its icy breath.

"You're praying, John."

"What?"

"You're praying."

"What am I saying?"

" 'God, please save my lame ass,' over and over," she said, laughing.

"We're dead, Ginny. Aren't you scared?" and a series of strikes rocked the grassy flat above us. My ears were ringing. The rain was not touching us now. The drops would began to splatter on the tarp, then the stuff would be swept up and away over to the next coulee. CK, I remember it was called.

"I feel peaceful, John. Look at this light show. It's outrageous."

"You're nuts, girl."

"Girl?"

And another microburst detonated perhaps all of 642 feet above us and between claps of ungodly thunder I could hear her laughing, "Just plain nuts," I yelled but it was way too loud out for her to hear me. Then as rapidly as the weather jumped all over us it moved off to the east and north. The crashing turned to distant rumbles and the blinding flashes became distant horizon flickerings. The storm had moved off on "legs of lightning" as the Dead's Bob Weir once put it. We crawled from beneath the tarp and walked back up to our camp.

The tent was still here.

The Suburban was still here.

We were still here.

"Wasn't that great, John," she said while throwing everything stored in the tent, along with the tent, in the back of the car, like an immense stuff sack. I helped, tossing a bag of charcoal, two five-gallon water jugs, the Coleman stove, and the chairs in the rear of the rig from about fifteen feet away. We stuffed the loose edges of the tent on top of all this, stakes, dirt, clumps of sage, cactus, and all.

"That was really something, but let's get the hell out of here and drive to Malta. A motel room sounds like paradise to me. The weather's building again, too. God cut us a break once, but not again, I think."

The lightning and thunder were once again growing all around us. I guided the Suburban back the way we came. The air was cooler now. In the upper sixties. Thousands of jackrabbits dashed across the bright arc of our headlights. Owls swooped right in front of us gorging on moths and large bugs. Then from up out of a narrow draw two racks rose, growing taller and taller and taller. Beneath them enormous eyes glowed yellow-green. As the two-track cut back briefly toward the slice in the land I saw a pair of the biggest elk on the planet. The size of pickups and they just stood there. Seven-point and six-point racks. Unbelievably huge animals that slipped back down the draw without moving. Ghostly. Unreal. The rest of the dirt miles back to DY Junction and Highway 191 were filled with millions of large, leaping rabbits, owls, clouds of bugs and moths, a band of antelope that leaped high above and across the road in the stagelight glare of our headlights, a turtle chugging down one of the tracks, nighthawks, and on and on. People zip by this land in the heat of midday and see it as lifeless. It is anything but that. The lull in the insane storm action brought the place alive, as if a crazy switch had been flipped. Surreal. Unreal real. Insane. The Breaks just exploded with life. They exploded like the storms. Even the grasses were glowing, some green, some fluorescing browns and tans. Alive. And the storms were closing in now and the rain began to fall and we made it to Malta by 2 A.M. as the bars were letting out and happily drunken cowboys, ranchers, Hi-Line hipsters, and plain townsfolk poured out and happily tottered to their pickups. We found a motel and the lady in the office seemed glad to see us; and the room was paradise. We slept until late morning when a passing freight train thundered down the tracks right behind the motel, horn blaring away, heading west, heading west.

"When he bit me I had to stick 'im," blurts the mildly manic voice at the end of the static-clogged, buzzing phone connection. "The sucker was twenty-five pounds. Tagged that red-and-black streamer I told you about, but when I got 'im to the bank, he got those razor teeth in me and tore up my neoprenes all around the ankle. He had to die, John. So I stabbed him with my knife, but Tazun got some great photos."

I get calls like this several times a year from Missouri Breaks native Powell Swanser and his wife Tazun. Slightly jumbled and excited dispatches from esoteric regions of the state concerning blown-out windshields while spring turkey hunting; twenty-five-hook catfish rigs constructed out of aluminum complete with self-baiting attachments; crazed and huge rainbow trout up near the Rocky Mountain Front—the usual stuff. I first heard from Powell years ago when he'd read a story of mine about a little-known run of giant browns that move up a small stream in far western Montana. Since that time we've traded information, some of it valid in nature, about our eccentric searches for wildlife and even wilder country. And, a minor detail to be sure, Powell is also the best trout sculptor in the world. Even he admits that, but back to the call at hand. "Powell, where the hell are you?" I ask, not really expecting a coherent answer. "Tazun and I are at the Rosebud," he practically yells and I am worried. This borders on a sensible reply. "I'm calling from Martha with the big tits' house. You know the one I mean. The pink ranch just above Flood Creek." I feel better. He's not making sense now. "Get your ass down here. The northerns are all over the place. We already filled a cooler."

"I can't, Powell. Talia and I are heading up to the Blackfeet Res to fish ice-out with Kipp, otherwise I'd be there," and I mean that. Powell and Tazun are two of the best big-fish (and turkey and whitetail and goose and so on) hunters I know. We always have a good time together, even now when we no longer break nearly as many laws as we used to—the stultifying restraint of advancing years trying to set in.

Powell has a long history out here. His family homesteaded in the Breaks, where he was born and raised . . . and . . . well, it'd be best to let him give his version of his life. And I know for a fact that some of this actually happened . . .

"I was born and raised in Jordan [the cultural center of the free world] and quite a bit of my upbringing was in the Breaks," said Powell around bites of a smoked antelope flank sandwich. "My people had a long homestead fifty-two miles northwest of Jordan, about nine miles up from Devils Creek. We ran sheep, horses, and cattle along with a bit of farming to try and pay the bills. Before I was even in grade school, they planted my scrawny little butt up on this big, ugly Appaloosa mare and said, 'This is your transportation and this is your job, boy. The cows are north. The sheep are south. Now go ride herd.' This went on through more years than I care to remember, until I was old enough to steal my first pickup and teach myself to drive. My old man was one tough cowboy and the head bronc buster for the Benny Binion spread out of Jordan. Binion owned the Horseshoe in Vegas and Mother was crew cook for the old gangster."

There are other stories, like Powell watching his grandmother beat away dozens of mostly feral house cats that were climbing the outside walls of their cabin trying to get away with the hundreds of skinned catfish fillets nailed to the structure that were drying in the sun as a hedge against future hunger.

"Cats attacking cats and my wildcat grandmom goin' after them all," Powell says, laughing. And there are tales of stalking gigantic elk with seven-point racks only to have the animals vanish into thin air, no tracks, no droppings, no nothing at the end of some desolate, desiccated sandstone and clinker cul-de-sac. And to hear Powell tell it, that's not all that appears and disappears in the Breaks. But I've spent enough time in this country to have encountered my share of spooks, spirits, strange lights, and ineffably weird feelings.

When Powell discovered that there really was going to be a book called *Coyote Nowhere* he got all excited and began barraging me with tales about life in the Breaks. The latest came via the mail in an envelope made from scrap paper and duct tape. The return address was: Swanser, Roast Cards From The Edge, Somewhere In Eastern Tim Buck Gumbo. He opened the letter saying he'd read an article of mine recently and that if I kept it up, someday I could be a real writer. As weird and farfetched as many of his tales seem, the few I've had the strength and foolishness to ground to truth have proven to be stunningly accurate. The world most of us pass through is a weak shadow compared to what a few souls experience.

"If ya want more Jordan color, the old Bear End Bar, now gone, across the street from the Hell Creek Bar, will definitely flatter yer palate. I was sitting in there one night when my uncle [Ma's bro, Art Ware, a legend from Jordan to Miles City] rode his horse through the door. Everyone got spooked. Ya didn't lip off to Art when he was strapped [wearing a gun] and drinking. He once called out the local sheriff and deputies for a balls to the goddamned wall shootout in the ditch ten miles out of Jordan. And this night he was STRAPPED. He tied his old mare to the bar rail, pulled out his ought six and .41 mag., laid them on the bar, exclaimed in a calm, powerful tone of voice, 'I have come in peace. I would like refreshments. She likes beer [the mare]. I would take a whiskey and I don't give a good goddamn what kind.' The bartender never blinked. Art's saddlehorse was served a Bud and Art was served a shot. Art hadn't seen me in eleven or twelve years since I'd been out of town down in the southwest. He sat at the bar sipping and looking at me in the mirror fifteen feet down the bar through the crowd for over an hour. We never spoke. Finally he said, 'I've shot and buried better bastards than you and I've been to Hollywood, too, you long-haired looking bird, but if you'll wander down to this end, we'll have a sip together. I'm buying and I know you know goddamn good and well who I am, doncha?' Well old Art went on, sayin', 'I'm just in from a special FBI blackbird mission.' That was code for him riding in from his ranch at night and shooting golden eagles out of the trees 'cause they were killing his sheep by the dozens. I didn't have the balls to refuse him, so we wound up having quite a whoop-de-doo that night."

Of course one story is never enough for Powell, even in letter form and the next, which I've since discovered is mostly true, also is subtitled "The Second of Volumes of Stories."

"Art and his cronies were out in the country at Hell Creek partying and one of the pack fell over dead with a heart attack.

Confronted with a perplexing and original situation, they [all drunk, of course] loaded the body in a pickup, piled in, and headed for Jordan. Going up a steep grade, just as they were meeting *ALL* the wives heading down to the fish camp to join the boys on the trail, the tailgate of the pickup flew open, the body rolled out, and the carload of hens ran over the body. And in the car was the dead guy's wife, and if that wasn't bad enough, Art made all the women feel even worse by convincing them that they ran over the poor fucker and KILLED HIM!"

Powell and the Breaks. One mirrors the other. The land influences the life of those who live on it and clearly Powell was influenced in a most serious way. You can see the Breaks when you look in his charged eyes, and I see Powell whenever I'm wandering down some lost coulee or atop some blasted bluff in that country.

Last I saw Tazun and Powell was on Halloween. They'd stopped by to say "Hello," dressed in full camo and preparing for a two-week, on-the-road bird-hunting expedition. They'd recently completed the long-threatened modifications on their old Coleman canoe. Formerly red, it was now jet-black and sporting a pair of airplane wing fuel tanks for pontoons. Each seat was complete with storage areas for rifles and shotguns. There was plenty of room for ammunition, coolers, and foul-weather gear.

"People did triple takes when we blasted by them on the highway," Powell exclaimed with a trace of crazed pride. "Their damn eyes bugged out their heads." Tazun looked at me and laughed her quiet laugh.

"Great to see you guys again, but we gotta be goin'," yelled Powell as he and Tazun, smiling as always, climbed into the black van. "Sure as hell hope the damn thing floats. Haven't tried her out yet," and off they went into the night. The canoe did float according to the letter, though they also managed to run it aground on a sandbar in the Missouri River somewhere out in the Breaks. Onward and upward.

"In later years I designed custom furniture and ran a twelve-man shop. I owned Wooden Horse Manufacturing for twenty years until one day I returned to the shop to find my crew half plastered, sitting in a circle on the floor drinking quarts of beer," and Powell gives one of those looks that says all there is to say about our species. "They were all on strike with a list of demands that were never met. I fired everyone, liquidated everything, and went to Australia.

"I spent time there, New Zealand, and especially Fiji. I married an East Indian girl from a tiny town called Tavua, up in the sugar cane district of Fiji's big island, Viti Levu. I've been back to Fiji six times and spent quite a bit of time there," says Powell as we continue the conversation in his backyard. A marauding band of small, gray caddis flies helicopters past us in a crazy flight that seems headed for imminent extinction out in the middle of not-too-distant I-90. "Bet the browns are eating those," he says before continuing with his saga. "I was caught up in two military coups, lived in the jungle, fished sharks, and discovered a koro (Fijian village) deep in the rain forest. I was the first white person that a lot of the folks in that koro had ever seen. I finally succeeded in getting my wife to America, and then proceeded to get into my artwork.

"It was a tough haul for a few years. There was a lot of living on venison, potatoes, and water but I finally started getting some breaks. After years of trying to get next to Norman Winter, an agent from Beverly Hills, I never received a single response," and Powell pushes his hands out palms up and shrugs his shoulders. "One day the phone rang. I picked it up. Norman was on the other end. I about had a coronary. He had seen my work in a Palm Springs gallery and did back flips. The next day I was on a jet to LA. He really helped turn things around for me.

"One day I'm covered with dirt, glue, and sawdust, sitting in my studio with no prospects for the future, the next day I'm in a tuxedo at a black tie affair in the Beverly Hilton drinking champagne and telling dirty jokes to Jimmy Smits, Charlene Tilton, and Sinbad. Norman introduced me to Carlos Santana and Bea Arthur as his Montana farmer friend, 'outstanding in his field.' I'm sure he was real proud of me when I ended up in a fight with Rodney Dangerfield later that evening that led to him getting tossed out of the place. I've been lucky with celebrity clientele. Michael Jackson has some of my work as do Ken Norton, Johnnie Carson, Darryl Zanuck, George Bush, and others."

Powell's work has gained recognition from other sources, too. His full-sized King Salmon sculpture was chosen by the Robb Report as one of their "World's 25 Most Exotic Gifts." One of his rainbow trout pieces was selected to represent the State of Montana at the World Trade Show in Tokyo. He illustrated Gary LaFontaine's book *Proven Patterns*. Both the Peta Pavlosk Museum in Moscow and the Smithsonian have requested work for permanent display. The Michelangelo Galeri at Caesar's Palace in Las Vegas headlines Powell's work and is shooting a commercial around his brook trout sculpture for national distribution.

"I have seen and appreciated wildlife art around the world, but never before have I actually witnessed such an unusual ability to stop a wild animal in time," said art critic Dr. Noritoshi Mabuchi in *Japan Economist*.

This could go on for a while longer, but Powell is really only interested in this recognition to the extent that it helps his art generate enough money for he and Tazun to continue this work and also to keep on roaming the far-flung reaches of Montana.

Describing Powell's work is difficult. Words don't touch the electric feeling his sculptures have. As the artsy dilettantes are wont to say somewhere east of Montana, his work is "kinetic." He says his sculptures are "mixed media" pieces, the bodies hand-carved from black walnut, fins of filed brass, gill rakers and teeth from hand-filed steel, cattails of oak and iron, and oval bases once again from black walnut. Other materials include polished white marble and acrylics. Each piece weighs fifty, sixty or more pounds.

All of his fish, the browns, brook trout, rainbows, goldens, and northerns, are based on fish he and Tazun have caught over the years. The pieces are dynamic—fish leaping up through the air pulling clouds of white and silver spray into the sky with them. The water spray is made of a combination of resins and other materials that is a well-kept secret process and quite possibly patented. Hundreds of hours go into each work. When Powell is on a run working nonstop for days and nights without end he is lost from view, from the world. Sometimes he doesn't even hear his phone. No big deal you say, except for the fact that he has the ringer wired into an air raid siren and it's damn loud.

Powell and Tazun truly live the life of those creative souls who wander among us. Their home is one of a kind filled with palm trees fabricated from old highway guardrails and bullet-riddled stop signs, a massive table carved from a single piece of exotic tropical hardwood, ancient guns, knives, bullets, bottles, photographs of famous outlaws his father and grandfather hung out and drank whiskey with, and there are the skulls, lots of skulls, including one of a buffalo that Powell found years ago embedded in a layer of exposed sandstone tucked away in a lost-from-sight coulee along the Missouri. The bison skull's age has been estimated by reliable sources at over a thousand years old. And there are some dinosaur fossils he found as a child while wandering the Breaks. All of this stuff and much more is set and displayed in adobe niches woven throughout the main room. One winter the two of them redid the entire main living area in southwestern adobe and velvet. What the hell? It works and it helped get them through a Montana winter. The whole place is like that. The backyard features a custom-designed cooking and BBQ area sweetly titled the Cannibal Cafe. And there are other undertakings in progress too arcane for print at this stage in the proceedings, anyway.

As for current sculpting projects, Powell has completed a sizable green sea turtle, *Chelonia mydas*, and already has orders for several of them. He is also designing a South Pacific jellyfish, and he is working on a piece for the aforementioned John Talia, he of marginal Bitterroot River angling renown. This features a huge brown pouncing on a ten-inch brook trout. I'd told Talia about Powell's skill, but he was skeptical until he saw the stuff up close. Then he called me and used words like "unreal, awesome, no one else comes close." That's Powell's, and Tazun's, work. Tazun is quiet, invisible when she chooses, but Powell makes it clear that without her most of what he's accomplished would never have happened.

"I tell ya, John, she's tough and she can outshoot or outfish either one of us," Powell said one afternoon while we were stalking a couple of feeding browns on the river behind his place. "She works as hard as I do and if I don't keep an eye on her, she'll go until she drops, that's if I don't go down first."

Tazun is self-effacing, modest, and a beautiful person in every sense of the word. When she hears Powell talk like this she gives him a look that clearly says, "Give us all a break, please," and her brown eyes sparkle with that combination of good humor and resolve common to fine women everywhere.

Ginny and Tazun opt for watching some hideous English period romance movie on the VCR in the adobe room. So Powell and I swiftly head off to the Clark Fork to harass some browns. The river is still high from late-spring runoff. The weather is dark, wet, and full of lightning that flashes and booms in the Sapphire Mountains to the south. We climb into Vankenstein, the couple's flat-black all-purpose van. The thing is filled with tools, fishing equipment, guns, coolers, and camping gear. The inside panels are lined with animal furs—deer, antelope, coyote, badger. There is a game-spotting platform built onto the roof and a hydraulic lift on the rear to aid in loading gear or downed meat. Powell crashes, slides, and skids down and through a muddy two-track that leads to a braided section of the river. We're both already

rigged up and we march ever onward to the roiling current. Even
at this just-below-flood-stage level, the water Powell has picked
is so good that large browns power up from the turbid depths
beneath dirty foam eddies and hammer one of the two patterns
he's designed. He's using his Junkyard Dog—a marabou muddler
on a bad acid trip concoction. I'm using his Outlaw Hopper—a
deer-hair hopper tied with psychotic looking white hair and a
dark, paranoid green, woven-yarn body. On these patterns I've
caught huge fish in streams that supposedly only held small trout.
This evening the fishing is slow but we manage to hook several
browns from sixteen to nineteen inches.

"Not bad for a couple of confirmed derelicts, John," says Powell
with a grin filled with glee, madness, and the joy of hanging way
over the edge every second. "Let's hit the tavern. There's a guy
there I want you to meet. He's made millions digging and hauling
gravel. He's a great guy and . . ." Powell pauses for a few seconds
while looking me straight in the eye with a wicked gleam. "Now
don't get concerned on me, here. He's a real sick cookie. Not only
does he have all of your books"—and Powell's laughing big-time
now—"not only that. But get this. He thinks they're good. Can
you believe that shit?"

"Takes all kinds, Powell," I say, and as we sail back the way
we came on that swampy two-track, bound for God-only-knows-
where, we make plans for meeting in the Breaks at Cat Creek, of
course, to fish for catfish next spring.

Highway bridges cross the Missouri River in or near Breaks country, but at a few places gravel and dirt roads end at the river and
the only way to the other side is by ferry. Not the big Staten
Island or Seattle to Vashon Island variety. Ships that haul dozens
of cars, trucks, and buses at a time and feature food and drinks
and sheltered surroundings. The ferries that ply the Missouri are
perhaps forty feet long, half as wide, and are propelled by a gas

engine that pulls the craft back and forth along a thick steel cable suspended above the muddy water. These crossings are located down below the broken bluffs and are operated by solitary individuals who live on the river's banks next to the crossings. One such place, the McClelland Ferry, is about a mile east of where the Judith River dumps into the Missouri from the south, a spot a couple of hours, give or take depending on the weather and road conditions, south of Havre and the same distance north of Lewistown, which is located at the geographic center of the state.

The ocher-brown rutted dirt road weaves its way among tall stretches of deep green grass growing luxurious in the deep brown soil deposited by the annual spring floods. The river flows smoothly with a slight rippling on its surface caused by the force of the current. Small whirlpools and standing waves mark submerged boulders and sunken cottonwood trunks. The Missouri looks to be a few hundred yards wide along here. Up ahead we can see an old trailer and several outbuildings. A sign saying that the free ferry is open from April through October cheers our spirits. A pair of medium-sized dogs, a black Lab cross and a black-and-white cross that looks to have some border collie in it, greet our arrival with wagging tails. We stop the Suburban at the edge of the river near the ferry. Soon a woman in her late sixties wearing a long khaki dress and a navy-blue sweater approaches us. She is working on a Camel straight, which she finishes and grinds out in the dirt. She smiles when she sees us and introduces herself as Grace Sanford. She guides me and the Suburban onto the ferry, fires up the engine, and we are off. The current tugs at the barge, pushing us slightly downstream, the ferry pulling on the cable. Grace steps from the small pilothouse and we strike up a conversation.

"I was born in a log cabin two coulees to the west of here," she says while lighting another smoke. "I've worked the ferry for seven years now and my daughter helps me in the summer," and Grace smiles, eyes twinkling behind her glasses. Looking back toward her trailer she says, "A newspaperman living on a shoe-string built the small house near the trailer under a big cotton-wood out of scrap lumber."

I ask her how much traffic she sees and Grace says anywhere from one car per day up to "eighteen or nineteen." She goes on to say that the Discovery Channel and *National Geographic* have done stories on the ferry and her, and that a filmmaker from Bellevue, Washington, did a documentary that Grace didn't like, adding that it was not "sympathetic" and made the female oper-ator of another ferry upstream "look fat." She also says that the previous operator at McClelland quit at seventy because of a bad heart and because the only fast way out in case of an emergency is by helicopter.

Soon we near the southern bank of the river and Grace deftly guides the barge up to the shore. Before we drive off she lights another smoke and offers some advice.

"Be careful. One woman went in a ditch up there," and she points to a nasty turn in the road that climbs swiftly along the edge of a bluff that rose along a rugged, sage-choked coulee. "I was on the phone for hours until help arrived and fortunately she was alright. So, have a safe trip."

She starts the gas engine once more and we watch as she and her two dogs chug back across the river.

A little later in the summer and once again it's near sunset in the Breaks. This time just south of Fort Peck Reservoir and slightly east of the Mussellshell River where it drains into the lake. We're perched on a skinny bench of land studded with ponderosa, prickly pear cactus, sage, and tall green grass. On either side of us the land falls away, dropping raggedly down into torn, fantas-tically eroded canyons that stretch for miles east, west, and north to the water. The evening is hot. In the eighties. The air is clouded with blue-gray smoke that turns the sun into a faint red-orange disk that seems to hang above the tortured landscape eternally. Its movement down behind the land is imperceptible. The wind kicks up and the smoke grows thicker. The air tastes of burned grass and pine. Wildfires are raging across the Alberta prairies a few hundred miles north. Drought time already on the northern high plains. Unless something absolutely unheard of happens, like say a sustained hundred-mile-an-hour wind from the north, the fire will never reach us. Even if the inferno moved south it is unlikely that flames or sparks would make the trip across the miles of water of the reservoir. Still, the feeling is eerie, unsettling, as if we were on another planet. Ginny is nervous about the fire, so I climb a crumbling clay and sandstone cone that rises a couple of hundred feet above our precarious camp. The sun dies dull red behind a line of pines. I look north in the gloom and can't see any orange glow on the northern horizon. The flames, if they are coming, are a long way off. I can see for miles up here, even through the smoke. I slip and slide down the powdery slope of the cone, my boots breaking through the parched soil and sinking in several inches. Puffs of tan powder burst up and are immediately swept away in the night wind. Ginny is standing nervously by the Suburban. I give her a hug and we decide to sleep in the back with the car pointed back down the way we came in just in case we need to make a frantic getaway. We fall asleep and when I wake to take a leak around 3 A.M. the wind is blowing coolly from out of the south. The smoke is gone and the blackness above is packed with stars, so many they cast bright shadows on the ground. My piss casts a wavering arc across the ground. I finish up, climb back into my sleeping bag, and fall back asleep.

The dawn breaks clear and crisp. Ginny is already up making coffee.

"See, Ginny. Just the Breaks fucking with our heads like always."

She smiles, nods, and says, "Let's head down to Lewistown and fish Big Spring Creek."

The Fort Peck Reservoir covered with ducks as seen from the north side of the Breaks.

9

FORT PECK RESERVOIR

IF WATER IS THE REAL GOLD OF THE WEST, well then Fort Peck Reservoir in east-central Montana is one of the region's largest veins of the stuff. The earthen and rock dam that holds back this huge lake is 5 miles long, 250.5 feet high, and maybe 100 feet wide at its crest. Maximum width at the base is 3,500 feet. Earth fill to make the structure amounted to 125,628,000 cubic yards along with 1,200,000 cubic yards of concrete. The dam is so big—a large grass-covered dike looking like a contoured bluff with its own wide, two-lane highway—that the first time I drove across it many years ago I wondered where the dam was. A common confusion. It's just so big it doesn't look like a man-made structure.

The dam came on-line in 1940 and closes off a wide gap in the Missouri drainage between two enormous bluffs and backs up the river for 134 miles all the way into Missouri Breaks country. There are 1,520 miles of shoreline at normal operating level with a surface area at maximum pool of 246,000 acres and a storage capacity of 18,688,000 acre feet. About 6.5 billion gallons of water per day are released generating 2.8 million kilowatt hours of electricity.

Those are just numbers that give only the slightest suggestion of the scope of Fort Peck Dam and Reservoir. Looking out over the inland sea from a windy vantage point on the east side of the dam, the water stretches off forever, the deep blue glistening in dendrite-shaped bays beneath a never-ending series of coulees and bluffs. The massive generating towers and the even larger spillway are dwarfed by the scale of the reservoir. The man-made structures look like toys compared to the immense layout of the arid land that is mainly grass, cactus, sage, ponderosa forest with sprinklings of low-lying common juniper. Dry Arm stretches for thirty or more miles to the south. Large fishing boats look like specks out on the water as they troll slowly back and forth at the mouth of the arm. Dry Arm is an ancient riverbed that Lewis and Clark came across two hundred years ago, an immense—everything is immense here—dry wash that once was an ancient river. Now it's part of this system and buried under many feet of ice-cold water provided from the Missouri River as it drains nearly sixty thousand square miles of land from the vast snowfields of the Rocky Mountains to tiny springs bubbling away out on the desert high plains.

Standing here in the sun and warm wind I cannot get a handle on this place. I cannot arrange the immensity of all of the water and land so that it fits into my mental map of Montana and the rest of the northern high plains. For the first time in this country the incredible breadth and expanse of the West hits home. Sure I get some idea as Ginny and I drive across hundreds of miles of prairie or along the front of never-ending mountains or encounter coulee after coulee, bluff after bluff, sage flat after sage flat, but this panorama is brain overload. All I can say is that the blown-away size of this place is beyond comprehension. To live out here without going mad a person must submit to the land and all its power. Ego just doesn't cut it all alone in the middle of all this barely populated vastness.

Lewis and Clark first explored this country in 1804. The old Fort Peck trading post was built in 1867 on a narrow ledge of shale about thirty-five feet above the river. The front of the stockade was so close to the ledge that it could be used as a landing for sternwheelers as they made their way up the Missouri. I can see whiskey-sodden traders tumbling into the river. High water washed out the fort in 1870.

Fort Peck Dam was the first dam built in the upper Missouri River basin. President Roosevelt authorized the project in 1933 and thousands of Depression-broke individuals moved to Montana for work. More than seven thousand men and women signed on to build the dam in 1934–35 and employment peaked at eleven thousand in 1936, a massive influx to this region where city populations were in the low thousands. Eighteen boomtowns popped up in the area and a mini-rebirth of the Wild West ensued and the township swelled from a few hundred to forty thousand.

Major Clark C. Kittrell, who served as the Corps of Engineers district manager at Fort Peck in the thirties, said of the dam project, "No engineering job of this magnitude had ever been attempted with so short a time for planning."

New techniques were developed including dredging slurry from the river bottom and pumping it through large pipelines as fill for the dam when the water drained off. The "core pool," as it was called, ran the length of the dam. Railroad cars then hauled rock and fill material over temporary bridges, dumping their cargo on top of the layered embankment of the dam. A massive slide, detailed in Ivon Doig's recent book *Bucking the Sun*, caused the deaths of a number of the workers. A large, waterlogged portion of the dam slipped a quarter mile out into the water taking men and huge machines with it.

We'd driven up to this vantage point from the now small town of Fort Peck, now with a population of 325, a far cry from the thirties as explained in *The WPA Guide to 1930s Montana*:

Fort Peck (6,000 est. pop., 1938), a planned city, seems strangely misplaced on the vast prairie. Built by the Government as a permanent town near Fort Peck Dam, today (1939) it has rows of barracks to house construction workers and a boulevard of stores and shops. South and west of the town is a maze of roads. The dam building activities fill the valley.

Not so today, though people in Fort Peck and in Glasgow twenty miles away have high hopes that a proposed Imax theater complex would return the place to its former glories. We hear them talking about the situation in gas stations, grocery stores, bars. One can only hope, I guess. Maybe Jack Nicklaus will build a real neat championship golf course here someday complete with a condo-plagued gated community. There's always hope.

Today the main form of income in the area is a slowly growing sport fishery. Walleyes bring the majority of the anglers both from instate and around the country. Fish over ten pounds are common and a hybrid of walleye and sauger, the fighting saugeye, is also caught in this range and a few pounds larger pushing the envelope of the world record ever further. Smallmouth bass up to six pounds are taken around the rocky points of the more isolated reaches of the reservoir, and this means way out there, since most of this country is isolated. Chinook salmon and lake trout in the thirty-pound class are taken by trolling large lures along the edges of the reservoir or down in a hundred feet or more of water.

Sturgeon and very large rainbow trout hold in the clear Missouri below the dam where the river is close to a mile wide as it oxbows its way toward the North Dakota border. At the head of

Fort Peck Reservoir the river is a warm-water, turbid flow filled with ling (a freshwater relation of the cod), catfish, northern pike, and a few confused trout. The sediment, which will be Fort Peck's eventual utrophied undoing, settles out in the reservoir and the river flows clean for many miles below the dam.

Most of the reservoir is surrounded by the Charles M. Russell National Wildlife Refuge with 236 species of birds sighted including upland sandpipers, mountain plovers, sharp-tailed grouse, Merriam's turkeys, sage grouse, Canada geese, northern harriers, pinyon jays, Sprague's pipits, burrowing owls, and long-billed curlews. There are also flocks of migrating waterfowl.

According to one brochure I read about 61 percent of the refuge's million-plus acres is sage brush-greasewood-grassland. About 36 percent, mainly on the western half of the refuge, is dominated by ponderosa pine-juniper type lands. Less than 1 percent of the refuge is considered riparian area, the remainder was inundated by the dam.

One evening around a fire at a camp above the reservoir some seventy miles down the Bones Trail Road I finally began to put all of this land and water into some vague semblance of perspective. I did so by recalling days wandering in similar country, a day spent floating the Missouri below Fort Peck Dam, and the time we were spending here on the northern shore of the place.

Five or six years ago Bob Jones, mutual friend John Talia, and myself headed out to this far from anywhere country to try to catch the rainbows swimming below the dam. A fisheries biologist acquaintance, who was studying both the sturgeon (pallid, I believe) and the rainbows, said that, at that time in 1994, the trout averaged over seven pounds and that he and his crew had turned up several of over a dozen pounds. He'd heard of someone hauling in a nineteen-pounder. I'd seen pictures of two rainbows taken by a moss agate collector who used his spare time to catch these fish using bait that he drifted near a large whirlpool that formed at the head of an old, rusting, sunken barge about a mile downriver from the dam. He claimed one rainbow was ten pounds and the other eight. They looked at least that large in the picture.

So with all of this in mind we headed over in Talia's older white, three-quarter-ton Suburban that we call the Great White. We were pulling an Avon raft behind us. Avons are common sights along streams like the Clark Fork, upper Missouri, Big Hole, and Jefferson, but out in this arid land, a place where most people fished from motorboats for the walleye and the always raging saugeye, the raft was an uncommon sight. Driving into Fort Peck from Glasgow, ranchers and fishermen would do double and even triple takes as we serenely negotiated the road with Talia confidently at the wheel. When we pulled into the parking lot of a bar-restaurant overlooking the water, curious faces peered at us from bar and restaurant windows. People pulling up for a quick drink stared and laughed out loud.

We had a few belts ourselves, then went off in search of a put-in for the raft. We drove down past the massive spillway, a concrete chute larger than a couple of football fields and with enough capacity during peak runoff to blow away the Dakotas in a wash of water. Then down a dirt road to a likely looking put-in except there were large white signs with blaring white letters saying that this section of river was closed to protect spawning rainbows. We shrugged our shoulders, each drilled a can of Ranier. Some of us even had a pull of cheap, very cheap, Evan Williams bourbon. At least the label said it was bourbon. The swill tasted more like varnish, but the case we'd worked over earlier on the trip hadn't killed us. We must have driven a hundred miles up and down a four-mile stretch of the Missouri looking for landings to launch and pull the raft out of the water. Back and forth in clouds of dust along gravel roads, dirt roads, and ill-defined two-tracks. We'd get close to the water, but that was it. The Evan Williams road bottle was taking some serious hits in the process. Finally Talia pulled into a ranch yard, got out, and was heading to the house when an ATV came whizzing down a dirt field and pulled up in a cloud of dust. A modern-day Lone Ranger, it seemed. The guy, in his early forties, dressed in faded black jeans, blue T-shirt, black cowboy boots, and a John Deere ball cap, introduced himself as Toby. Short, stocky, and tanned with the hint of the red burn that everyone has who spends any time out in this country. He listened to our woes with a wide, sympathetic smile.

When we asked if there were trout in the river he said, "Why yes. I've got a ten-pound rainbow and a thirteen-pound brown mounted over my fireplace. I've caught bigger, but don't care much for them myself. I prefer walleyes. Good eating. Or catfish or paddlefish. [Prehistoric, boneless monsters with bill-shaped snouts. They exceed one hundred pounds but eat plankton and are taken by snagging. They look like dolphins with beaks. The meat is excellent grilled over mesquite.] But, heck, if you want to float the river and catch some rainbows, be my guest."

And he spent the next hour showing us a couple of dandy put-ins and a perfect takeout and promised to leave his ATV down there for us to run a shuttle back to the launch point. We all smiled and shook hands. Bob, in one of the most gracious acts of generosity I've ever seen, pulled a virgin bottle of Evan Williams from one of our cases and handed it to Toby. We thought he was going to cry (not Bob, Toby), but he choked out a heartfelt "Thank you very much," and we said we'd be back down early next morning.

Well, we'd touched Toby, alright. That night at the bar and the restaurant Toby was our new best friend and he introduced us around to all his old best friends. He bought us drinks. We

bought him drinks. His friends bought drinks. Eventually everybody was buying everybody drinks. We had a high old time and
even managed to order a superb dinner of deep-fried walleye
caught that day from Fort Peck. It was pretty dark out by the
time we all staggered out of the inn and across the highway to
our sumptuous digs at the local motel, a ramshackle, beat-up place
that featured TVs with blown-out screens, bobbers attached to
monofiliment for flushing toilets, and three hundred species of
mold growing along the edges of the windows and all over the
bathrooms.

Five-thirty came early and when we reached the river one of
us was conscious. Talia, of course. He'd stuck to beer and two
shots of brandy. An icy late April wind was whipping up the
river, but we managed to launch the raft with only minor mishaps.
I spilled a beer. Bob dropped his in a foaming crash. Talia pulled
us swiftly out into the current with strong strokes of the oars and
then that current had us. For the rest of the five-mile float that
took only three hours, Talia broke his back trying to hold us
against the powerful flow of the Missouri, to retard our rapid
downstream progress so we'd have a decent shot at casting to good
holding water.

Bob and I cast large streamers, woolly buggers, saltwater patterns, and huge dries with no luck, except for one time when
Jones riffled a cast bank tight, began stripping it in, and something silver and red and enormous tagged it, snapping the twelve-
pound tippet as if it were thread.

"That was one hell of a fish, Bob," offered Talia with a slight
smile. We never saw another trout, but it didn't matter. We
floated over five-, six-, maybe seven-foot sturgeon as they worked
their way up the graveled streambed singly or in small groups.
We watched sandhill cranes lift off from nearby wetlands with
huge bluffs and buttes rising behind them. Bands of antelope
grazing on the new grass looked like tan-white-brown ants. Eagles

glided over the water looking for fish as did an osprey. We almost got sucked into the whirlpool by the sunken barge. The water spun with a roar as it sucked logs, limbs, a dead duck, nearly us, down its tightly spinning maw. Geese flew above in long skeins as they headed north, their calls the sound of spring. Whitetails grazed all along the banks. Robins chattered and argued in the cottonwoods that were starting to show the beginnings of life, as were the willows with their bright yellow-green bark and the flaming red alders. The air warmed and the Missouri just kept flowing with an even-tempered intensity that was frightening. Fall overboard and forget it. You'd die.

We pulled into the takeout and the ATV was there waiting for us. We ran the shuttle, dropped off Toby's rig, and headed up to the inn for a few post-game drinks. Toby was there to greet us and was genuinely disappointed that we'd failed in our mission.

"Come back in a couple of weeks when the water's warmer," he advised. "Then you'll catch the rainbows. Maybe a big brown, too, and if you'd like, I'll take you for some walleye."

We said we'd like to and had a drink or two more before heading down the road to our next fiasco, leaving Toby in our dusty wake waving good-bye until he vanished from view in the mirrors.

That's a bit of this place. The huge river, its big fish, the game and birds, the rolling country, and the honest, friendly people. That's a part of it.

And there's this place at the bottom of a rough, narrow road that skirted hundreds of feet of striated badlands as it snaked its way down to the water. The country is harsh, dry, severe—cactus, sage, the greasewood, a few skinny cows munching on the dry, tough grass and the land holding forth all around us with its layers of brown, ocher, tan, pink, gray, black, and light green soil and rock. Dry washes that have carved out jagged canyons over eons of rainstorms and snowmelt rip and claw their jumbled way back into the Breaks far across this narrow upper portion of the reservoir. Groves of ponderosa carpet much of the land. Deer tracks pockmark the sandy, charcoal-colored shoreline. High clouds pull in gathering storms behind them in the west. Rips in the weather show blue sky and the sun breaks through a large crease and turns the still surface of the water silver. The air is scented with sage, dust, and dry. Thousands of ducks swim slowly along shore or out in the middle, their wakes spreading out in a sequence of widening V's that flash like hot gold as the sun aims toward the horizon. Many of the ducks dive down below the surface only to reappear again many feet from where they disappeared. In a few moments they bob up like big corks and resume their course. A few coyotes talk to each other in the hills behind us. The wind has died off and the storms are staying away. The only sounds are the crackling of the fire we built from old fence posts and sticks of long-dead sage that we found lying around on this little bench we're sitting on above what I now call a lake, and the chirping of some crickets. The surface of Fort Peck is smooth as a mirror and reflects the weather and a few stars that peek through the clouds. Ginny and I look up from the coals now beginning to show their radiant colors in the gathering dark. We smile and look out over the water to the far, broken country that we'll probably never set foot in. Weathered, blasted land that glows softly white in the star and crescent moonlight now cast down from a clearing sky. Magic stuff. Mysterious. Scary in a wild way.

And that's another small part of this place. The lonesome, awesome landscape that looks lifeless in the heat of day when we are driving up on top away from the water, but is alive with these ducks and deer and invisible crickets and even scraggly cattle. Water truly is the wealth of the high plains, even this incredibly large artificial reservoir, maybe especially this artificial body of water.

That's a piece of this vast land. Cut it down to size. Visit some new stuff every year and return to old places until a sense of recognition and respectful familiarity starts to grow.

That's the way to do Fort Peck . . . the way to do the West.

A tiny tributary of Alberta's Ram River west of the town of Rocky Mountain House and just east of the Canadian Rockies.

⇜ 10 ⇝

ALBERTA—WEST

THE BIG TRUCK IS ANGLING TOWARD US in the mud. We are fishtailing toward it. The semi is hauling tons of oil rig equipment and the driver is letting the rig make its own track. The thing's tires are over a foot wide and taller than our car. Try as I might the Suburban will not respond to any of my turnings of the steering wheel. I figure that we are soon to be dead, horribly mangled in the crushed and burning remains of our car. I don't feel any fear, only a sense of frustration at not being able to control the motion of the Suburban. The semi continues toward us, now only one hundred yards away. A mud-splattered oil company crew-cab pickup slogging along well behind the truck sees what is going on, what is about to happen, and tries to slow down. He almost goes over the edge and down a steep embankment into a muskeg swamp. The truck and its heavy load loom like a seagoing oil tanker through our windshield, blotting out the horizon of low clouds, rain, and dense forest of pine trees. Seconds away from the end of all this I imagine a small headline in the *Livingston Enterprise*, our hometown paper back down in Montana a century from where we are now. "Local Writer and Photographer Killed in

Blazing Alberta Crash." One way to go out, I think. Maybe my books will sell better when I'm gone and in that instant the Suburban's tires catch in the clinging gumbo and pull us over to the far side of the road. The oil rig passes by in an avalanche of brown slop that drenches the car and coats the windshield. I have no idea where the edge is, a common situation, and blindly aim us toward a wide spot at the top of this rise that I think I'd remembered seeing when we first started up this hill. Holding on to the wheel with my right hand, I flick on the windshield washer with the other, and through the smeared, brown mess I see that we are inches from plummeting into the swamp ourselves. The car keeps its traction and I ease away from the side and slowly we top the rise where I pull over at the graveled entrance to a gas field. I get out and stand shin deep in the mud. The white pickup is slipping and spinning below us out of control in the middle of the sixty-foot-wide road. No trucks are coming the other way. The guy has a chance as he reaches the bottom of the hill in a sideways splash of mud and gravel, corrects his course, and powers up the next hill. Ginny is standing outside shakily trying to light a cigarette. Behind her I can see a pair of tall stacks with long orange flames blasting from their tops. Natural gas burn-off that hisses in the sodden quiet of the logging-ravaged forest that grows here along the slopes of the province's share of the Canadian Rockies. The forest sweeps down off these mountains in a dark green bordering on black wave that washes across wild river drainages, rugged hills, and over us and out for many miles until it washes up on the vast Alberta prairie.

"How do you like Alberta this time around, Gin?" I ask as I suck on a smoke myself. "Four days of steady rain and exciting driving, no fish, no light to photograph in. What the hell, springtime in the Rockies." It is late June, cold, wet, unpleasant.

"You saved us, John," she says. "Great driving. That guy at last night's campsite was right. The big trucks go where they want and if someone dies, so what?" and she pauses to sip some coffee. "Can you get us out of here?"

I have my doubts but nod and say, "No problem. We'll take it easy and the sky is getting lighter. The rain should let up. We pick up Highway 40 in another twenty miles and the map shows that is a better road. This forestry trunk job is bullshit."

She shakes her head and mutters, "God, please let us live."

You hear tales of how bad driving in the back country of the Rockies can be, but this road is a death trip. We've been on the thing for only an hour slogging along at twenty, thirty, sometimes thirty-five miles an hour, carefully picking our way through the thick mud, and edging over to avoid the steady stream of trucks hauling tractors, pumps, pipe, or felled trees to Highway 11 bound for other oil and gas fields, lumber mills, or Rocky Mountain House one hundred miles away to the south-southwest. Last night the park manager where we'd spent the night camped along the Pembina River warned Ginny that people were killed on this road every week. The huge trucks couldn't or wouldn't maneuver to avoid collisions. They drove where they pleased, smashed cars and pickups without stopping, and kept going. The road belonged to the extraction industries even though it was public. The rest of us hapless bastards could fend for ourselves. One hour of this and I am beat and we still have 300 kilometers (about 190 miles) to go.

I've been coming up to Alberta for years for the great fishing for rainbows, graylings, browns, brook trout, bull trout, and cutthroats. That's why we were at the Pembina yesterday. For the grayling, a silvery fish with a prominent dorsal fin that fluoresces with turquoise spots and yellow stripes, the entire body warming to light shades of purple when the fish are hooked. We didn't catch any. The June rains had blown out the river even though most of the spring runoff of snow from the mountains was gone. So we decided to head north toward Grand Cache to try for the grayling and bull trout in the Smoky River. Never been there but

I'd heard stories of excellent fishing for lots of big fish. Onward and upward. At twenty-five miles an hour we'd be there in eight hours, around 6 P.M. Plenty of daylight to find a secluded place to spend a night or two, set up camp, and cast to eagerly rising grayling using small dry flies. Fantasyville once again.

Through the fishing season of 1996 nothing much had changed up this way. Sure I'd noticed the oil boom change in Rocky Mountain House, a small place of several thousand friendly people located on the banks of the North Saskatchewan River. Originally constructed in 1799 by Hudson's Bay and North West Companies, Rocky Mountain House was the last fur trading post constructed along the North Saskatchewan River from the flow's mouth on Lake Winnipeg, and then upstream for over eight hundred miles nearly to the edge of the Canadian Rockies. Following the joining of the two fur trading companies in 1821, Rocky Mountain House fell out of use and was even abandoned for a short time. But today there is more traffic around town and the driving is a touch more frantic and reckless. And oil roughnecks are all over the place. In the motels, bars, stores, standing in parking lots leaning up against their outfits smoking cigarettes and shooting the breeze. But the change didn't seem that dramatic in '96. Sure, I'd cringed at the large clear-cuts in the deep pine forest with its attendant stream of logging trucks. And I'd shuddered at the deep open pit coal mines, but none of this rapacious activity seemed any worse than down in Montana or Wyoming. Go with the damn flow I must have figured back then. I guess I wasn't looking or the pace of the industries had kicked up a notch or two all of sudden.

I hate to see good country destroyed for the sake of a buck, for greed and excessive wealth. I know that there is lots of wild land left, and that there are lots of committed people working to save what remains. It's just that sometimes it seems like every time I turn around some formally pristine area is now a housing development or is being torn up for coal or clear-cut for its timber or sucked dry for its water. My reaction to these things is instantaneous and always filled with anger. That's the way it's always been with me and will never change.

Last year when we were up here to do a trout story for *Men's Journal* magazine, things were really changed. The oil, gas, coal, and timber industries were hacking and gouging the spectacular wild country with serious intent. Rocky Mountain House was swarming with oil company people and rigs. The locals acted stressed, even angry, a sure sign of change. And so far this year I can see that these greedy lunatics are completely out of control and damn well aware of the fact that no one is either looking or about to put a crimp in their madness.

The whole scene is turning ugly and depressing, but ever the optimist I believe that at least the rain can't last much longer. The precipitation has been coming down in sheets since we crossed the border at the Chief Mountain station on the east side of Glacier National Park. The woman there gave us a thorough going over with questions and penetrating eyes. She reminded me of an FBI agent I'd run across in my long-haired youth. *Damn, woman,* I'd thought at the time. *We're only coming up here to fish, take some pictures and notes, and have a good time. Lighten the fuck up.* I regretted not saying this to her or her twenties-something punk cohort who kept looking at us with what I assume he assumed was a withering glance. Give people a cute blue uniform, the vestiges of authority, and a border station of their own, and they go nuts. I kept my mouth shut. We like Alberta and want to come again. Up north of Pincher Creek, a town founded on mining years ago and now as much tourist place as anything, we drove along the Oldman River looking for a place to camp. This river was blown out, too. Overflowing its banks with brown water colored by rain-drenched landslides, it was unfishable and who wanted to spend time out in this monsoon anyway? Apparently a lot of Albertans, who were hunkered down beneath immense blue tarps at every wide spot in the road. Motor homes. Campers. New pickups. ATVs. All of the people were sitting around huge bonfires, and I mean huge, all reclining in lawn chairs (the ones that weren't standing out in the rain), drinking from cups, mugs, jugs, and I assume they were quaffing beverages a bit stronger than coffee. Happy (or drunk) as hell under the tarps as the rain poured off the plastic in gouts. The fires roared away in the rain that turned the forest into a misty, dull green nightmare. Smoke from the fires hung like thick blue fog around the trees. We turned around and found a motel room in Pincher Creek.

We walked uptown looking for coffee and a meal when Ginny spotted a couple of teenagers working on big mugs.

"Hey, where'd you get that?" she abruptly asked one of them. A little road buzz firing through her veins, it seemed. The kid looked at her with wide-eyed, dilated pupils (drugs?), fear, and amazement, back at his coffee, and then said quickly as if he were talking to a cop (much tougher, boy, a redhead), "I paid for it," and then the two kids beat it around a corner.

"I guess I was too forceful," she said.

"A bit, but well intentioned," and we went into a restaurant and had some Chinese food and weak coffee.

The next day we fought the rain for several hundred miles up to Rocky Mountain House where it was snowing so we rented another motel room. We went nuts trapped in the place and early in the morning we headed out to the Ram River driving through fantastic foothill country with the Rockies towering above us, the upper flanks covered with fresh snow. Each place that looked promising for camping and even fishing, though the water was already on the rise, had either a motor home or a camper or both and one or more brand-new pickups parked nearby, most of them carrying new ATVs. Blue tarps were stretched over the immediate camping areas at all but a few spots. Fires blazed away.

"Albertans take all of this seriously," I said.

Eventually we found a place tucked into the trees by the river. The rain came down in buckets and we sat by a smoking fire huddled beneath our small blue tarp, we were trying to get in the spirit of this thing, sipping thick black coffee. The river was now unfishable, and the next day we headed through the downpour north to the Pembina. The rain never let up, but the park manager came by and sold us some dry wood. John Whitehead was his name and he was a good guy. Medium height, slightly built, in his thirties, wearing a wool watch cap and wool coat, he talked about his neck of the woods, how good the grayling fishing can be later in the year, and hoped the weather would break for us. When we told him about our plans to keep going north he looked at Ginny and cautioned her about how bad the road was, and as we soon discovered he was telling the truth.

"I have mixed feelings about all of it," he said while wiping the rain from his mustache with a red handkerchief. "On the one hand it's good for the economy. Most of us have new homes, trucks, and campers, eh. But on the other hand the industry is unstoppable and they are destroying my woods. It's good for the economy, but bad for the land. I don't know what can be done about it."

He shrugged and said he had to make a run to the dump up the road at Robb, where we are headed today in the mud, and that he wanted to be there well before dark to avoid dealing with the trucks at night. He wished us luck and raced off in his old, banged-up little pickup.

So, somewhat recovered from the near miss with the truck and immortality, we climbed back in the Suburban and drove on. I had a better feel for what the car would do in this gumbo and drove a bit faster than before, carrying enough speed to push through the muck and be able to maneuver to some extent. A few large semis came close to us, but the drive went better.

Everywhere we look thousands of acres of forest are clear-cut, the land shaved as if by a gigantic lawn mover. Every drainage is hammered. There are still vast tracts of untouched forest closer to the mountains, but how many years does this country have left? Open pit coal mines are everywhere. The land scarred to depths of hundreds of feet. Miniature mountains of pulverized rock piled all over the place. Seismic roads and access tracks lead to oil and gas fields cut into the forest in an enormous grid obviously laid out with forethought and precision. Alberta is under siege big-time and no one seems to care, except for John and a few others. The rest of the people have good-paying jobs; brand-new Dodge Rams, Ford Explorers, Chevy Z77s; motor homes and campers with names like Prowler, Intruder, Executive's Choice, Rustler, Shadow, Scamper (our favorite—"Oh, look, it's a Scamper," and I'd mutter, "Piece of shit.") and Escaper; ATVs by Suzuki, Honda, Yamaha, and so on. And everybody clearly has lots of money and is very pleased with their newfound prosperity. Who can blame them? When you've been broke all your life you don't usually question the motives of the cat at your trailer's side door when he comes calling with a fistful of money.

The song by Joni Mitchell, the one about paving paradise and putting up a parking lot, keeps running through my mind, only what is going down in Alberta makes that image seem quaint. More like they raped paradise, hacked off its limbs, and left the body to rot out in the wind, rain, and mud.

Coming around the bend the gravel road we are now on widens dramatically and looking toward the mountains I can see that whole ridges have been carved off. Flanks of the Rockies have been blasted away. Piles of gray blasted rock tower above us. Huge machines move coal toward an enormous power plant. The Gregg River Power Plant. The scope of the devastation is unfathomable. I've never seen anything like it. For miles the land is blown away, hacked up, decimated, and for what? Coal to fire steam generators that produce electricity. An entire section of the front range of the Canadian Rockies is in the process of being leveled for coal. The slopes leading up to the plant are covered in bright green grass that obviously has been planted by the company. A lone deer stands in the grass. The buck looks up from its feeding and stares at us with wide, dark eyes and flicks its tail. I wonder if it's on the payroll.

And it only gets worse. Alberta is still a flat-out beautiful place and the people are as friendly as any in the world. Ginny and I once thought of living here. Not anymore. We drive through Grand Cache, a formerly wild frontier town now buried alive in tacky new banks, motels, gas stations, and restaurants. Oil company rigs are parked everywhere in packs like wolves, exactly like down in Rocky Mountain House. The wild energy of good country still roars down off the east slope of the Rockies, but this place is already gone, but it doesn't know the shape of things yet. It will.

And the wide highway that follows the Smoky River from a few hundred feet above the valley floor opens vistas of carnage that blot out the remaining mountain and forest splendor. Seismic roads cutting off in straight lines. Vast clear-cuts scar the forest like virulent acne. A coal-fired power-generating complex that spews black dust over thousands of acres of pines and birch has turned a huge wetland into black mud, sections of the Smoky River into brown-black crud, and across the river on the east side another coal operation is doing more of the same, the blackness stretching on and on.

Goddamn, this is grim and I unfairly hate Albertans and jus-tifiably hate the corporate bastards that oversee all of this hideous destruction . . .

While I write this chapter I come across my notes for this horrible day, a vision of hell for me, and find:

"Wild country relentlessly being hammered to its knees by extractive industries. They want it all no matter what the cost to the environment and spirit of the land. Just like Montana and Wyoming, only more so."

I wrote that while sitting at our campsite at Musreau Lake Campground. The day was sunny for a change. The light glittered and sparkled as it played with the new green leaves on the birch trees. We were in the middle of a prime stand of uncut temperate forest that would eventually give way to the boreal forest of the northern part of this province and the lower half of the Northwest Territories. The lake glistened cerulean with speckles of golden sunlight. The place, despite holding more than a hundred campers, was quiet at 6 A.M. Some squirrels chattered away. Small birds chirped in the ground cover. The wild roses (Alberta is called the Wild Rose Province) were budding up. The fire crackled nearby. I took a sip of coffee and recalled a conversation I'd had recently with guitarist Amos Garrett.

Amos is a genuine piece of work. One of a kind. A gifted guitarist who one reviewer said, ". . . plays a guitar like God when He's drunk." And he sings with a whiskey-throated voice that is filled with the depth of honest hard living and concern. Amos is also an over-the-edge fly fisherman and upland bird hunter. In one of the first letters I received from him he included a couple of photographs . . . of his hunting dog, also a film canister with three streamer patterns called Ganders that drive big trout to distraction. Years ago he played in Ian and Sylvia Tyson's Speckled Bird band. Went to Woodstock, and recorded and toured with Maria Muldaur, blues legend Paul Butterfield, and has recorded with, among many others, Stevie Wonder, Emmylou Harris, Bonnie Raitt, and Todd Rundgren. His latest album is called *Off the Floor Live* and was recorded at Edmonton's Sidetrack club. He is frequently seen wearing a hat that an Inuit gave him when he was in the Northwest Territories. The ball cap has a working clock on front with the question: "What time is it?" and on the back the answer: "It's fishing time." That's Amos and he makes his home near Calgary, quite near the Bow River and its fat rainbows.

"Alberta is a very, very wealthy province compared to Montana, but that comes with its own baggage," he said. "The provincial government is making millions in oil taxes and that just comes in the mail," and he laughed but it wasn't one of joy. "Maybe there's ten to fifteen million dollars from sportsmen. That's paltry. So there are deaf ears in Edmonton [the capital] when Trout Unlimited or Ducks Unlimited asks for, say, a fish exclusion device to screen off trout from being drawn up by pumps sucking irrigation water.

"I don't think we have the federal programs, the three-letter acronyms, that you do down there that are great. You do much more for the trout and the upland birds than we do," he added. "All trout streams have built-in enemies and in addition to the obvious ones like mining, timber, oil, and gas, we have irrigation to deal with. Wheat is two dollars a bushel now. We've had a string of bumper crop years. Because prices are so low now with the surplus, a farmer needs twelve to twenty sections to make it. Before then, in times of drought before all this irrigation that is drawing down the rivers and sucking up the trout, one or two sections was all a farmer needed, then he went south to Arizona for the winter."

And Amos told me about his TU group spending long days netting rainbow trout out of irrigation ditches after they'd been sucked out of the Bow River by the big pumps. One hundred thousand of them and there were plenty more that he and his friends couldn't save.

"The outdoors clears my mind from my art, especially when I'm hunting behind my German shorthair. By the end of the season my legs are like iron, but come winter everything falls apart," and he laughs at this.

The only optimism about the extractive industries that Amos could muster was, "The best thing about running out of oil is no more oil companies."

And that's the deal with oil companies, coal consortiums, and timber giants, when the minerals and the trees are gone, so are the companies and all of their money. They're looking to ravage someplace else for a quick, transitory buck. And all of the people with the new homes and pickups and ATVs will be broke and the provincial banks will repo all the toys. That's how it goes on the high plains. And what's left? A blasted, torn-apart, ruined landscape that's had its guts and spirit slaughtered for the sake of greed and profit.

I recall what Dr. Brian Horejsi of Calgary said in the summer 1999 issue of the *Networker* published by the Alliance for the Wild Rockies based in Missoula, Montana:

> On this day of reckoning Americans cannot trust the future of endangered bear populations to another land or another government. The future lies in your own backyard, your own institutions, your own public lands. To look elsewhere for salvation is to commit ecological and scientific suicide.

Horejsi was speaking of the fate of the grizzly bear, but I'm considering the fate of everything. Canadians justifiably worry about our treatment of the land and we worry about theirs. I guess the whole sick situation comes down to everybody cleaning up their own backyard messes and moving on from there. Maybe in the next variation of my life I can just go from pristine wonderland to outrageous paradise with no worries about the destruction of the land. I'd like that.

I paused in my egocentric thinking and looked out over Musreau Lake. Trout were rising to large mayflies. The fish were making wide rings on the lake's surface and I could hear the sipping of the larger trout. *Plip. Plip. Plip.* Then the sound of outboard motors ripped the silence, and loud voices yelling to "Bring the beer. Don't forget the bait. Where are the skis?" Within minutes the lake was filled with noisy, fume-belching outboards pulling water-skiers or racing off to the far shore to fish or just roaring around in circles. Over the roar I could here the whine of ATVs starting up and a mix of radio, CD, and tape player racket. I looked out at the lake. The trout were gone somewhere down deep.

The forest drops down to the banks of this small river that first tumbles down from the Canadian Rockies many miles to the west before sinking into muskeg only to reappear in the soft, rolling edges of the foothills where the stream now flows dark emerald beneath the dark firs and silver-green spruce. Willows and alders grow along the green undercut banks of tall grass. The river curves in easy arcs as the water winds its way toward the prairie. Logjams are piled up in some of the narrow bends. Pines, knocked down when high water washed away the soil holding their roots, the trees still living, stretch across the stream at places, the limbs of green needles streaking the surface of the flow. The clear water bubbles brightly across narrow riffles of colorful rock and pebbles, sweeps silently in deep runs along the banks, or forms deep pools that are more sapphire than the green. Deer graze in the forest. Birds sing. Tracks of small mammals sharply mark the moist banks. Fresh tracks from a grizzly push deep into a silt bed on the inside of one bend. A first true day of summer with its soft, warm wind. Large brown mayflies are rising up from the river, or already swirling in their timeless up and down mating dance high above the surface. Down below, long, dark, thick shapes hold inches below the surface or quickly rise to the surface and with a gentle yet quick opening and closing of their jaws take the mayflies still trapped in the surface film of that water. The browns, some of them over five pounds, flash golden brown flanks with deep red and black spotting as they shift and turn in the river feeding. This all-connected motion drifts on all day and well into the cooling dimness of evening. The unspoiled river flows peacefully through the countryside as do a number of others in western Alberta. The ones that still remain wild.

The Cypress Hills of Alberta in October. Reesor Lake is on the right.

11

ALBERTA—EAST

THE COLD WIND THREATENS TO SWEEP US OFF over the high plains of eastern Alberta and then across Saskatchewan. From our lofty vantage high in the Cypress Hills the land stretches off flat and washed-out brown to the east and the south. Ranch ponds sparkle in the distance whenever the sun peaks through the high cirrus cloud cover. The early October windstorm is blowing cold weather down from northern Alberta and the interprovincial park is empty except for a gang of road workers trying to make hot patch stick in some chuck holes back up the road. Down below us Reesor Lake has whitecaps on it but no fishermen. Thick montane forest grows right to the western shore—white spruce, trembling aspen, balsam poplar, paper birch, and willow. The deciduous trees, now leafless, stand out as gray patches within the stands of green pine. On the other shore all of the long, green grass of summer is now a dull tan and brown, the stuff buffeting and rippling in the wind like the water on Reesor.

The land feels empty at this time of year, unlike when we drove around the park in early August when the place was jam-packed with campers. Few campsites were available then and those were tucked well back in the woods along with hordes of mosquitoes and open range cattle that had covered the bare ground around the fire pits with their sloppy droppings. At Elkwater Lake, park headquarters, the small lake was crammed with speed boats and jet skis last summer. Hundreds of tourists clogged the visitor center and cars were backed up at the combination gas station-general store. A line had formed by a pile of wood that campers had to purchase if they were to have fires that night. Walkways through the woods around Elkwater were paved and illuminated with strings of lights. The entire feeling of the place was that of a frantic need to cram in as much forced recreation and quality time outdoors as time would allow. No one seemed happy. They all seemed stressed and angry. Perhaps they wanted to go to Disney World. I had the feeling that they were already there. The many thousands of acres of tree-covered hills and the open fescue grasslands were choking with people and their machines. A constant hum of recreational vehicle engines filled the air. I could hardly believe that this was once the wild, untamed country described by Wallace Stegner in his book *Wolf Willow*. A land of wide-open spaces, vast forests, and fierce weather as described in his novella *Genesis*, where a blizzard of unmatched proportions wails down out of the Arctic in a torrent of wind and snow and nearly kills off a band of cattle drovers.

I was eager to experience this country after reading Stegner's book and my enthusiasm continued to grow as we crossed the border at Wild Horse north of Havre, Montana. The rangeland rolled off in all directions. The Sweet Grass Hills dominated the skyline in the west. Herds of cattle were everywhere. The farther we drove north the better the country became. The highway dove down a long swooping valley and then climbed rapidly up a long rising bench. Silvery sage and tan-green grass stretched off in the distance. A small creek worked its way through a tough, eroded valley. At the crest the forest covered the western flanks of the gently rolling Cypress Hills that are 4,800 feet above sea level at their highest and as much as 1,500 feet above the valley floor. During the Pleistocene Ice Age the Hills escaped glaciation, and as a result, a wide variety of plants and animals are concentrated in the area. The Blackfeet call the Hills *Ketewius Netumoo* or "the hills that shouldn't be."

"We've found it," I said aloud to myself as we drove along the crest of the hills, grasslands drifting off on either side of the road before confronting the forest. "This is going to be alright."

It wasn't. The highway dropped down through the trees and on my right I saw a modest ski area, rope tows, denuded slopes, the works. And soon we were trying to negotiate the narrow streets of Elkwater without running over addled tourists dressed in garish tourist garb or be crunched by trucks hauling firewood, boats, or foodstuffs into the townsite. The park along the lake was manicured with wide paved walkways. Dogs and little kids ran all over the place. If you walked on the grass, when signs didn't prohibit this activity, you had to watch where you placed your feet. The Cypress Hills in the heat of summer battle were a scene of organized mayhem. I wanted to get the hell out of there. The motel room in Havre the night before beat this—the cracked ceiling, the loud, drunken guests next door, the traffic, the plumbing that didn't work. Even all of that beat this. Beautiful country overrun with overorganized recreational lunacy. Exquisite country ruined by over-managed, overorganized recreation is no better than clear-cuts or strip mines.

So when Ginny and I drive up again in October I am prepared for the worst. Even with temperatures in the forties and the wind raging, I thought the Hills would still be a shambles. I am wrong.

The view from up here is magnificent. The place feels wild and relatively unspoiled. I begin to see why Stegner loved this place and the time he spent growing up here in his youth. Elim-

inate the visitors and the land comes back alive, as is true throughout the high plains.

The Cypress Hills have a long history. A number of miles east of
Reesor Lake was the site of Fort Walsh in the Battle Creek Valley.
This is also where members of the Nakoda tribe, wrongly accused
of stealing a horse, were gunned down by wolf hunters, Metis (a
distinct culture that is a mixture of Native and French Catholic
traditions that first developed along the Red River in Manitoba
and they number about twenty thousand in the province), and
whiskey traders in 1873. The fur traders and whiskey traders had
established posts throughout this country. Before 1870 the area
was truly lawless and more or less under the jurisdiction of the
Hudson's Bay Company. The killing of the Assiniboine Indians
quickly became known as the Cypress Hills Massacre, not so much
for the number killed, but to arouse anti-American sentiments in
eastern Canada. The violent act by semi-U.S. citizens against Canadian native people forced the government to take swift action
by forming the Northwest Mounted Police, the Canadian Mounties. (I found it interesting that in the park's brochure, *Hills' Hap-
penings*, no mention is made of the Metis' involvement in the
killings while every other source I read did. Revisionist history?)
The Mounties established a series of forts and outposts throughout
the West following this incident. In 1875 Fort Walsh was built
under the supervision of James Morrow Walsh. For the next eight
years the men and officers at the fort worked at taming the un-
controlled behavior of the traders. To put this time frame in perspective, a year later Custer and 265 men were killed at Little
Bighorn.

Following the Battle of the Little Bighorn, as many as five
thousand Sioux along with Chief Sitting Bull fled the vengeful
pursuit of U.S. government troops and crossed to the Canadian
side of the 49th parallel. The Sioux normally camped between the

Cypress Hills and Wood Mountain in present-day Saskatchewan. The tribe competed with Cree, Assiniboine, and Blackfeet hunters for what few buffalo remained on the grassy plains. By 1879, with the buffalo gone, the Canadian government attempted to starve the Sioux back to the U.S. Despite the tribe's wanderings back and forth across the border, the Canadian government referred to them as "American Indians." By 1881 Sitting Bull moved his starving people back down south.

Since that time of violence, trapping, and whiskey trading, the region, along with most of southeastern Alberta, has come to rely on cattle and vast wheat-growing operations. So much grain is produced here during good years that the huge silos can only store a portion of it. The rest of the grain is piled in buff-gold-colored mountains next to the storage facilities, leaving it to either rot or blow away in the ever-present wind. Because the Cypress Hills and the rest of this country are so far from the clear mountain streams and lakes of the western portion of the province, most of the water is warm and turbid, playing host to fish species such as catfish, sauger, largemouth bass, and some very big northern pike. Recreational fishing is not a big industry here as it is farther west. Hunting for birds, elk, mule, and whitetail deer as well as upland birds such as pheasant and sharp-tailed grouse provides income for the communities, but that's about it aside from the ubiquitous oil and gas industry. Grizzlies and bison, being plains animals by nature, used to roam this land, but they've been gone for many decades as have the buffalo wolves that were trapped out here at the turn of the century. Pump jacks, pipelines, and storage tanks are scattered throughout the country, and the smell of the gas is ever present in some areas.

If there is one voice that is synonymous with the Canadian West and Alberta in particular it is that of singer and songwriter Ian Tyson. Tyson, who lives on a ranch south of Calgary, has recorded numerous albums including his latest release *Lost Herd*. Songs like "MC Horses," "Four Strong Winds," "Navajo Rug," "Someday Soon," and "Springtime in Alberta" have become standards in this country and made him a legend in the music business. Listening to his music it is easy to hear his love, commitment, and concern for the high plains of his province. His voice mirrors the wind-swept, harsh weather of the majestic Canadian prairies, and he has a passion for good cutting horses and open country.

His words in a keynote speech he gave at the 1997 Cowboy Poetry Gathering in Elko, Nevada, strike home:

When "Kid Russell" (western artist C. M. Russell) along with Phil Weinard and Long Green Stilwell lit out of Helena, Montana, for High River, Alberta, in May of 1888 the only indication that they had crossed the border would have been the remains of the stone cairns left by boundary surveyors in '73. It's doubtful they caught Charles's watchful eye, having been mostly rubbed out by buffalo and range cattle . . . the rocks scattered.

The irony of this is not lost on me as I fill out the H-1 and P-2 forms required if I am to sing songs in Elko, Nevada, with the musical and political correct information . . . My visa stamped and approved in Sweet Grass, Montana, I climb in my truck. I'm thinking as I head south of an old-time U.S. Marshal, Charles Hard, of Fort Benton. One time in the '70s he was pursuing whiskey traders up the Whoop Up Trail when he overtook them somewhere near Medicine Line. A discussion ensued as to what country and jurisdiction they were in. "Hell, Marshal, you're twenty minutes too late, we're in Canada, you've no jurisdiction here. The line is back there at the north fork of the Milk." Old Marshal Hard headed back to Fort Benton empty-handed.

Twenty years after Chas Russell's idyllic summer in Canada

the open range was gone and the open border closed. The arrival of the Canadian Pacific Railway and the homesteaders combined with Canadian nationalism and fear of American "manifest destiny" gave reality to a political line that bisected the geographic unity of the northern plains.

With that in mind I asked Ian if things have improved any since that time.

"Ranch land is being broken up into smaller and smaller parcels," he said. "A woman with a half section near us has her place up for sale and if it goes the land will be divided into small tracts. We hope this doesn't happen. It's not a happy situation. People think that there is an endless wilderness in Canada, but that's not true. We try and not talk about the situation all of the time. It bums us out. It's a constant litany."

And the spread of the oil industry led him to say, "There is so much oil exploration that it is killing the land."

But Tyson's songs are of the West and cattle and cowboys and the romance that goes with all of this and he still sees some of that remaining.

"The West has been very good to me. It's a place carved out for me and I ride with people from here to Mexico. The government has been involved in this for a long, long time," he adds. "Most of them are good, hardworking people, but they have their agendas all screwed up.

"I hear younger kids talking with an environmental frame of mind. I hope that's the case. The environment seems high on their list of priorities. The older ranch people have kind of given up around here. The young will make the difference. You can take from that what you will."

Big cities are a plague and nowhere is this more evident than in the West from Salt Lake to Denver to Edmonton to Billings to Cheyenne and to Calgary.

"We have to figure out how to stop the growth in Calgary," Tyson said of the city that is 800,000 strong and growing rapidly. "It's Denver ten, fifteen years ago. If you want a blueprint of where Calgary is heading, it's Denver. Everything is down there telling you what you need to figure things out."

I could tell that my questions on the state of the environment in Alberta and the West were getting Tyson down so I asked what living on the plains means to him, how does he feel about the grandeur.

"After my kid comes home from school this afternoon, we'll saddle up and bring in a hundred head while on horseback," Tyson said with enthusiasm. "We'll bring the cattle in like the way it always was and have a good time doing it. That's the best I can say it."

One of the points Tyson brought up in his speech to the cowboy poets mirrored my own thinking. We've managed, through our various governments and bureaucracies, to carve up the West with a myriad of lines and boundaries drawn on stacks of maps. These lines translate into a lack of freedom of movement. No longer can we saddle up like Charlie Russell did 120 years ago and ride the open range all the way from central Montana into Alberta. We have to stop at border crossings and answer questions about where we live, where we were born, are we carrying guns, alcohol, or tobacco, how long are we going to stay, and on and on. And if we look suspicious or fit some paranoid computer-generated profile, we will be asked to pull ahead and park in some stall and have our car and possessions searched. Arbitrary boundaries laid down for the sake of commerce, law enforcement, and whatnot.

The land doesn't recognize the boundaries. Rivers flow where they will. The Milk River heads on the eastern slopes of Glacier National Park before drifting out onto the plains and swinging north into Alberta for a while and then jogs down south back into Montana to merge with the Missouri. Grizzlies come and go from Montana to Alberta as they wish. So do elk and migratory birds. The Rocky Mountains are the same geologic structures in Montana as they are in Alberta. Living in Cheyenne, Wyoming, and loving everything about that state and all the while saying, "I hate Montana. It's ruined," exposes this lack of awareness concerning the interconnectedness of the land. The Powder River in Wyoming is no different when it flows through Montana. Same for the Milk as it glides through Montana into Alberta and back into Montana. A black line drawn on a piece of paper doesn't alter this connectedness. We are obsessed with taming and controlling the land, but we can't. We can and do ruin it for ourselves and other species, but we don't control the country. That's beyond us. It is pointless. Landslides bury towns as at Frank Slide west of Pincher Creek. Rivers carve new channels. Storms destroy crops and towns and kill some of us. Tectonic plates shift and entire mountain ranges slide miles out onto the high plains.

We just don't get it.

The drive down from the top of the hill winds through birch and pine. Most of the leaves are gone or blowing down and swirling about the winding, narrow road, the brown and tan leaves whipping about in devil winds, downscale tornadoes that bounce around kicking up dust, grit, and detritus throughout the plains. The high cloud cover blows off and the sun brightens the countryside. The thick limbs and remaining yellow leaves form a sparkling canopy over the road. The lake shows a deep blue with the whitecaps offering a foaming counterpoint. The last time we were here the shoreline was lined with anglers flinging lures, worms, chunks of hard salami, and whatnot in attempts to catch the rainbow trout that swam here. Float tubers paddled away trolling flies out in the middle. Still more anglers worked from a peripatetic armada of canoes. Wood smoke from dozens of fires drifted thickly across the water. Music choked the natural airwaves. Today everything is changed. No people. No vehicles. No fires. Only the deafening silence of the wind as it blasts down from the tops of the Hills and whistles across the lake. The valley resembles a fjord with its steep slopes shooting up from this narrow crease of water that is actually a reservoir backed up by an earthen dam. Crossing the dam leads to a ford of Battle Creek. You drive through the six-inch-deep water that is perfectly clear now unlike last August when the stream flowed a cloudy turquoise caused by dozens of people wading in the creek. A moose vanishes into the woods below the dam where it was feeding in a marsh. Its large rack kicks aside pine boughs as it trots from sight. Three green-winged teal zip past riding the wind, their beating wings whistling through the sky. A grouse (ruffed) runs up a hill, its mottled browns, grays, and blacks blending with the ground cover. Rose hips glow bright red as they swing from prickly branches.

We drive up to a campground, now empty except for the blowing leaves and a few whitetail deer. We have lunch at a picnic table. We enjoy the solitude and the warmth of the sun. I finish eating and walk down to the creek. The tiny stream drifts without much current along a colorful gravel streambed. The shore rocks are gray, dull brown, and faded maroon, but the stones in the water flash gemlike turquoise, emerald, ruby, silver, topaz, gold. A pack of rainbows holds behind a downed pine that stretches across three-quarters of the width of the stream. The fish rise cautiously, no doubt still traumatized from all the angling attention they received earlier in the year, to delicately sip midges that are buzzing along the surface of the cold water. The trout are from six to twelve inches with a couple in the fifteen-inch class. Large trout for this slip of water. I move a couple of steps closer for a better view and the sound of my steps sends the nervous rainbows scurrying for cover. I glimpse parts of them—heads, quivering fins, flanks—holding beneath a mossy bank. The olive-green moss grows like a large, fat sponge and drapes over the bank and into the water. Tiny mushrooms grow in the duff of pine needles and leaves. A large boletus mushroom, its yellow cap worm-eaten, pokes up through the soil.

As I move upstream I spot lots of rainbows holding in shallow pools or holding close to cover like the downed tree and undercut bank. No matter how carefully I approach they scatter before I can close the distance to less than twenty feet. These fish would be difficult to catch, even with tiny flies and slender tippets. I sit on a deadfall and wait for the trout to resume feeding. Fifteen, twenty minutes. No fish. They know I'm here and are tucked in tight to their cover with no thought of exposing themselves to my predaceous intentions. Walking back downstream through a forest of aspen and pine I see that none of the rainbows has returned. Very spooky fish.

We clean up our lunch and drive back toward the crest of the Hills and the return drive to Havre. The land feels empty, lonely, and relieved. The wind is perhaps a giant sigh of relief that all of the manic tourists are gone. The Cypress Hills can rest now for another six months. The land can sleep and regroup as it hunkers down in the calm of a raging, bitterly cold winter. To the northwest a wall of purple-black storm clouds is moving down on us bringing rain, falling temperatures, and snow. The land sweeps away in a wash of hills, coulees, and valleys full of grazing cattle. We stop to look and can make out the silhouettes of the Sweet Grass Hills, three hazy purple cones, far away. In the few minutes we spend at this overlook the approaching storm has rushed miles closer, the menacing clouds dominating the horizon. The weather is coming on us quickly.

I pull the Suburban out onto the broad highway and run the thing up to 110 kph. We race winter back to the border.

Great Slave Lake in Canada's Northwest Territories, not far from the town of Hay River.

❧ **12** ❧

THE TERRITORIES—
FAR NORTH HIGH PLAINS

POWER MANIFESTS ITSELF IN MANY WAYS. Ted Turner buying up the West for his own pleasure under the guise of raising bison and saving wolves. The Rolling Thunder B-52 bombing of Vietnam. The World Trade Organization cutting the world's financial pie into pieces for a select few corporations. The examples are countless, but what is going down here in the Northwest Territories is in a league of its own. No rules followed. No quarter given. Hell, no damn awareness of any human perception of strength. That's small-time stuff to this country.

We are camped deep in the boreal forest, spruce, birch, other trees rising high all around us, more than a quarter mile from Louise Falls on the Hay River about fifty miles south of Great Slave Lake. The Hay River is nothing special as the Territories' rivers go—several hundred feet or more of wide, deep, swift, deadly current boiling brown-water style with an intensity that kicks up one to two-hundred-foot whirlwinds of dirty white foam that spins and twists far above the water's turbulent surface, the riverine dervishes flashing in sun-driven rainbows of spray, the whispy foam curling and floating in widening spirals rising above the massive falls that crash and thunder over several hundred feet of eroding limestone shelf. Not bad as rivers in the States go. Bigger than the Yellowstone, swifter than the Missouri, and so on, but merely normal for this land. The Mackenzie flowing silently, powerfully west out of Great Slave on its thousand-mile trip to the Beaufort Sea above the Arctic Circle is six miles, maybe more, wide in places. The Horton races above treeline through wind-blasted rocky plains and tundra flats, then finally winds along the base of Smoking Hills before it dumps into the Arctic Ocean. The Hay, well, the Hay is kind of medium-quality water-intensity-wise for this country. Still, small-time or not, our partially full coffee cups shimmy and vibrate in the rocky soil more than a thousand feet from Louise Falls. And the roar of that chocolate-brown water, water that pours with such force over the limestone that sheets of curling spray boil back up to the tumbling water's crest, is an all-present rattle and hum that grinds through our guts, through our spirits. The Territories are serious country and the Hay River is telling us so as it cruises north to Great Slave while the white-hot, cooked-through-and-through, late-evening blue sky sizzles with an electricity not known down Alberta way or south across the border in Montana.

We've only been in the Territories two days and already the immense, immeasurable power of the place has knocked us out cold, humbled our naive sense of place and proportion to the extent that we move through this ancient, perpetually undisciplined taiga (Russian for "swamp forest") with our heads bowed, our feet making slow, measured, respectful steps as we walk too stunned to be anything but silent.

Montana is heaven on earth for a few of us, but the Territories are heaven, hell, and mind-ripping, blown-away, electroglide, screaming energy from another time zone, another planet.

This landscape is so far out there it has to be home for the terminally in search of unspoiled, outraged country. Those such as ourselves.

Nothing prepared us for the overwhelming nature of this country. Plowing through the mile upon mile of never-giving-an-inch forest in northern Alberta did not give us a clue. We work our way up that Canadian province to the town of High Level, population 2,921, located twenty or so miles north of the Paddle River Metis Settlement, something like our Indian reservations. High Level is a place that, according to a woman working at the Shell truck stop there, is "good for nothing but catching up on your sleep, eh." The spot is little more than windswept dusty barrens hacked from the forest, a lonely wayside community of gas stations, an A&W, assorted other greasy food road joints, a new and hopeful-looking tourist information center. A big sign points the way to a nine-hole golf course lying somewhere out in the snarled madness of the bush. I bet Tiger Woods and the rest of the PGA automatons ain't played no course like that baby before. "What's par here, man?" "Gettin' back to the clubhouse in one piece, kid." Motels that look like any end-of-the-road, nowhere bomb shelters you've seen everywhere else lie scattered like neon-lit 1990s tombs next to the highway.

I top off the tank at around two bucks Canadian per gallon as a hot wind blows dust in my eyes and up my nose. "Where in the hell am I taking us?" I mutter.

"Up through more damn, claustrophobic forest, that's where," says Ginny as she returns lugging a couple of bags of ice from the convenience store portion of the Shell high-octane experience. She doesn't look happy, but we are this far and I am determined to make the Territories.

North of town a few miles I pull over to look at a stream. Water's a key to the nature of any land and I am desperately looking for guidance. Within seconds moose flies the size of steroid-driven grasshoppers begin dive-bombing me, insect jaws wide open, the voracious creatures taking chunks of pate and neck flesh with each buzzing-loud run. I look at the nameless creek. Is there any discernible current in this thing? Sort of cloudy, dark brown water curls from the density of muskeg and trees on my left and then curls into the density of muskeg and trees on my right. I pick up a small stick lying in the dirt, gravel, and other detritus too ghastly to name by the side of the road and toss it in the stream. The wood just sits there as the moose flies haul pieces of me away into the fen- and spruce bog–choked woods. The stick doesn't flow in any direction. It just sits there. Then, no, wait a minute, the wood drifts six inches, now a foot to the left. Then it stops for a bit to catch its breath before surging a solid two feet to my right in a matter of perhaps forty seconds. For a few minutes this continues, back and forth, until the moose flies drive me, partially devoured and bleeding, back into the Suburban. No current to speak of. We are high atop an enormous spongelike plateau covered in trees and populated by vicious flies that could more than likely absorb a direct hit from a 28-gauge. High Level my ass. We head up the road. It is around 7 P.M., or high noon around here, listening to Ibrahim Ferrer and the Buena Vista Social Club belt out Bruca Manigua on the car sound system. Cuban music in the North Woods. Makes as much sense as anything. So I figure what the hell. We'd bomb our way up to Hay River perched on the southern shore of Great Slave Lake. Get a room. Cruise the town, turn around, and head back the next morning at least being able to say, "Northwest Territories? Damn straight. Ginny and I were up there last June. Damn good pike and pickerel fishing, but not much else except for enormous man-eating flies." Yeah, we can do that, the two hundred or so more miles and the time. We can do that.

But the reason I'd gotten this far into this is because of my occasionally accurate road instincts that kept saying, "Man, there's something up there about the northern high plains waiting for you. Get on up there. Stay with this." I am listening and we keep going, and all of a sudden a peace and sensation of power start flowing through me like the first time I saw the Sweet Grass Hills down in Montana or the Missouri Breaks or the Atlas Mountains in Africa. That rush. The one that comes when I know I've stumbled onto intact, righteous, mean, powerful land. The sun is still well above us.

High Level? Maybe.

And as I roar past the streams now, they have changed. Not the languid, torpid, turbid dirge of a few miles back. The water is clear black, a wild, unmanageable darkness that races through big steel culverts beneath the Mackenzie Highway and then flies around curved mossy banks into the forest, white foam lines bubbling along the energetic current seams. Serpentine root-beer floats. And the sky is bluer now. Not sky-blue, the color you see when you look up everywhere else. The whole forest, the clear shot of the highway tearing through the trees, the air, all of this is awash in a blast of the purest electric-blue light I've seen anywhere. A silent, roaring wave rolling and surging over and over us and growing stronger as we near the Territories. Twenty miles away. Intense light growing brighter. Five miles. Blue light that is around us and wailing through the landscape. Finally reaching the border and a sign proclaiming "THE NORTHWEST TERRITORIES—WHERE THE ADVENTURE BEGINS."

No shit. The place is on fire.

Coming home to a place I'd never been, which I've babbled countless times before whenever good country knocks me out, but this is it, in spades. I absolutely know, can see with my eyes, feel with my spirit, that this place is what I'd always been seeking, had always fantastically imagined. Huge. Unspeakably wild. Scary as hell. Heaven on my perception of earth.

There really is such a place. It exists and I've been here for all of five minutes and feel like I've been here forever.

So, like I said, nothing prepared us for this place. Not sweet home Montana. Not poor, beautiful Alberta dying under a relentless, greedy siege of rapacious exploitation. Not Wyoming. Not Iceland. Not Morocco. Not nowhere.

Ginny is scared by the insane energy of the land. Sanely so on her part. The unfamiliarity of the place, the unknown, the wildness, should have frightened me, too, but I am either brain-dead exhausted from the road or too stoned on the Territories or both to be scared.

We pull into the tourist information center parking lot at the border and go in to gather a bag of brochures. Information being power. Sitting next to us is a pair of 1960 something VW vans with British Columbia plates. Battered body work, oxidized, dull, flat paint finishes. Beads hanging from the rearview mirrors. Macramé hemp curtains. The works. Standing next to one of the vans is a young woman with piles of long, curly brown hair that drapes over her shoulders in large twisting tendrils. She is wearing an ankle-length crimson velvet dress, off-white lace blouse with matching crimson velvet vest, and turquoise and gold jewelry. A queen. Her mate drifts out from inside somewhere muttering about how he hopes they can find leaded gas, an uncommon fuel these days, soon because they are "runnin' on fumes." He is wearing weathered dungarees torn at the knees, a long-sleeved beige union shirt, and thick Rhasta dreadlocks. The queen smiles and pats his shoulder. "There, there, now," she seems to be saying. Two others complete the quartet of wayfaring hipsters. A black man dressed in jeans, Bass moccasins, and plaid shirt and his mate, a striking Oriental woman dressed all in black—jeans, boots, silk blouse, and leather vest—follow closely behind. A quartet of youthful wanderers up here checking out the Territories. After lighting a cigarette, I look their way and the queen looks through me with kindness even though it is clear that I am beneath her station. Week's growth of beard. Twenty-year-old Cubs hat pinned with old woolly buggers, holey black jeans, Parks Reece T-shirt, and well-broken-in, white Converse high-tops. She recognizes my existence but that is it. I am forty-eight years old and they are riding the crest of early twenties bliss. These aren't any Winnebago-hauling, ATV-lugging tourists from Utah up this way to check off another through-the-windshield location. These are freaks. I know I am home now. I share a glance with the Rhasta and he grins and shrugs his shoulders as if to say, "She IS the queen and a lot of fun, but quite a handful." I smile and wonder if he's met Ginny inside, who now appears with two cups of coffee, twelve inches of brochures, and a mangy off-white husky in tow.

We pile into the car, leaving the dog sadly behind, and head for Hay River about fifty miles up the road. A quick thunderstorm drops the moose flies and mosquitoes somewhere out of sight and we drive with the windows down, the moist, cool air blowing in our faces. Suddenly Ginny sits upright and exclaims, "John. You were right about coming here. Listen to this," and she reads from the sacred *Hay River Recreation & Tourism Guide.* " 'Great Slave Lake lies at the point where the rugged Canadian Shield meets the Interior Plateau, the northern terminus of the Great Plains. This meeting of two very diverse geological regions gives Great Slave Lake a unique nature and a bit of a split personality.' "

No big deal to most people, but we are working on a book about the northern high plains and I've been wondering how I can fit this little jaunt into that narrative.

"I knew so all along," I said.

"Sure," she says, and we drive on. The luck of fools and derelict writers never ceases to amaze me.

As we near Hay River we catch sight of the water as it cuts

its way through an immense, steep-walled limestone gorge. The river runs powerfully and fast with long, thick strings of foam that curl in large midstream whirlpools. A sign to the right announces Paradise Gardens Campground. We drive on into the town, past a modern airport with a couple of DC3s marked Buffalo Airways Ltd. parked near the runway. The highway potholes its way through the new part of town. The brochure informs us that the old part of Hay River had been blown and shoved away by a massive ice jam during an ice-out years ago. Then we cross the West Channel of the Hay River and follow the East Channel around and through what is left of the old town. Dusty street. Tough-looking bars with rough-looking pickups parked outside. Some of the buildings' pink, yellow, red, blue, and orange neon lights work. "Iz y s B r nd rill," "M son Ale," "Fres ish Fri d N y," or more properly Izzy's Bar and Grill, Molson Ale, Fresh Fish Fried Nightly. The Territory license plates on the pickups are white with blue trim and cut in the shape of polar bears. We continue on the narrowing and deteriorating road to a campground marked on one of the maps obtained at the tourist information place. We find the provincial place but it is nothing more than a cluster of narrow parking slots cut into the brush. Bugridden and no view of Great Slave Lake.

Tourist brochures are all well and good but the deceitful souls who put them together have the uncanny and arcane ability to make an auto salvage yard look like Zion National Park. The Hay River bit of fictional verbiage can hold its own with any of them. The campground is filled with pickups marked with company insignias of various mining, barge shipping, and industrial companies. A place for transient workers to stay on the cheap and, most likely, on the duck. The brochure proudly champions the Hay River Territorial Park and shows a wild, scenic picture of Great Slave Lake filled with peaceful waves and piles of driftwood. What lake? And the quaint fishing village at the end of the road mentioned in the brochure as offering fresh-caught inconnu, whitefish, lake trout, and northern pike daily is nothing more than a series of rough-hewn tables surrounded by rough-hewn houses, noisy kids, and barking dogs and sinking into a sand dune there reclines an old, beaten-up wood building with a sign hanging by a rusty nail or two purporting to be The Museum of Fishing.

I should have known but am too road-buzzed from sixteen hours of driving to acknowledge the tourism bureau hyperbole factor. I am tired, mentally down on the inland seaside village of Hay River and life in general. Ginny suggests the Paradise Gardens and we head back out of town. Midnight and it sure as hell isn't dark yet and I need a good meal and a nap.

As soon as we leave town and begin cruising through the tall stands of white spruce and birch separated by gatherings of small black spruce, begin running alongside the river, the buzz returns. Towns and cities everywhere are often the worst of what a place has to offer. Crowding even on the small three thousand population scale of Hay River is a distillation of what kills off the land. The sad, potentially violent bars, often sadder motels and adjoining restaurants, the chamber of commerce hype, all of it is not what the West and the Far North is about. Open spaces, wild places, and not damn electricity-powered grunge that overrides our natural perceptions that are scanned thousands of times per second by our brains at a frequency that is at best muddied or more often canceled out by the frantic zip of TVs, neon lights, toasters, computers, Musak, and the rest of it. The "boogey electric" as jazz flutist Roland Kirk used to say, adding, "Clickety-clack, somebody's mind's gone off the god-damned track."

The Paradise Gardens sign points the way to a wide dirt road that swings dustily down to a peninsula of tall trees and impressively bountiful, well-manicured gardens and orchards.

Apples, onions, rhubarb growing eight feet tall with thick leaves of deep emerald-green, onions with three-foot rich green cylindrical tops, robust bushes of what we later learned were Saskatoon berries, a thick carpeting of grass connecting all of this, perfect whitewashed garden sheds and homes. Simply put, heaven. This is Ben and Fran Greenfield's Paradise Gardens Campground. It is now 1 A.M. and a big black cat wanders out the open door by the office sign. A husky, though stooped, man in his sixties moves slowly, very slowly, out of the house opposite. Jeans, plaid shirt, and tennis shoes. At first we think he's had a stroke, but as time goes by up here we learn that everyone moves this way. The strength of the country is overpowering. To live here, to accomplish anything, a person must submit to the will of the land and in the case of the Territories that involves an unconscious shift to a much slower physical gear. Not mental. The wonder and mad mystery of the place zings and zaps audibly through the airwaves like a softened hiss of a rattlesnake. I am bone-dead tired but my head is wide awake as if I were on some very clean, hybrid psychedelic. A very high place Canada has going up here.

Ben smiles at us and Ginny goes inside to register. The cat and I hang around outside talking about the state of the mouse and rabbit crop. I walk over to the riverbank that stands thirty feet above the water that flows silently through the wide stream course and makes a casual, looping bend before circling back around the north side of the property. The river is power. The way the current moves with subtle boilings and whirlings of unseen undertows says so. I look down at my feet. The cat is perched butt-down on one of my tennis shoes, also watching the river, then looking up at me, then purring softly. Its tail switches languidly back and forth. I hear a wooden screen door close and turn to see Ginny and Ben looking at the Saskatoon bushes, talking and laughing. I smile at Ben and he smiles back with an expression that clearly says, "What took you so long to get here?" All I can think is, *Damned if I know*, and Ben smiles again before disappearing into his home. Down the road that leads to where we will camp I spot an older woman in baggy jeans, cotton shirt, and sunbonnet (at 1 A.M.) working along the rows of rhubarb. Ben's wife Fran. She doesn't look up as we drive slowly past, but I feel as though she acknowledges our presence all the same.

"A stoned place," I think.

Ginny says, "I know."

Where we camp is nothing more than a wide-open grassy field lying between the forest on one side and bordered on the other sides by fields of fruits and vegetables and well-groomed orchards. The campsites are merely widely separated areas with fifty-five-gallon oil drums cut in half and mounted on steel legs for combination grills and fire pits. There are also white picnic tables. Perhaps a half-dozen sites in all. A bucolic setting even with the whine of mosquitoes that leave us alone after a spraying of Backwoods Off. The sun is just below the treeline now as we set up the tent and make dinner of pasta and Italian sausage, a salad, hot tea, and Mounds bars for dessert. There is one other group here, a family of Albertans. While the wife and son unload a staggering amount of gear from the back of the small Datsun truck—tents, sleeping bags, grills, gas stoves, axes, chainsaws, tables, chairs, dozens of coolers, TVs, lanterns, a small inflatable wading pool, blankets, quilts, sacks of groceries— Dad soaks a pyre of birch with lighter fluid, tosses a match on this, setting off a huge blaze that grows larger and larger as he keeps dragging logs and deadfalls from the woods. He gathers wood when not attending to his personal conflagration. The fire is such that even if it had been dark out it would have been light enough to read. The flames surge toward the sky as the ambient light of day dims slightly, like the vague beginnings of dusk, but by the time we crawl into the tent the sun is glowing orange behind the trees in the north-northeast. Sunrise approaches. The sounds of our friend's fire crackle and pop across the meadow. Two-thirty A.M.

I sleep like a dead man and when we wake in the morning it is already ten-thirty. The sound of birds is everywhere. A golden eagle screeches far above us. Loons call their eerie song from a calm eddy on the river. Mourning doves coo along the gravel road. Ravens squawk from the tops of tall pines. An assortment of nuthatches, sparrows, chickadees, and bank swallows swoop, flit, and titter from the fruit trees and bushes. The mosquitoes are silent and large swallowtail butterflies lazily glide up and down above the tall, thick grass. High bands of cirrus clouds sheet across the southeast horizon and blue sky pushes in from the north. The day is warm already with a mild breeze. The air ruffles the bright purple flowers of fireweed, the reds of new blooming Indian paintbrush, the softest pinks of prickly wild roses, and the yellows and whites of sweet clover. This place is paradise. I'm sure winter can be the opposite of this, even with the otherworldly blazings of the northern lights flashing overhead, but I'm not interested in this reality right now.

I walk down to the river that pours silently toward Great Slave Lake. Even though the orchards, home, and gardens are right behind me I feel as if I were in the middle of the wilderness. The rock and sand banks rise high above me on the far shore. Huge spruce and aspen line the banks. A moose crashes through the undergrowth across the river and a pair of osprey glide downstream looking for a meal. One hundred yards from our camp, less than a mile from the Mackenzie Highway, and there are no sign of humans anywhere. Amazing. I drag myself away from the river so we can head off to explore town and perhaps, just maybe, catch a glimpse of Great Slave Lake.

As we enter Hay River we cruise past a series of service stations and weathered, largely unoccupied motels. At inlets, channels, and bays of the river and lake large ore barges and tugs are tied up with immense cords of rope or the ships are rolled up on thick wooden ties for dry-dock repairs. The place resembles High Level to some extent except that the buildings are older and more weathered. Wind-battered is more like it. And even in this decay a sense of energy, of something always about to happen, swirls around the large-planked docks and around the enormous, battered propellers of the dry-docked vessels.

At the tourist information center, another new building like the one in High Level, we learn that barely three thousand people visit Hay River each year, that the far-ranging Dene Indians have their cultural resource center located in the forest not far outside of town. We look at photographs of enormous lake trout of sixty, seventy pounds, forty-pound northern pike, five-pound Arctic grayling, and big inconnu, or sheefish, and whitefish. All caught by wide-smiling, ecstatic anglers or so the photographs would have us believe. My tourism BS detector is back up to speed today and as a result I'm skeptical of all information disseminated in this place. The lady behind the desk appears kindly and she, too, smiles a lot, but I'm suspicious. What's her con? What is she trying to pitch? Halcyon weather, generous people, a resort community à la Cape Cod? We'll see. But if the photos are to be believed, Great Slave Lake has the big fish to prove it really is the world's tenth largest freshwater lake and sixth deepest at over two thousand feet. Outside, clutching still more brochures, we bump into a couple in their late sixties from Troy, Montana. They say they are having a "Fabulous time" (they're probably shills for the tourism bureau) and produce two miniature tennis rackets strung with thin-gauge electric wire and powered by a handful of D-cell batteries that they use to kill the moose flies with in fierce volleys during cocktail hour. "You guys should go buy some. They'd be great for your kids. The place is just down there," and they point to a small shack sunk into the ground in the shadow of a decrepit ore barge along by the east channel. They stare bulging-eyed and grin at us and we say we'll go there right now and we leave in a hurry. Whatever you hear about the silliness of North Dakotans, don't be misled. Montana has its share of world-class bozos, too.

A right turn brings us to the new townsite, which is dominated by a high-rise business-office building of seventeen stories. "The tallest building in the Territories," the brochure exclaims. It is a chipped and peeling pink-beige stucco that has all the charm and ambiance of those abandoned apartment complexes outside of Chernobyl. There are new banks, a grocery store, indoor skating-curling-hockey rink, a donut shop, laundry, and a bookstore with a fine selection of north woods and Arctic titles. They don't have any books I've written or any written by my friends except for *The Cowboy Way* by McCumber. Well, why would the locals want to read about Montana fly fishing, violent westerns, Montana murder mysteries, or African hunting stories. I can see this much. The entire downtown encompasses only a few blocks. The dense boreal forest looms on the outskirts, ever present.

I go into the bank to use the ATM to get some Canadian cash. Beautiful paper money in shades of vermilion, lake, aquamarine, and coins called loonies with brass centers and bright silver borders. ATMs way up here. Magic money everywhere. Tomorrow is July first. Canada Day. Like our July Fourth . . .

. . . and we are back in town the next day waiting for the parade, standing on a corner of the main drag in the shadow of the tallest building in the Territories. The breeze is cooler here by Great Slave and tinged with the smell of diesel fuel from the tugs and other large boats and the fecund, cloying smell of fish. Flocks of seagulls circle the streets, the birds raucous and always on the lookout for a stray bit of food or garbage as they flap and hover in the moist air. Then, suddenly, out of the blue, un-believably loud ambulance and fire truck sirens drill our ear-drums, then louder still the fire siren on top of the firehouse goes off, then red, blue, white, orange, and white lights begin flashing all over the place. The hundreds of people gathered for the Canada Day parade cheer and yell, the mass of them ripples like the waves on the lake. Five Royal Canadian Mounties cloaked in flaming crimson coats, black breeches, and blacker still knee-high boots lead off the procession. They march stiffly and perfectly in step, the middle Mountie a swarthy, hard-looking dude of six-six or more. Then follow the fire trucks crammed full with kids, the ambulances packed with kids, floats awash with kids, a desultory rock band slouches on a trailer pulled by a new, hot yellow Dodge Ram pickup, the school marching band, and assorted stragglers dressed as dalmatians, moose, yetis, and God-only-knows-what bring up the rear. Tor-rents of brightly wrapped hard candy are tossed at the parade watchers by those in the parade, some of the candy launched with a vehemence at certain individuals that may indicate past grievances or wrongdoings are being addressed by the children, dalmatians, moose, and yetis. Who can tell? The noise of the si-rens, mufflerless trucks and late-model hot rods, the bands, and screaming people is as deafening as an NBA playoff game. In what seems like an ear-shattering, eye-blinding eternity but is no more than ten minutes, the parade is over, all the people who watched the mayhem vanish, and the town of Hay River is strangely, weirdly quiet. Where has everyone gone? We look at each other and shake our heads and then do the sensible thing and strike out in search of the donut shop . . .

. . . but that was tomorrow. Today the teller counters and banking machines are lined with Dene Indians cashing checks, withdrawing money, trying to withdraw money, hitting up friends for dough, and so on. They are all in various stages of drunkenness, a serious and depressing problem up here among the native peoples. Outside they are leaning against the bank passing bottles wrapped in brown paper bags from one shaking, nicotine-stained hand to another. I'd been there in the bottle for a way-too-long period in my life and the brief return to that feed-the-beast-all-day hell sends a nasty shiver up my spine and through my gut. I hustle back to the Suburban where I gather Ginny and our laundry and drive off in search of the lake. She has scored a bag filled with rich, greasy, cream-filled, chocolate-covered, sugary donuts. The booze memories begin to fade and have completely vanished by the third one. Down to the sea crazed on donuts. Live free or die. And I take a bite from another donut, sugar buzzed all to hell.

So it is back down the road to the fish market and museum in search of the as-yet-unseen lake and halfway there we pull down a sandy two-track that winds through the trees and hopefully leads to the lake. We park and start walking. Topping the rise of a modest dune we get our first view of Great Slave, three-foot waves rolling up the brown sand, deep green water breaking over rocky reefs, and farther out the dark blue inland sea stretching to the horizon. The shore is littered with driftwood. Limbs, logs, and entire trees are piled and stacked in a chaotic arrangement up and down the beach. Small pools of water hold schools of ninespine stickleback minnows trapped until the next series of larger waves sets them free. The wind is blowing cold and hard from the north, turning a warming day in the shelter of town cool. All along the northern horizon the sky is light blue. Behind us the bands of cirrus are gunmetal gray and silver. There is a pervading sense of isolation and tremendous loneliness here as we stand in the sand looking for miles out over the frigid water. Great Slave Lake is nothing like the Great Lakes of the Midwest. Similar in size and depth, but those five waters are largely surrounded by industrial cities like Chicago, Detroit, Milwaukee, Cleveland, and Buffalo and millions of people. What surrounds this? Hay River and the slightly larger community of Yellowknife on the far shore. No superhighways and countless cars, trucks, and buses honking and crashing into each other. No Sears Tower, Terminal Tower, or major league ballparks. No glitzy restaurants, rapid transit, slums, or smog. Only trees, water, and wind.

As the sacred brochure intones Great Slave is situated partly on the edge of the Canadian Shield and partly on the Interior Plateau. During the Wisconsinan glaciation from fifty thousand to ten thousand years ago the great Laurentide Ice Sheet covered virtually all of eastern and central Canada to a depth of two miles in places. As the climate warmed and the ice retreated an enormous lake, larger than Wyoming, called Glacial Lake McConnell extended from present-day Lake Athabasca to Great Bear more than a hundred miles north of where I'm standing. Great Slave is nothing more than a remnant of that vast glacial pool. Some remnant. Four hundred fifty-six miles long by fifty wide and covering 10,980 square miles. In winter the ice freezes over the surface here six feet thick with ten-foot-high pressure ridges that extend for thirty miles along the frozen surface. The lake is rarely ice free until mid-June or later. Spring warming causes rising water levels that can flood out townsites and push massive chunks of ice into the forest leveling tracts of trees. Sand ridges marking former shorelines of Great Slave are found as far as fifty-five miles away.

These facts are entertaining but do not give any true sense of the raw power of Great Slave Lake. I cannot imagine being on a ship way out there in seventy-foot seas whipped by hundred-mile-an-hour winds raging down from above the Arctic Circle. Magnitude 6.6 to 6.9 earthquakes have rocked the region as recently as 1985. Summertime temperatures approach one hundred degrees and winter levels plummet below minus eighty. From late June until the first frosts of August the flies and mosquitoes drive the wildlife, both human and animal, mad, often sucking trapped victims blood dry. Killer storms kick up out in the middle of the lake in a matter of minutes. Many ships and men have been lost in these sudden strikes. Great Slave Lake is unpredictable and unforgiving.

We walk down the beach dodging the waves and climbing over and around the driftwood. A mangled fishing trawler lies shattered far up in the trees. Beams splintered. Hull smashed. Prop mangled. Farther on a moist area of sand sucks Ginny down to her knees. She stands there looking at me with a frightened expression. "The land wants me," she yells. I pull her free and we continue walking, stopping every now and then to examine small mollusk shells in green, blue, and brown hues. She moves on to photograph this place.

Sometimes, if you have slightly mastered the arcane art of seeing without looking, the land shimmers and radiates intense shades of electric blue. I first noticed this uncommon phenomenon one summer in the Sweet Grass Hills along the Montana-Canadian border. Waves and streaks of bright, deep blue light rolled down the crest of Middle Butte and shot in airy streamers between subtle rises in the land. This went on for hours and I've watched the display in other places since then.

Looking out to the larger waves breaking on the reefs hundreds of yards from shore the light appears again. Subtle, fleeting at first. Aquamarine shading to azure flickers across the crests of the crashing water. Looking west to some distant islands shimmering miragelike in the distance, the light blazes intense blue shooting in sheets all across the watery horizon from west to east. Bands and waves of this earthly light shimmer and blend, growing in intensity until the blaze shoots in great bursts far into the sky and boils overhead, finally washing up against the reef of cirrus clouds, the blue light crashing and breaking against the diaphanous barrier.

Great Slave Lake is the focus of this immense energy that reveals the unimaginable wild, intact nature of the Territories. The light continues to radiate for long minutes before slowly dying down in a series of diminishing pulses and horizontal bolts of white-blue. Then the light is gone just like the parade watchers.

Ginny returns, eyes WIDE open. She's seen the light, too. We walk up the beach, over the dune, and back to the car.

Blackfeet tribal members Joe Kipp (right) and his father Max in Joe's backyard near Cut Bank Creek.

֎ **13** ֍

BLACKFEET COUNTRY

ALL OF THE BUILDINGS ARE EMPTY, LIFELESS. Windows broken
out. Doors torn from their hinges. Furniture long gone.
Plumbing gutted. The barracks constructed in the fifties to house
the servicemen who manned this radar station far out in the middle of nowhere on the windy high plains of the Blackfeet Indian
Reservation of northern Montana are nothing more than empty
shells today. The huge steel structures that supported the radar
dishes and contained all of the electrical equipment are stripped
bare. They stand out bleakly on the rise above the barracks guard-
ing nothing now but the stark loneliness of the bluffs, buttes, and
wide valleys that are still brown in early May. All of this was
built just south of the Canadian border near the port of Del Bon-
ita, way back when the U.S. was on the watch for Russian ICBMs
that would nuke the country back beyond the Stone Age. This
facility and others like it were discarded before the supposed missile threat ended, discarded for newer, more efficient forms of paranoid tracking devices. In fact, the entire high plains region was
a nuclear zone. Testing facilities in Nevada, these stations, and
enough missiles were buried beneath the ground in silos to an-

nihilate the earth many times over. At one time Montana was one of the top ten nuclear powers in the world. The sovereign domain of Big Sky Country had enough warheads sunk within its rocky soil to take out all of Europe. Many of those missiles are gone now, too, but enough remain to cause a global ruckus. I wonder what the Blackfeet had thought of all this. The not-so-long-ago warriors of the high plains, now trapped in a windy prison not of their own design, might have found the fact that the U.S. government—the entity that took away their freedom, destroyed their way of life, and confined them to this wide-open hell in the first place—had been using their lands as part of a Cold War, a manufactured conflict beyond their comprehension, I was sure.

The day is warming as the sun moves across the sky and each day a little farther north. New shoots of fresh green grass are poking through the thick matting of last season's dead growth. Pockets of buttercups and small lavender flowers I can't identify light up the hill with splashes of color. Even this early in the spring, which comes late in this country, I can feel the approaching heat of summer and all the freedom that comes with it.

I'd spent last night sleeping on my pad, in my down bag, inside one of the radar buildings, up on a second floor littered with steel beams, scraps of sheet metal, and lengths of Romex cable. The night wind howled and moaned through slits and creases in the walls of the place. I nervously killed off most of the night shining my flashlight around the inside looking for ghosts and ghouls I'd hoped I'd never see. The place was filled with the morbid vibes of what went on here. If the men working at this station forty years ago did indeed detect a salvo of Russian missiles their only purpose in life was to send the message to the powers that be so we could fire off our own rockets and mutually finish off the world. That kind of insane purpose surely affected everyone here and the horror and fear remain. By sunrise I was a depressed, wired wreck.

The fresh new day wipes all of this away. A breakfast of fried trout I'd caught in the nearby Milk River yesterday, bacon, orange juice, coffee, and a Jamaican cigar revives my spirits by the time I climb into my rig, which I'd stashed between the barracks, and set out for a cross-country jaunt across the reservation aiming for Duck Lake and its enormous rainbow and brown trout, which should be easy to catch at this ice-out time of the year, and especially following a long, dark winter of relatively little food. The wide gravel road built to service the radar base swiftly degenerates into miles and miles of deep ruts, barely identifiable tracks, spring-fed, muddy gullies, and rock-studded lanes. The land spreads out before me in broad vistas. To the north the rolling plains of Alberta grain fields stretch off into the purple haze. Ahead of me the land kicks and bucks for miles in a progression of benches, buttes, and the sweeping valley of the Milk River. Cattle graze everywhere. Hereford. Angus. Calves only a few months old frolic in the fields. I am frequently forced to slow to a crawl and work my way through the animals. They stand or rest in the middle of the road, lurching and jumping up at my approach, then stare at me with bovine ignorance or maybe bliss. Eventually the cows bound off up a hill or across a field with a thudding of hooves and a spray of soupy cow shit. The calves, particularly the young bulls, try to force standoffs, but even their diminutive brains realize that what I am driving, what is easing their way, is a lot bigger than they are, so finally they give up the game and run off to join their mothers, bawling as they go. The Rocky Mountain Front towers in the western distance, the mountains shimmering as the sunlight blazes off the vast winter snows piled up along the peaks and many feet thick in the alpine valleys and cirques. All of that water will come down in the next month or two as the weather warms. Billions of gallons will pour down narrow creek drainages, merge with other swollen streams, eventually join rivers like the Milk, St. Mary, and Marias and all of this water will flood its way either to the Gulf of Mexico, the Hudson Bay, or the Pacific. Blackfeet country was the location of the triple divide where water eventually makes its way to three separate oceans. Immense land.

After opening and closing a number of wire gates, nearly getting stuck in a swampy crossing, fording the raging Milk River that is no more than a foot deep where I pass, finding myself going down a lane that leads nowhere, and stopping on the edge of a grain field to have lunch and soak up the view, I finally find Duck Lake Road where I turn north and drive to the large body of water in search of trout, praying that the wind stays at its modest thirty-mile-an-hour pace. Much stronger and the waves at Duck will be too rough for wading out to the cruising fish and the gale too rough to cast in.

I top the rise of a long bench and as I drive along its crest I look down at the lake. Windy and wave-capped for sure, but for now at least fishable. Chief Mountain stands out by itself near the Alberta border. Chief is the farthest eastern extension of the overthrust belt, an enormous plate of pre-Cambrian rock that slide miles out onto the plains, which are mainly a deposit of Cretaceous sandstone and shale, and glacial moraines carved out by the retreating glaciers at the end of the last ice age 10,000 years ago and the Bull Lake ice age 70,000 to 130,000 years back. The mountain is on the far edge of Glacier National Park and sacred to the Blackfeet who call it, roughly translated, "He Who Stands Alone." I think of my long-time Blackfeet friend, Joe Kipp, and the first time we fished here . . .

. . . The edge of the retreating ice was about fifty feet from the shore. As the stuff melted and broke up we could hear large booms and a sound like a train makes when it pulls the slack out of a mile of freight cars and the couplings slam together. Beneath all of this racket, almost subliminally, shattering ice crystals tinkled like millions of small bells. Chief Mountain was a black monolith outlined by the setting sun that turned the rest of the land bloody gold. The ice-free water in front of us was so clear we could see cruising fish twenty feet down.

"Watch this, John," Kipp yelled as he waded out into the frigid water. The air temp was in the fifties but the water was near freezing. We were wearing thick neoprene waders, long underwear, sweaters, and fingerless mittens. Late April is a time of warmth and magnolia blossoms down south. Up here on the northern high plains the climate is a mixture of winter that refuses to leave with all the miserable determination of a dead drunk at a late-night party and equal parts of the joys of warm weather. Kipp worked his line out over the ice and landed a Hare's ear nymph several feet on the ice. He then began inching it toward the water in sporadic, quick jerks. What the hell was he doing? I'd only met him yesterday and up to this point he seemed like a likable, reasonably sane, happy guy. Well, the truth of a man's personality always comes out in good country, sooner or later. I guess now was as good a time as any to learn about Joe.

"We call this ice fishing, John," and his laughter mixed with the crackling ice and tinkling ice crystals.

I watched as he pulled the fly right to the edge and then jerked it into the water. The moment the nymph touched the surface a submarine shape raced out and in a boiling swirl of red, green, and chrome nailed the fly. Kipp set the hook and the rainbow tore back underneath the ice.

"He's tail walking now, John." He's always used my name with great frequency. "Upside down on the bottom of the ice," and more laughter flew across the ice. Eventually he brought the fish to shore and I was there to admire it. Nearly two feet of pure, hard, colorful muscle.

"A small one, John. Maybe six pounds," and he turned it loose.

"We'll catch bigger ones at a lake I'm taking you to tomorrow, and the really big fish will be out when you come back in May."

A lake tomorrow? May? I thought I was leaving tomorrow to drive back to Whitefish, a beautiful mountain town nestled among the Swan, Salish, and Whitefish Mountains with the peaks of Glacier rising even higher to the east. Unfortunately California developers discovered the place, and now what was once Paradise to me is overrun with yuppie skiers and golfers, the town clogged with crazed gridlocks of very expensive vehicles—the usual suspects—Tahoes, Expeditions, BMWs, Jags, Mercedes, etc. Condos and private communities are springing up like poison mushrooms, but that's the past. And where I lived when I met Joe. Now I live somewhere else.

I tried my hand at this ice fishing and took a couple of rainbows of around three pounds that pounced on my fly and "tail walked" beneath the ice. Joe pronounced my efforts as "Not bad, John." Then we made the hour drive back to Browning where Joe lived and I had a motel room.

Browning is a tough place. The weather is mean—brutally hot, brutally cold, almost always brutally windy, and the poverty is evident. Buildings in ill-repair or abandoned. Many of the cars and trucks are battered, old, and even abandoned. Men, and women, line up in front of places that sell liquor early in the morning, hands shaking, time standing still, cigarettes shared. A hard-time place that Kipp and others are trying to change but they have a way to go, forces to overcome.

"The Indians, the chief year-round patrons of the stores here, in summer provide the local color relished by the tourists. They carry themselves with dignity and gravity that hides considerable amusement over their roles as entertainers. Many a patronizing eastern visitor would be shocked by the natives' private comments on his antics. Since most of the Blackfeet have been educated in government schools and speak good English, attempts to address them in pidgin English may result in embarrassment."

That was taken from *The WPA Guide to 1930s Montana*, and the seemingly understanding and humorous tone of those words, really more an attitude of condescension and superiority, has changed little today. To my eyes it's worse. Now the place is filled with "wanna-be Indians," fools who think they've discovered spiritual enlightenment, whatever that is, and want to learn the Blackfeet ways. They pull up in their forty-thousand-dollar cars, step out, and inquire where they can find someone to "perform a sweat" for them or teach them the ways of the Indian. They all want to buy their salvation with a checkbook and from people they are sure will gratefully accept the pocket change they offer in return. Makes me sick. Countless books are being written and pimped by whites about the ways of the Indians. I've known Kipp for years and still don't have a good clue about what he's up to most of the time. Even worse, movies like *Dances With Wolves*, which should have been called "Dances With Mediocre Actor's Ego," (Kipp laughs whenever this piece of tripe is mentioned) masquerade at telling the Native Americans' "real story." All of this self-serving, sappy shit and the people that purvey it need to spend a winter out on the high plains, maybe in Browning, with no money except what the federal government doles out to them each month. All of this after the IRS has confiscated all their land, possessions, and money for back taxes, of course. I'd like to see the movies that Costner and Redford manage to crank out after that.

The next day we caught those bigger fish on a splendid blue-sky, seventies day. The Rocky Mountains blasted into the sky behind us and the prairie seemed to have greened up overnight. I came back in May and caught so many large fish that my arm cramped, and even though the fishing on the Blackfeet Res is rarely as good as it was that first time, Kipp and I have become close friends. That was thirteen or fourteen years ago and we're still the same clowns today that that we were back then except I've lost even more hair, we've both added a bit of weight, and we both quit drinking—unknowingly at nearly the same time. Joe because he believed he needed to set a better example for his people. Me because I needed to set a better example for myself, but I digress. We both still smoke cigarettes, though.

Today Kipp is forty and one of his tribe's healers and leaders. He said the tribal elders told him he had "to get going" as far as this work was concerned because his people don't live very long and his time was running out. He started laughing and so did I.

Kipp is serious about setting an example for his people and leading them to a better life through self-understanding and imparted knowledge about how to deal with white culture. He runs a successful fly-fishing guide operation (if you're a pain in the ass he won't do business with you again), guides some bird hunters, runs his cattle ranch, and with his wife Kathy, who is a schoolteacher in Browning, raises their children.

The confinement on reservations has caused pain, misery, and even the total destruction of some segments of North America's native peoples. Alcoholism, drug use, and violent crime are symptoms of this lack of freedom and death of spirit, something that plagues the majority of the country these days. The Blackfeet are now in the process of trying to reclaim more of their original lands. The reservation's present size is a significant depletion of the original Blackfeet territory. Early treaties in 1851 (Treaty of Fort Laramie), 1888 (Sweet Grass Hills Treaty), and a treaty in 1896 ceded land from the tribe that later became Glacier National Park. Tribal officials have broken off talks with park officials and instead are dealing directly with Washington.

"The bottom line is that we weren't hearing from the decision-makers," said Bill Old Chief, chairman of the Blackfeet Nation, in a November 27, 1999, article in the *Missoulian*. "Every time we brought something up in the negotiations, the people from the park wanted to go running off to Washington or Denver to get a decision. Finally we said, 'Why are we talking to you guys? I'd rather hear it from the horse's mouth.' "

Park officials counter saying that the Blackfeet have free entrance to Glacier. Quite the deal. They get to visit their home turf at no charge. What the tribe wants is the right to run cattle there, preferential employment on park projects, and a share of the park's income. They would also like to settle disputes about the park's boundary.

The buffalo represented an essential resource to the Blackfeet, providing food and materials for clothing, lodging, toolmaking, and food. With the depletion of the buffalo in the 1880s, the Blackfeet became dependent upon the federal government for supplies and food. With the coming of the Catholic missionaries, educational systems, government rules and regulations, the tribe had to make even more changes. Stock raising was emphasized in the early 1900s, but with a drought in 1919 combined with low beef prices, many of the Blackfeet had to give up their allotted lands to pay their taxes. The Indian Reorganization Act of 1934 brought on more land loss by placing Indian lands into trust status.

Throughout and despite all of this the tribe has made steady progress. The development of natural resources has raised the People's expectations. Culturally many Blackfeet traditions have been renewed. The Sun Dance, sweat lodges, and the Blackfeet language have all made significant comebacks after years of neglect by education and government officials.

So with all of this history and all of these issues and goings-on, Kipp decided to commit himself to helping his people. His business concerns are examples of how the Blackfeet can coexist in the white-controlled economy. His home is located on the banks of Cut Bank Creek down in a narrow valley that's "out of the wind, John." His cattle graze on the windswept, grassy benches above his home. He steers clients through the million-plus acres of the reservation to some superb (though a good deal of the time extremely windy angling for tough-to-entice rainbows) fishing. He occasionally guides bird hunters. He teaches the old ways and language of his people, and he devotes large amounts of his time and energy to healing the physical and spiritual ailments of not only his people, but outsiders, "If they come with a sincere heart."

And beyond all of this, Kipp drives me crazy with his dry, subtle humor.

"All come on, you know we're both crazy and talk about things that nobody else will listen to and if they did, they'd lock us up," and we drive on to another lake or hidden stream. There've been times when the two of us have played out our running joke of Kipp threatening to kill me if I don't get him first because of long-running disputes between our cultures, times when, in front of clients who don't know either one of us all that well, Kipp's said, "Walk ahead of me, John. If a grizzly comes out I'll shoot you and then the rest of us will have a chance to get back to the truck while the bear works you over," and I'll reply with an angry face, along the lines of "Screw off." We stare each other down to the horror of some anglers from New Jersey before breaking into smiles and laugh loudly when one of them asks, "How long have you two known each other? . . . Are you brothers?"

Perhaps. In a way, but then we're both crazy and really believe that the land is a conscious entity filled with lights and spirits and power beyond our abilities to describe it. Yeah, we're brothers that way.

Mid-October and Kipp and I are working the matted grass bluffs and coulees of the reservation just short of the northeastern boundary, not all that far from the abandoned radar station. Five minutes walk down this rise and we'd be in Alberta, that is until we are chased off or apprehended. We're hunting sharp-tailed grouse and Hungarian partridge if they show themselves. The day is warm verging on hot, upper seventies. The sky is cloudless, deep autumn blue. The wind is light, uncommonly so. I move off to the top of the next hill and began walking to the edge of this piece of topography, to the edge where it slopes down into a winding, small valley of tall grass. All of a sudden sharptails blow up in my face. Dozens of them flying in all directions with whirring wings and frantic ratcheting calls. The buff-colored birds fill the sky. I raise my Beretta .20-gauge over-and-under and touch off both barrels more out of instinct than anything else. Not a feather is touched. The grouse land over the edge a quarter mile away.

"Nice shooting, John," Kipp yells.

I walk on. From the edge of the incline a lone bird shoots up and rides the western breeze right past me. I raise the gun, pick up the grouse, swing through its flight course, and pull the trigger. Time slows way down. Expands. I can see the high plains stretched out for a hundred miles before me, shining in the sun, and the Sweet Grass Hills, freshly covered in a dusting of snow, as I finish my swing. I barely hear the shot or smell the gunpowder, and watch as the sharptail rolls to earth in a small cloud of feathers. The bird hits the ground with a soft *whompf*. I walk over to pick it up, still warm, a crease of blood issuing from its beak. Browns, tans, mottled whites, grays, some blacks. Perfect camouflage for this country. I stuff the grouse in the game pouch on the back of my vest and move on. Kipp is closer now and watching my actions. Another grouse kicks up the same as the first. I raise the gun, follow its flight, seeing the golden land. I swing through the sharptail and see again the Sweet Grass Hills dominating the eastern horizon, but I do not pull the trigger. The grouse sails along the bench, then drops down the far edge out of sight.

"I could have killed that bird, easy, Joe," I say.

"Maybe you didn't want to, John," he says as he walks up to me.

That was five years ago and was the last sharptail I've killed. I no longer have the burning desire to hunt upland birds as I did before that day. Maybe I will again next fall, but until I do I'm not going out and killing the grouse, Huns, and pheasants. I have no idea what happened. Some internal switch just flipped in another direction. I still get the urge to go walk the fields behind a good dog with good friends every time September rolls around, but I never do so. Most of my friends hunt. They do it well, walking, stalking, killing cleanly and quickly, respecting and honoring the fallen animal. I have nothing against hunting. I'm just not up to it right now. What happened?

Kipp has spent a lot of time explaining the origins and history of his people since I've known him. The Blackfeet have lived on the high plains for centuries, all but a small portion of the time without horses. Vast land to travel on foot, not to mention bringing down a ton of buffalo on the hoof. Some people believe that they are the earliest Algonquian residents to migrate from the east, possibly the Red River Valley of Minnesota.

For three centuries the three Blackfeet tribes have been known to white men as the Pikuni or Pigean (Pay-gan'), the Kainah or Blood, and the Siksika, Kipp's tribe, the Blackfeet. The three tribes are politically independent, speak the same language, and have mostly the same customs, intermarry, and battled the same enemies. Their name, Blackfeet, may have derived from the fact that some of their moccasins were made with black earth or the ashes from fires. Pigean refers to those who possessed torn robes or were poorly dressed. The Blood used to paint their robes and faces with red earth, which is still part of some sacred rituals today. Or possibly the name derives from warriors returning with blood on them after attacking a band of Kootenai Indians that had crossed the mountains to hunt buffalo in Blackfeet territory. Kipp says of those long-ago battles, smiling all the while, that his people would wait until the Kootenai had finished hunting and skinning the buffalo, then Blackfeet warriors would swoop down and kill all of the Kootenai except for "the good-looking women," taking them as slaves and making off with the buffalo hides and meat. The Blackfeet have always had a fearsome reputation among the various tribes of the high plains. As for the name Kainah, it means "Many Chiefs" and the people prefer that name.

Napi, the Old Man, was the creator of the world and all that lived in it. Kipp told me that Napi rose from a chimneylike cave in the Sweet Grass Hills and refers to the peaks of the Front that rumble down along the horizon as Napi's Launching Pad. In the beginning the world was entirely covered by water. One day Napi sent animals to dive and find out what lived in the depths. First duck, then otter, then badger dived without success. Then he sent muskrat who remained under the surface for a long time before returning with a ball of mud. Napi blew upon the ball and it swelled until it became the earth. Napi then piled up rocks to make mountains, dredged valleys for rivers that he filled with water, and covered the plains with rich grasses. He also made timber grow in the mountains and valleys, and roots and berries on the plains. He then made the animals and birds, and from a lump of clay he made a wife. The two of them designed the people and decided how they should live—men with the first say, women with the second.

Old Man said, "Let the people have eyes and mouths in their faces, and let them be straight up and down." Old Woman added, "Yes, let them have eyes and mouths; but they shall be set crosswise in their faces." Old Man said, "Let the people have ten fingers on each hand." Old Woman said, "No, ten fingers are too many. Let them have four fingers and a thumb on each hand."

Old Man and Old Woman could not agree on one point. Should the people live forever or should they die. Old Man said, "I will throw a buffalo chip into the water. If it floats the people will die for four days and live again; but if it sinks, they will die forever." The chip floated, but Old Woman said "No" again. "I will throw this rock. If it floats, the people will die for four days. If it sinks, they will die forever." It sank. Then it was agreed among the two that it was better this way. If people lived forever they would never feel sorry for one another.

At first the people were hungry and cold, before the Old Man showed them how to collect edible roots and berries, how to make wooden bows and stone-headed arrows, how to use weapons, traps, and deadfalls to kill buffalo and smaller animals for food, and how to dress animal skins for clothing and shelter. A slightly different version according to Kipp is that Napi spoke with all the animals and plants about the need for them to give the people things to survive—flesh, roots, hides, etc. That's why the Blackfeet pray before a hunt and consider the act of killing sacred.

After all this the Old Man climbed a high mountain and disappeared. Kipp also says many believe that he is under a white rock deep in the Atlantic Ocean.

This year it's October again as we drop down from the bench above Kipp's home and pull in front of his ranch-style home. A pair of dogs greet us with wagging tails and wide grins as Kipp comes out the door smiling.

"How's it goin', John," and we shake hands. "So this is Ginny. I finally get to meet her."

He's heard about her for years, but they'd never met.

We go inside and Kipp fixes us lunch while telling us he's flying to Atlanta tomorrow morning to visit his daughter at school. He's busy, but on the phone last night when I called him from our motel room in Havre he said not to worry, that he couldn't wait to see us. So we're here.

The talk over lunch is about the grizzlies that are wandering out onto the reservation from Glacier Park. Kipp says he's seen six near his home this year and in 1998 the tribe was forced to remove fourteen, meaning some were killed out of necessity and fear for the public's safety. And he talks about a person who was killed by a grizzly and officials referred to what was left of the victim as "partially devoured remains."

"Partially devoured remains," he says with disgust. "All that was left was seventeen pounds. Partially devoured . . ." and he lets it slide.

"Everyone is telling us we have to help ourselves, but the state won't let us hold a trophy elk hunt at ten thousand dollars per elk," he says with more disgust and some anger. "We have hunters waiting in line and that money would help the tribe. Same with a trophy grizzly hunt to remove problem bears, and the environmentalists are against that one, too."

Once a bear, any bear, becomes habituated to humans and their food—garbage, cattle, people—once it's tasted blood, that bear needs to be taken out. Relocating the offending animal even one hundred miles away does no good. It will be back within days. Animal rights freaks, and that's what most of them are—ill-informed zealots hell bent on turning what's left of the wild, natural world into theme parks or zoos—along with way too many members of environment organizations, most of which do more to preserve and enhance their corporate entities than save the land, have taken up the cause of the grizzly rarely armed with the facts. The same white "wanna-be Indians" also wanna let the bears have carte blanche anywhere the bears decide to roam. A nice thought 150 years ago. Not today. Too many people living along the edge of the mountains back into where the grizzlies have been shoved. The bears are on the verge of mauling, killing, and eating Blackfeet, the people that the wanna-bes write the checks to so they can become spiritually enlightened beings. I never thought that someday I'd be in a society that puts people's lives and needs ahead of the bear's, but the self-absorbed, self-serving nature of so many of the thralls in the environment milieu is too much. Give me a break.

We lose the bear subject after a while and Kipp smiles when

he tells us beef prices are going up and then takes us out to his sweat lodge where we discuss this and that personal stuff, and he explains what he goes through when he fasts.

"The first day I feel fine, really full of energy," and his eyes sparkle behind his glasses. "The second day I'm weak. The third day my demons come out and I've got plenty. The fourth day I'm really weak and can barely walk off the mountain [he fasts at the top of one of the buttes that dominate the skyline in this part of Montana]. It's a dangerous time to come off of there."

And Kipp tells us that 65 percent of the tribal fishing permits sold go to Flathead Valley residents over west of the mountains around Whitefish and Kalispell. And that once they find a lake that is on and filled with big fish, the fishing and size of the trout is cyclic in the reservation waters where trout can grow as much as an inch per month, once the "boys from the Flathead" find such a place, they make it their own and work it to death.

"At Little Goose Lake I used to get clients thirty good fish a day, then the Flathead boys found it," Kipp says with a wry smile. "Now I'm lucky if we get four rainbows."

Kipp's father Max shows up. He's sixty-five years old and full of energy. We talk about the weather, the approach of winter, how an old bow he made from a red birch tree was destroyed decades ago in a house fire, and how the beavers were flooding his son out and that he'd better do something about it. The beavers have damned sections of the creek and the water is rising. Joe says he'll trap them out and destroy the dams soon enough. Max asks what he can do to help while his son is gone, then wishes him a safe journey, gets back in his pickup, and drives off.

We talk some more and Kipp really tries to bend my arm to go see some great pheasant cover, but I know he has a lot to do, so I beg off and we prepare to leave, but not before planning for the three of us to fish next year at ice-out. And he tells us of a sacred place where we can camp in the Sweet Grass Hills and tells me where to leave a couple of cigars for Napi. Tobacco is part of many Blackfeet rituals. And finishes this by saying "My Old Man enjoys a good smoke," and he is smiling, but serious. I promise him I'd leave a Dominican and a Honduran so that the "Old Man" can taste tobacco from a warm climate during the cold winter. Kipp likes that.

"I'll let you know when the fishing gets good," Kipp says through our car window. "And be sure and bring Ginny. She's a lot more interesting to talk to and a lot easier to look at."

He laughs and walks back to the house and we drive back up the road.

Some people never change. Like Kipp, thankfully.

Now it's September, a September from another year. I'm standing out on a ridge that overlooks the confluence of three creeks that began up in the Rocky Mountain Front that towers above us a few miles away. Bob Jones is talking with Kipp about a magazine article he is doing. It's about bison and the high plains. A gale is coming down from the high country. The peaks are wrapped in sheets of spinning black clouds that tear away from the summits and race down on us bringing stinging rain and sleet. Maybe it's above freezing, but it feels below zero. Kipp points to a hill a half mile away and we see the bison. Dark brown shapes moving slowly down out of the wind. We move much closer and watch as the bulls, cows, and calves feed in a sheltered draw. A couple of lead bulls spot us, give us a hard, long look, then resume feeding. These animals were brought down from the Bloods' herd in Alberta. The Bloods are also Blackfeet. We count the animals.

Thirty-seven.

"Not many, John, but it's a start."

Thirty-seven.

They used to have tens of millions out here.

Middle Butte in northcentral Montana's Sweet Grass Hills at sunrise.

~ 14 ~

THE SWEET GRASS HILLS

THE LAST OF THE LIGHT WAS GOING, drifting away with an orange-gold edge that crept lazily up the cone-shaped butte while silently pulling purple and steel blues behind as the sun dropped away behind the Rocky Mountain Front one hundred miles to the west. In windy land that always seemed to be blowing somewhere, strangely, the air was flat calm and so was the surface of the small lake, no ragged waves whipped white by eighty-mile-an-hour gusts roaring across the prairie and shooting up the draws. Though in this uncommon stillness the water was far from lifeless. Countless rainbows dimpled the surface. Little ones of six inches, medium ones, and here and there large fish of several pounds or more. Sippings, splashings, and slurpings—the sounds of fish eating without a worry in the world. They were casually feeding on some small bug of mayfly dimensions, probably some mutant callibaetis subspecies spawned by the incredible isolation and stark-raving loneliness of this place. The last of the summer's heat was dying a peaceful mid-September death out here above Montana's Hi-Line not far below the Alberta border. The Sweet Grass Hills—West, Middle, East, and the slightly lesser entities of Mt.

Lebanon and Haystack Butte. Middle towered above us casting a serious reflection on the still water. The evening was turning cool. The trout seemed to take no notice of this or the fading light show. They just kept sipping away making their liquid, crystalline sounds. Soft music swiftly sucked dry by the waves of tan grama and buffalo grass holding motionless. Miles and miles of the stuff languidly fading into autumn.

I launched a cast of about seventy feet out ahead of a rise made by a worthy trout and got lucky when it sucked down the fly, setting the hook in its voracious vehemence. Feeling the bite of the point galvanized the rainbow into a series of leaps toward the far shore, water spraying in sheets. The fish crashed across the lake, putting down everything in its path except for a group of mallards that lifted immediately into the air with beating wings and disturbed *quacks*. They were out of sight over a near ridge in seconds bound for quieter doings in some other puddle.

The fishing went like this until deep dark and I kept a few smaller ones for dinner. I liked the taste of trout sautéed in olive oil and butter with a handful of slivered almonds thrown in. Salt, pepper, and a squeeze of lime juice and that was that. Walking up the rise from the lakeshore I looked up and saw the sky filled with stars hanging in three-dimensional relief against the blackness. A crescent moon was showing itself silvery as it rose west of the faraway lights of the railroad town of Shelby. Coyotes howled in acknowledgment from the tops of flattened hills. Ginny and I cooked the fish in a pan on a Coleman stove. No fires here. Too dry and no wood to speak of, except for wiry tangles of sage. No trees out here in the huge openness.

There really wasn't anything special to this place. Nothing much to it. A trio of volcanic-shaped buttes, three towering cones, standing alone together out here like a miniature mountain range. There are other places we know about, had spent time in like the Missouri Breaks a few hours away. A place where the river flows large and silent. Where elk the size of draft horses rise up out of

brushy cuts in the land around sunset. Where thunder and lightning appear from all directions all at once out of nowhere and
pound the land with such intensity that praying for survival seems
the natural thing to do. We'd had times there where even bouncing
and lurching across a bone-dry dirt two-track required four-wheel
drive if we were to reach a little-known lake filled with voracious
three-inch largemouth bass. And there was the morning in that
country when we woke to the sound of a pickup truck slamming on
its brakes near camp. A government biologist was heading out to
the field. We were pulling an Avon raft we'd used to float the Missouri below Fort Peck Dam and other lesser flows. The anomalous
sight of the craft out here made the woman driver look once. Drive
off. Stop. Look again. Repeat the sequence, then roar off to a plague-
infested prairie-dog town. She obviously preferred studying the
Black Death to possibly dealing with lunatic fly fishers ensconced in
the middle of a desert. Or there are all those lakes along the Front
over by Augusta filled with overweight browns and just as fat rainbows. We've caught plenty of those with the rocky reefs of the
mountains holding silently in the background.

So where we were now is no big deal, even if a Canadian mining
company eventually has its way and tears the gold out of the butte
rising above the lake we just fished. We can go elsewhere and for
that matter even come back here and catch these fish while we
watch the butte being leveled with tons of explosives, and then see
the blasted rock hauled away by a horde of massive earth-moving
machines. It is all the same to us. As Annie Dillard said in an article
for Harper's, "We arise from dirt and dwindle to dirt, and the
might of the universe is arrayed against us."

That gets it. No big deal.

After eating the rainbows we stand in the star-bright darkness
looking at the shadows we cast when far in the distance we spot
headlights climbing and dipping, moving in our direction like a
spastic searchlight. A car or truck is heading toward us on the only
road in, a dusty job that wandered through wheat fields and range-

land. We watch as the car approaches. It stops every now and then to open and close a barbed-wire gate before moving ahead. Eventually we can hear the faint whine of its engine, the sound drifting unnaturally to us. The air is so clear up here that we can see ranch lights many miles away and the observed car's approach over a period of thirty minutes or so. We wonder if the vehicle is full of sex-crazed, carousing teenagers from nearby Sunburst or, even worse, ax murderers looking for random victims like us. We've been random victims all our lives. In fact, we are quite good at it. I long for the .357 Magnum I'd left on the kitchen table yesterday. Eventually the car, an old Japanese beater from the sounds of the muffler and the rotten exhaust smell, drives by us and stops nearby at the next gate in the road. We hear the muffled bass booming of the sound system, not at all like the booming of night owls slicing through the air above us. Then the car backs up and turns around. *God. They're leaving,* we think, but are wrong as usual. The car rolls by, pulls down to the water not far from us, and stops.

All is quiet, even the car's music. Then the inside light flashes on and stays that way. Then goes off. Then on again. This continues for an hour or so. Ginny walks over to our rig and grabs a pair of binoculars. She creeps to within yards of the car and begins spying on the car's occupants. I slip up behind her and take a look through the glasses. When the inside light goes on I can see a pair of guys, in their twenties, passing something back and forth. A cigarette lighter flickers on and off and clouds of smoke fill the interior. The image is so cloudy it looks like one of my photographs. This activity goes on well into the night. The moon, now a copper slice, is dropping down toward the southeastern horizon. We finally give up and sneak back to camp reasonably assured that the two smokers of what obviously isn't pipe tobacco—a smell of something much more aromatic, herbal, reaches us on the slight evening breeze—aren't out this way to do us wrong.

"Almost one hundred years of living between us and look at what we do for amusement," I say with a laugh.

"It's pathetic, John," and we both laugh and then crawl into our cold sleeping bags. If the two in the car are indeed dope fiends, as a rule ruthless individuals every one of them, they are too well tuned by now to bother us. If we have grievously slighted their character and they are merely ax murderers, well, out lifeless, sightless heads will be looking out on wide-open Montana for eternity.

The intense light of a new day's sun flashing over the eastern hills wakes us. It is nippy out and there is frost on the ground, but at least our heads are still attached. Looking down to the lake we notice that the car is gone and so are our un-met friends. Following a breakfast of thick Ethiopian coffee, Krusteez pancakes covered with butter and Vermont maple syrup, and some bananas we head down to the water for a dip. Midmorning and already eighty degrees. Another blown-away gorgeous late-summer day. We strip and jump in the water. Definitely awake now. As we paddle around like confused springer spaniels, tiny trout nibble at the hairs on our bodies. I hope that the sun's intensity will keep much larger trout holding tight to the lake's bottom. After a while we climb out and dry off in the warming air. Not a cloud in sight. Nothing. And then small rise forms out in the middle. Little fish. Then more and more. Larger ripples. The wind is still a dead issue but the lake is dancing. Perhaps we'll chase the rainbows later, for now we prefer being voyeurs once again.

"The Sweet Grass Hills contain their own revelation. Sacred places such as the Sweet Grass Hills are the foundation of our survival. The Sweet Grass Hills are not sacred in the way a church is, not as a holy relic or the plaster statue of a saint. The Hills are sacred as a source of life, and it was the spirit of life within them that the people worshiped. The Indian People said, 'In the flesh of the Earth, as in the flesh of the body, there is this spirit.' They are one," said Curley Bear Wagner, Cultural Coordinator for the Blackfeet Nation on a Native American Sacred Sites Web site.

Mining companies have filed claims on nearly twenty thousand acres of public-owned surface and/or subsurface lands surrounding the Hills. This was accomplished under the archaic 1872 General Mining Act, which costs the mining industry boys, at the most, five bucks per acre. Countless attempts to strike down or reform the Act have met heated opposition from representatives and senators more than a little bit sympathetic to the industry. One of these good old boys is Montana's own Republican Senator Conrad Burns, who, since elected, has never missed a chance to help out the mineral extraction and timber industries at the expense of the land. And so, for a very long time, there have been three of them standing alone out here looking like volcanoes that pushed up through the ground of the shortgrass prairie when no one was looking. Up this way by the Alberta border a hot wind shoves the browning grasses back and forth all day. Distant yellow fields of canola and fading emerald lakes of wheat ripple far south to Shelby and off west to peaks of the Rocky Mountain Front, snowfields blending with the miles of hazy, simmering air. A small pond below camp sparkles clear blue and sunlight flickers from its wave-broken surface, the water spring-fed and cool. Small rainbow trout leap from the surface chasing midges. Dragonflies cruise just above the water hunting down the same insects. In country that seems desolate, barren from a distance, life is everywhere. Yellow-and-white butterflies bounce around. So do gray-and-orange ones. Red-tailed hawks, Long-billed curlews, pelicans, mallards, and nighthawks dip and glide on hot patches of air or curl upward riding the easy force of lazy whirlwinds. Sharp-tailed grouse kick up from moist draws. Spotted ground squirrels prance about like pets. Badgers growl from beneath the ground when their burrows are approached. Coyotes chatter and howl back and forth around evening. Later, a crescent moon hangs in the sky along with a rising Jupiter and some bold stars not afraid of the moon's brilliance. This land is not dead at all. It is alive in many ways.

The three buttes tower above the prairie, lower flanks covered with blue grama, buffalo grass, and sage. Also, tall stems of sweet grass stand in isolated spots. Above this is dark gray, almost black, igneous rock, consisting of mostly feldspar, rock that rises steeply in ragged chunks and loose sheets for hundreds of feet, formed more than 50 million years ago, the surrounding softer stone cut away by ice during the Bull Lake Ice Age. The buttes are like miniature island mountain ranges far out in nowhere.

Still the land is alive with a hum that sails beyond electric. That is why this place is sacred to the Blackfeet and they fear for its vast spirit. In a way I know why. Why they feel so strongly about this place. Years ago I saw sticklike figures dancing on the northern horizon at sundown and later that night large trout leaped above the pond taking my fly before it ever hit the water. Wild, unexplainable doings. There is serious power here, not the false juice that comes from owning fancy cars, gaudy jewelry, or a big house. The real thing.

Perhaps not for much longer. Rapacious mining interests from both Canada and this country want to level the hills and reduce the pulverized rock with a solution containing cyanide. The greedy bastards are after the gold that lies here in microscopic flakes. The mining industry doesn't give a damn about the heart of this country and what it means to the Blackfeet, people who have lived and worshiped here for centuries. Some of us who aren't tribal members love this place, too. Gold, money, power, conquest. The same perverted steps to the same old, sick dance. Level the Little Rockies. Plan to do the same along the headwaters of the Blackfoot. Destroy this country we're looking at. What's the difference? There's plenty more mountains just over the horizon. Who'd miss these three rising out where nobody really lives? Dead country to the mindless thieves. Except for the gold. That's all the fools can see. The Blackfeet believe, actually they know, that if these hills are cut down the spirits that live here will vanish. They'll fly far away. Imagine going to church, dropping on your knees, and praying to a God that no longer exists for you. No all-powerful being to hear your pleas for mercy and forgiveness. Empty doesn't quite get it. No redemption this time around, kid. Try again in the next life, if you make it that far. Maybe the miners will be stopped. For now, there's always hope, but don't bet on it. The industry has lots of money and owns lots of people in all the wrong places. They'll probably get what they think they want.

As we do every time we're in this country, we sit on the ground and look at Middle Butte, watching it change in shape and dimension beneath the moving light of the sun, the grass and rock shining with brightness. Both of us look along the low rises flowing south from the butte. A thin line of blue light, pure blue, shimmers just above the land and begins to explode into bursts of charged clouds of this unreal color. We look at each other. Are we seeing the same thing? Of course. Crazy being crazy we always see the same things even if nobody else does. What's the damn difference. You must believe everything you see before the dream spins real. We turn back to the view from here. Bolts of the light shoot back and forth among these grassy knolls and to our left a darker more intense blue sizzles up the north slope of the butte before rolling over the crest like a swirling storm cloud blowing over a mountain peak. These edges of landscape are alive with the blue. Light fires back and forth between the hills and this lone mountain, wave after wave for hours that seem like seconds and last forever. The light just keeps flashing and then the grass at the tops of the hills shines copper and gold. Flickering beneath is the glow that pulses with a rhythm far beyond any jazz, further along than any human beat. Time passes in a way and the blue slowly draws back into the earth as the sun begins to set, its light shading the country in soft oranges, reds, and purples. Smaller bursts and bolts shoot from the ground and then the glow is gone. For now.

What the two of us experienced, we've never seen before. A shade of blue foreign to art. Unknown to photographers. Out of the reach of musicians. Beyond words. The land resonating with two humans who cannot explain what they saw but will always recognize the light whenever we see it again.

And they always say it can't happen here, but it can. Multinational mining have filed claims to mine the Hills and according to a statement from Sacred Sites, "The BLM [Bureau of Land Management] is stuck in its 'mine-set.' Ignoring this overwhelming local and statewide opposition to the mining of the Sweet Grass Hills, the BLM selected as its 'preferred management alternative' an alternative that could directly lead to the permanent destruction of the Hills [Alternative C]. The EIS concedes that the BLM's preferred Alternative C would allow 'some or all' of the proposed mining activity to occur. It concedes that it can lead to an irreparable injury to the Sweet Grass Hills, and 'could result in the permanent loss of the traditional Native American spiritual practices associated with this area.' "

Screw the Indians one more time without feeling. Hell, they're used to it and while they're at it, screw the rest of us that love this place.

We open and close the last wire gate that grants access to a lake of ten acres lying at the base of Middle Butte. The land is owned by a large ranch, but the owners have graciously allowed anglers to fish for the lake's rainbows and to camp here as long as there are no fires. This time around in late June, Ginny, my son, Jack, and daughter, Rachel, spend a few days hanging out and catching countless trout from eight inches to four pounds on a nymph called the Bigg's Special, a pattern that imitates a damselfly nymph. At the right time of the year the bug takes rainbows on every cast here. The fishing is straightforward, brain-dead easy. I love it and never tire of the easy hunt. There've been days when I've taken seventy or more trout. A glutton, but I only keep a few small ones for breakfast.

The rancher comes up to check us out just as the four of us are leaving to head down to the Bears Paw Mountains over south of Havre. He is pleased when Ginny mentions that Rachel has spent several hours picking up cans, beer bottle caps, and other garbage. He points to a cabin a mile or so away at the base of the butte, the place surrounded by aspens, holding a spring, and sheltered from the wind.

"I keep the place for my family, for my grandkids," he says as he adjusts his beat-up, sweat-stained cowboy hat and straightens his coveralls. "We all get together during the summer and I string a big, old awning over those poles you can just see over there next to the cabin. We have some fine times there."

We talk a good deal about the trout in his pond and thank him for letting us fish and camp here. He is most interested when I tell him the size of some of the fish I'd taken over the years.

"What'd you catch 'em on?" he asks, and I rummage through my tackle bag to find some Bigg's Specials. I hand several to him and he holds them up in front of his eyes, examines them through the bottom lenses of his bifocals, twists and turns the patterns in the light, squinting as he does so.

"These skinny things really work?" and the rancher looks at me hard to see if I am fooling around with him. Fishing is serious business no matter what you do for a living and I'm not about to B.S. this guy.

"Yeah. They work good," I say. "Put a small split shot at the head, cast it out just past the weed beds, let it sink some, maybe a few seconds, then strip them in with several short retrieves, let it drop again, and repeat the process. They'll come up and take in the first few feet. Big fish, too. Three, four pounds." I demonstrate the motion with my hands and he imitates me with his, both of us standing out in the gale in the middle of one hell of a lot of open space, looking like neither of our medications are doing either one of us all that much good. He looks up at me, smiles, and adds, "I'll be sure to give that a try."

I pass the test. He believes me. We talk a little more, then he says he has to "be goin' to finish moving some cattle over to another field, behind that hill over there," that he points out with a long arm and a straight, tanned forefinger.

"See you again, soon," and he is off in his pickup, down the dusty road, then cross country to "that hill over there."

Not too many miles east of where we are camped lies another small ranch pond that was once filled with fat rainbows. I remember a time years ago when a friend and I braved clouds of savage mosquitoes to cast for hours in the brown water. We never turned a fish, never even saw a dead one floating belly up near shore. Later, while getting gas in nearby Sunburst, a spot in the road with a few homes, gas station, grocery store, and farm implement business, the man at the station informs us that the pond used to be good fishing but the "damned Hooters dynamited the dam and netted all the trout." That explains our lack of success. The water in question was located on a large Hutterite ranching operation, but because the state had stocked the water with rainbow trout, it was open to the public. The Hutterites have enormous ranches scattered about Montana, South Dakota, and Alberta. The Hutterian Brethren are a communitarian religious sect that originated among the Anabaptists in Moravia (now the Czech Republic) during the Reformation. They take their name from their original leader, Jakob Hutter, who was burned as a heretic in 1536. The ranches that they refer to as colonies are called *Bruderhofe*, and the members practice a conservative, austere lifestyle similar to the Amish. I've seen men fixing fence dressed in dark wool coats and pants, shirts buttoned to the collar, and the temperature well over ninety degrees. They found their way to North America as over the course of centuries they struggled to escape persecution in Europe by moving eastward as far as Russia before eventually migrating here during the years of 1874–79. There are now over twenty thousand Hutterites in Canada and the U.S. Their inward-looking sectarianism has engendered a good deal of hostility and ridicule from their western neighbors. My experiences indicate that they really do keep to themselves, though I remember a time when two of them pulled my old pickup from a muddy crossing near the Musselshell. I appreciated the help and it only cost my friends and I one hundred bucks.

"Remember as you pass by as you are now so once was I, as I am now so you must be, prepare for death and follow me."

—Jesse Rowe, 1887–1902

A dirt road winds its lonely way from camp, cutting through hills of tall grass that flow like water in the wind. The hills close in. Middle Butte disappears behind the waves of rustling grass. A slight crease of wetness shines between the cattails growing in the wash alongside the road. Mosquito Draw. Its namesakes are not around in this blow. Climbing steadily higher the path runs through an old, abandoned gold placer mine. The scars from the work are little changed. Not by wind, rain, snow, or time. Mounds of tailings surround small ponds of green water. Paired mallards swim in them. Piles of wood that used to be sheds rot into the bare ground. Metal framework from the machinery used to wash the gold from the dynamited rock lies twisted and rusting at odd angles that almost look like intentional sculptures. They frame a high-cloud, faded blue sky. Coming above all of this, out of Mosquito Draw there is a grave on the side of a hill, a hill that runs a long way up to another hill that pushes against a ridge that connects with Middle Butte towering more than a thousand feet above it all. The wind really kicks and wails at the grave site, cold blasts tear through the seventy-degree day. Sparse grass, small sagebrush, and prickly pear cactus grow in the orange-brown soil. The gravestone is gray granite, thin patches of lime-green and orange lichen mark the surface in random patterns but don't obscure the epithet. First glances, first readings, say the words are meant for those who wander past this spot that looks out across the high plains, far past West Butte glowering a few miles away, far off to the Rocky Mountains flickering in and out of sight in the miles of haze. The mountains dance like sedimentary ghosts when seen from here, the peaks in it for the long haul, like this grave. Maybe the words are really for Middle Butte, a place that might be already dead at the hands of gold miners, might be if the limiting conception of linear time is ignored.

The high plains, all of the millions of square miles of it, are as much about ghosts as anything. Dead dreams, dead innocence, dead animals, dead us. Images and entities that float throughout the land spinning their connected vibes everywhere a person turns. The Sweet Grass Hills are filled with these spirits. An easy overnight spent sleeping on a ridge turns into a never-ending horror show peopled with the demons of internal hells. Come here with bad intentions, a wicked mind-set, or just plain and simple singing the blues, and the Hills will intensify any of this, stretch all of the feelings out into a dozen hours that never seem to tick by. Eventually the sun comes up over the edge of Middle Butte and burns away the horror of recognition, the awareness that life could all be going very wrong for the most common of reasons—avarice, pettiness, lust, perverse thoughts—and driving away from this place seems like a surefire cure because of the prevalence of the naive belief that enduring bad situations is akin to growing stronger, but this fallacy is soon exposed in nightmares of dark, boiling clouds blowing down the butte's ridge in the always wailing, relentlessly cold gale, nightmares that gradually and with abrupt swiftness reveal their true form as that of a too bright light of day-to-day reality. There's no hiding, no running in or from the Hills. Once in, the switch is flipped on and stays on.

"As I am now so you must be . . ."

Trapper Dick Kenck, ninety-four years old, of Augusta, Montana, on the edge of the Rocky Mountain Front.

15

ONE OF THE LAST OF
HIS KIND—
SUN RIVER COUNTRY

"I CAUGHT MY FIRST BEAVER WHEN I WAS TEN BACK IN 1916," and so begins the tale of Dick Kenck, one of the last trappers who can remember a Montana that was as wild as the state tourism board would have us believe it still is today. Kenck is ninety-four years old and still going strong. There's a sparkle in his dark eyes and enthusiasm and fire in his voice. His less than six-foot frame is unbowed by age. His sun-browned, gnarled hands are steady and his walk is assured, purposeful. Hell, he still runs twelve miles of trapline in the winter and is apologetic that it isn't more. Twelve miles in the snow and wind that blasts along the raging Rocky Mountain Front near Augusta and Choteau all through the long, dark dead of winter in Montana. "I trapped weasels, muskrats, gophers, and stuff like that before beaver."

Kenck lives in Augusta, a small ranching community about twenty miles east of the Rocky Mountains, which loom like a giant wall on the horizon. Wild, contorted formations made up of slabs of Madison limestone over 200 million years old are mixed with slices of younger Mesozoic rock creating a massive scene of organized chaos. The wind roars down from the high country of the Bob Marshall Wilderness, funnels through the steep-walled Sun River Canyon, then blasts out onto the plains. The town is the setting for the Augusta Rodeo, one of the most free-form, popular locations on the circuit. The first one I attended was in 1973. State police were parked at the ends of all the roads leading out of town. You could come in but you couldn't leave until everything was over on Sunday. The place was as chaotic as the mountains nearby. An intense competitive mixture of bulls, horses, steers, and cowboys swirled in the dirt, dust, and mud in the arena below the old wooden stands with thousands of people yelling and screaming in the wind beneath a wicked sun, all night drinking and carousing, individuals on horseback riding up and down the main street and sometimes into one of the bars. All of it. Years ago when I interviewed duck decoy carver Bob Null back in Wisconsin I noticed an old poster from the twenties for the Augusta Rodeo hanging on his workshop wall. "I rode the broncos out there," Null said with the slightest of smiles. "That was one of the wild rodeos." Still is to some extent today, though the town, located beneath the shelter of hundreds of huge cottonwoods, is a quiet, easygoing place. This is Kenck's home.

And while it's unfortunately true that we live in a world where his way of making a living is far from being in fashion or politically correct, a loathsome term, as I sit here listening to a man who's lived in a West I can only dream of or try to imagine, there is one thing I am sure of. If we all went about our day-to-day business like Kenck, cleaned up our own messes instead of trying to control everyone else's life, all of us, society as a whole, would be in much better condition.

When white trappers first wandered into this country back at the beginning of the nineteenth century they came looking primarily for beaver. The same was true for Kenck at the start of the twentieth. Beavers and their smaller cousins, muskrats, build dams and lodges with a fervor often ascribed to the current greedy pack of arbitrageurs chasing their next ten or twenty million. Trees, lots of them, are gnawed down by the large rodents using retractable incisors that make short work of huge cottonwoods, downsized willows, aspens, whatever is handy. The dams flood a creek or small river drainage turning verdant emerald meadow into ponds and marshland. With man a recent fact of life on the prairies out here, men like Kenck performed a necessary function years ago, as they do today.

"Now at the time [around 1920] beaver were under a permit system and the game warden said you can take three beaver or five beaver, like that," and he leans toward me. "Well, this one large beaver was pretty smart and poachers had tried to take him plenty of times before, but they couldn't. Well I finally caught him by the hind foot in one of my traps which was located right on the way to school. I couldn't pull him out of the creek. He had a big rock on the trap, probably thirty, thirty-five pounds, you drowned him you see, well Dad went down and he had quite a ride and when we weighed him he was ninety pounds. Biggest beaver I ever caught. I caught 'em up to eighty-five. I've got some here that run seventy-five, eighty, but that one, oh, ho, he was like that. Took me four hours to skin 'im."

Kenck slaps his knee and leans back in his big chair laughing and staring out his living-room window past the cottonwood-lined streets of Augusta, past the golden brown grass hills of Augusta, past the purple-blue Rocky Mountains still holding snow on their peaks in late summer, past all of this far back into the years of his life in country that was home to vast herds of buffalo, the Blackfeet Indians, and the setting for A. B. Guthrie's classic western novel *The Big Sky,* Ivan Doig's *This House of Sky*, and the landscape that inspired Charlie Russell's paintings. The real West.

Harsh, windswept, hot, cold, dry, peaceful, beautiful beyond words, dangerous, deadly. Land of immense ranches measured in miles and hundreds of sections not in mere acres. Land so unforgiving and relentless that two hundred years ago Lewis and Clark barely survived their exploratory expedition here. Forget about finding an inland water passage through the Front and on down to the Pacific. A country filled with deer, antelope, elk, moose, wolverine, black bears, golden eagles, red-tailed hawks, coyotes, wolves, and enormous grizzlies that roamed wherever they damn pleased. Kenck sees all of this and more as he stares down the past. He turns from his distant visions and leans forward.

"I was born in Choteau in 1906. My dad was the first dentist between Helena and the Canadian line [one hundred miles north of here] practicing twenty hours out of twenty-four," he said. "His health finally went bad, his heart, so he had to quit. He had a little place on the Dearborn River, he and his brother, so he moved up there and later bought some more property. He had a cattle ranch there.

"For several years he raised fish and he planted the first fish above the diversion dam [about twenty miles west of town on the Sun River, which runs far back into the mountains into what is now called the Bob Marshall Wilderness]. There were three hundred miles of water and not a fish in it. With the dam there was a big falls and the fish couldn't migrate upstream," Kenck said. "So he got little fish from the federal hatchery and brought them in from Craig with a spring wagon in fifty-gallon barrels. He had a little foot pump to keep the water aerated and the trout alive. He got to where they couldn't go any farther with the wagon and then he'd put them on a packhorse. He put them in five-gallon cans and he'd take them out every time they crossed a creek, take 'em out and lay them down and let fresh water run in and cool the water. On top of them they had a tomato can soldered on and it had a screen on it and water washed in and aerated it. He said he lost very, very few fish and he hauled them back more than fifteen miles. He planted the first fish and they're still above the diversion dam.

"I packed fish up near Dearborn country, planted up the Dearborn and up Falls Creek and you take a packhorse, had the trout in those cans, and in a couple of years the fish were all over the place."

Life in the West goes easier for those with a pragmatic disposition. Romanticism and emotional attachment look good in the movies, but running a ranch, taking care of business, is another matter. Kenck's father knew what this meant.

"I was raised on the ranch. We had cattle and my brother and I had a bunch of sheep we raised from lambs and we got so we had about a hundred head of sheep," Kenck says with a proud grin. "We sheared them ourselves and lambed 'em out and everything, sold the withers to the meat market. The ewes we kept and of course that increased our herd. When Dad sold the ranch we had to sell all the sheep, of course. I didn't even know he had it up for sale. He come in one day and said, 'You gotta get rid of these sheep. I sold the ranch,' which was kind of a shock," Kenck added with wry understatement.

A puff of wind rattles the windows and I think back to the night before last camped out along the Sun River a few miles below Gibson Dam. We'd pulled into our usual campsite beneath the pines and aspen next to the aquamarine water around four in the afternoon. This is windy country more often than not. Gales racing along the Front from the north and out onto the plains often pass the hundred-mile-per-hour mark. It blows so hard out here that car windshields collapse with the force of the wind, the open country is mostly without trees, and snow rarely sticks to the ground, even in the dead of winter. As we drove up the canyon the Suburban rocked and bucked in forty-, fifty-mile-per-hour gusts. Setting up the tent was sporting and the force of the wind was increasing, the sound of it a roar as it howled through the narrow canyon walls that towered above us and raged through the limbs of pine needles and leaves. Branches and limbs were ripped from the trees' trunks with cracking sounds. Our cookstove blew off the table and into the brush by the river. The now full-tilt gale whipped sheets of spray up from the river's surface and far into the air. What was fifty was now seventy, eighty maybe more miles an hour.

"Let's get the hell out of here before we're killed," I yelled in Ginny's ear and we threw what we could into the car, leaving the poor tent behind. The last sight I had of it as we fled with the setting sun was of the rain fly flapping maniacally, straight out in the storm, and the body of the tent compressed flat into a rippling half-moon shape. We spotted a canoe and aluminum boat, both crumpled and submerged, foundering on the far shore of the impoundment near the diversion dam. I'd seen the two craft tied to a tree on shore below a group of campers earlier in the day. The thin rope they'd used must have snapped like thread in the storm. When we reached a motel in Augusta an hour later the weather was serene. Clear skies and a mild thirty mph breeze. Over coffee in a local cafe the next morning we learned that the cold air was dropping down from the high country of the Bob Marshall Wilderness as a high pressure system pushed in. Sustained winds of eighty mph with gusts over one hundred had been recorded at the weather station in the area.

Well, that's life along the Front, day in and day out. Wind over a hundred, temperatures over a hundred in July, below minus fifty in January, and snowstorms that come at you like a psychopathic killer, with no mercy, stinging sheets of vertically screaming snow and ice that cut the skin, freeze cattle and elk with impunity, and cause whiteout conditions where up is down and sane is three sheets to the crazy wind. That's the country Kenck grew up in, trapped in, and loves. A land of vast rolling hills, clear rivers, brush-choked, muddy-bottomed creeks, alkali flats that sizzle white under a hellish sun, mosquitoes and flies that live for your blood and flesh, sunsets flashing golden orange, pink, and crimson through banks and piles of cumulus clouds, nights so bright with the cold light of the stars that the land casts black images of itself, silhouettes that slide across the sage and grass and prickly pear with an eerie motionless movement that dances to the moon's wild tune with eerie yips and howls from packs of coyotes holding sway on distant bluffs, mountains flashing silver and the deepest purple on the horizon, the sound of huge animals working their way through brushy draws in the dark, elk, grizzly, moose, wolves. Nighthawks soar overhead booming away and you throw more wood on the fire and feel glad in a weak way that you brought along the .357.

That's Kenck's country and he loves it with a force of commitment that buzzes and hums even at ninety-four, perhaps more so. Nine-plus decades drive the powerful message of this land home.

"After the ranch was sold, we came here to town. I was going to high school in town. Dad had an office here where he practiced dentistry in his later years. He was around eighty and was a doctor, dentist, an undertaker, you name it," Kenck says. "He said, 'I bring people into the world, take care of them while they're here, and then I put 'em away,' " and he laughed at this.

"And you know there weren't many cars around here back then, cars or trucks. About 1914 was when the first cars came here. Two-seated outfit, a Studebaker, then a Maxwell, most you never hear of anymore. And most of our supplies after 1911 or '12 came by railroad. They were building the diversion dam and they used to freight from the town of Gilman to the mountains with teams of horses, but about 1922 the railroad came up here, all the shipping came through here and that was the end of Gilman," says Kenck and he looks off out the window again. "But Gilman was dying before that, after the reclamation left there was not much and then there was the Depression. During World War I the government encouraged people to buy more land and put in more crops and all this and that, then in a series of dry years people went broke and it broke the bank. Then the government encouraged the banks to loan money to these people and ended up with a bunch of stuff worth fifty cents an acre and they loaned five dollars an acre and that's still going on today," Kenck says with a long, ironic laugh.

Boom and bust is the true story of the modern West. Cut the timber until the trees are gone and then the timber giants wait for the pines to grow back before cutting them again. Cut the heart out of the mountains blasting and digging for gold, silver, and copper as bustling, prosperous towns spring up like spring wheat in the dampness of a warm spring, then die back as the ore pays out and then the mini-cities become ghost towns that slowly sink back into the ground beneath the sun and weather as no one watches. Or cattle prices skyrocket or wheat prices do the same, then the dry years come one after another and they call this place, the high plains, the drought-stricken, arid West and more people go broke and move on or blow their brains out behind the barn and on and on, and someday the glitzy ski resorts and all of the expensive fly-fishing guides will find out the West's ultimate truth, when the weather turns truly fierce for a series of winters or droughts kill off the trout (if whirling disease doesn't do this number first) and they'll go back to selling damn near anything you might want to buy or they'll move on or maybe they'll blow their brains out like others before them. Boom and bust.

Kenck picks up on my train of thought and says, "At the time they didn't know how to farm, would try on dry, worthless land far from any water and it's not so much different today. People keep making the same mistakes," and he slaps his knee to make his point. "When I was young there was an accountant from New Jersey had quite a family. Built a big bungalow, beautiful home.

Had a bunch of Jersey cows and started a dairy. At the time you didn't have many separators and stuff, you used big pans, you know, and your cream would come to the top and you'd skim it, you see. They didn't know what that scum was on top of the milk, so they just throwed that away. They only lasted about a year," and he laughs at this with humor and with a trace of anger at the arrogance and stupidity of people who would more or less drop into this country without a clue about any of it.

The more things change the more they remain the same doesn't always hold true in the West and Kenck's part of this country is no different.

"There was a lot more people in the country than there is now. What it took, to break an old-time ranch down, well as an example around here, you've got a ranch with land in five counties. This fella from back East bought the first place of 56,000 acres [about 87.5 square miles]. It was two big ranches combined and that sold as a unit, and then he bought everything adjoining."

Kenck looks away again and then turns to me with anger in his eyes.

"He killed the town, killed the community. I was in business here for forty-three years and the potential when I started was one hundred times what it is now, because every place that he bought, a family went out, gone." Kenck bangs his knee with a fist at this. "He said he's doing business here in town, but he goes to a factory and says I'll take so many carloads of this or I'll take so many carloads of that, you see. Shipped directly. He put in a lot of these pivot irrigation systems, oh, he's got to own I don't know how many. He went to the company and said, 'I want so many.' The company says, 'We can't build that many.' So he bought the company. They run several thousand head of cattle, four, five hundred head of buffalo, raise grain and hay. He's got land right out here, just across the river there aways. He was on Dry Creek [east of Augusta]. Now he owns all of Dry Creek. Full length of it.

Both sides. So it don't help the community one bit," and Kenck glares off across the prairie outside his window.

Kenck and those like him who have lived in the West most or all of their lives are open to newcomers, but they hate, and this is the right word, those who come highballing in here from the East or West Coasts and throw tons of money at a place to buy themselves a big ranch without giving a damn concerning their big business ways and how they may affect a community. Look in any of the glitzy western magazines that pockmark the racks these days and you'll see dozens of ads with beautiful color photos offering for sale properties along this line. "Historic ranch lies in central Montana's Little Snowy Mountains. This premier cattle ranch is famous for its livestock and wildlife and people. Over 47,000 contiguous acres, with beautiful hay meadows, over ten miles of creek bottom, vast timbered slopes, and hills of strong grass. This ranch offers superb bird hunting and big-game hunting and has one of the most respected names in the cattle industry. Its large size, varied terrain, and complete set of ranch improvements allow for an outstanding recreational and cattle ranching opportunity. $19,500,000."

So the realtors masquerading as ranchers or individuals grounded in the land dance around in their phony western getups replete with some kind of weird lizard-skin boots, thousand-buck suede jackets, and four-hundred-dollar hats. They are skilled in locating the very well-monied swells who want a Ponderosa of their own and these hucksters put out the word that is couched ever so carefully but bottom line says, "No shit, buddy, throw twenty mil at the land and it's all yours. The livestock and wildlife and people. Just between the two of us, we both know that this land and the hicks that live on it are nothing but commodities put here for our insatiable purchasing greed." And that's how it goes throuhout Wyoming and Montana and Alberta and the rest of the West. People try and buy a piece of this country without the willingness or even awareness that a person must spill his blood out here—physical, emotional, spiritual—to finally catch a glimpse of the majesty of the place, of what's really going on. They don't give a damn about the wind and the elk and the need of a smaller rancher for water that flows upstream through the nouveau riche billionaire's latest proprietary toy and without giving a damn for the real ones like Dick Kenck, who looks back at me and notices the fire in my eyes and smiles a smile of righteous recognition.

"Then there's the Salt Creek Cattle Company. They bought five ranchers in one year. They own land from Highway 200 to right around the edge of town here. And from the forest boundary [along the Front] to down close to Simms [about twenty miles east of town]. So between here and Wolf Creek [twenty more miles east of Simms] we've got that ranch, the Hutterite colony, Salt Creek Cattle, and also the big shot of the Sierra Club. The first ranch he bought was a cattle ranch. First thing that went up was a NO TRESPASSING sign adjoining the forest. No trespassing. That meant he had control of access to the forest," and Kenck looked both bemused and sad at this.

"Then he built some cabins back there for his friends to come on and then he bought the JB Long Ranch up here. No hunting. No fishing. No trapping. Well he got his control all right. Elk come down on that place, maybe two, three, four hundred head, you see. Well he didn't say too much about that, but no hunting, no fishing, no trapping. So wolves moved in, a big den, took ten of 'em out of here last year and moved 'em down near Yellowstone Park. Those wolves didn't know where the forest and park boundaries were so they went out and started killing cattle and they got killed themselves," and Kenck is angry about all of it.

"And no fishing, no trapping. Well the beaver moved in and it was a regular home for them. No trapping, remember," he says with a wry smile. "Now they're flooding these meadows and now they wanted a trapper to come in and estimate how many beaver they had. I laughed at him. How you gonna estimate for that jungle of fifteen miles of water? He couldn't even crawl through some of that brush. One of these days the wolves are gonna come in and clean out all that bunch of cattle. Grizzly bear. He's got grizzly bear on that place, too. And the beaver will flood him out. I know because I trapped for a fellow neighbor and one year I took out seventy-five beaver . . ." and Kenck looks at me with an expression that seems to say, "Do you believe the foolishness of some people," and then continues.

"In fact, last year they asked me to come and trap them some more. I hadn't trapped there for several years and he'd poisoned all the brush. Killed it. When he killed the brush he killed the food for the beaver so they moved out. And it takes years to bring that back.

"For over thirty-five years I live-trapped and transplanted beaver where they were doing damage like flooding meadows and county roads or filled in culverts or an irrigating ditch with sticks or something, so I would go and trap those when they were sleeping at night, take them back in the forest or out in the open country where there were no roads or ditches to bother and turn 'em loose. And then in a year or two they would be a colony and I could take a crop."

Kenck looks at the land and its resources like fur-bearing mammals as a sustainable resource as long as those who use it and rely on it for their living take only as much as the land can handle. Greed has no place in Kenck's life.

"Price of beaver coats went down, you see. One of those big beaver I got out of here last year averaged about twelve dollars. Takes me about two hours and a half to take care of a beaver. And then, of course, there's goin' out there and gettin' 'em and haulin' 'em and all that. You have to skin him and stretch him and dress him out. Well, all of that figures out to about forty cents an hour. There's only two of us here that are active trappers now. One of them works at a service station down here," and Kenck points down the gravel road to one of the two gas stations in Augusta. Kenck shows me a tanned beaver belt. The fur is lustrous, soft. It glistens in the light.

We're quiet for a moment and then I ask him about grizzlies and wolves, those overly feared and romanticized creatures of Hollywood movie distortion and tourist mania.

"Never had too much trouble with grizzlies, but when I was a kid we had a lot of trouble with wolves, but then the government come in and they poisoned them and shot 'em and trapped 'em and did everything to annihilate them. It took a hundred years trying to get rid of them. When they come out with 1080 [a poison] that knocked them out. There was always wolves here and fact is I saw seven in one pack. We saw them several times and then there was three later and they weren't far from the front gate and from me. Since then I haven't seen any in a few years or so, but I have seen their tracks and they've been close enough behind that I could see the toenails in the snow and a half hour later that track was that big around [Kenck spreads his hand wide open], melted out from the sun, so I was pretty close to them."

When you live in wild, largely unspoiled, underpopulated country like the Rocky Mountain Front, grizzlies, mountain lions, and wolves are no big deal. The impassioned, often hysterical pleas of the animal rights do-gooders make men like Kenck laugh, often with a tinge of anger. Why bring back something that is already here and why spend loads of taxpayer dollars to do something so unnecessary and potentially harmful, both to the region where the wolves are to be reintroduced and also to the wolves themselves. As Kenck says, "It doesn't make sense."

And as for the wolves in his country.

"I knew just where they traveled. They made a circle," and Kenck moves his hands in a wide arc. "Every so often they come back around the same way, within a mile or so, they would come back through that same area. When people found wolves up here, up on the game range [located about ten miles west of town] they found a pair mating and they reported it. You'd a thought the United States Army and Navy had moved in here," he says with a shrug and a smile. "Airplanes and cars and trucks, pickups, you name it. It was just a constant racket. You turned on the radio and they were talking to each other all the time. They finally got one wolf and put a radio collar on him. Well for about a year there was about four or five of 'em [wildlife biologists] with these little radio antennas checking on them. Plus airplanes and helicopters and other stuff. Those wolves multiplied and were under full protection [by the Endangered Species Act].

"Got to be quite a bunch of 'em, you know, and they took ten out and that slowed it up some, but they also killed about twenty cattle and they caught those wolves doin' the killing. One of the airplanes was flying around. They were counting deer is what they were trying to count. There was a couple of wolves there chasing a cow, so they buzzed them two or three times, but the wolves never quit. They killed that cow. So they reported that and that's when they took ten out of here. There again a helicopter, a pilot, and the shotgunner using a tranquilizer gun. What does all that cost? Millions and millions of dollars spent on it and there's no accounting for it at all. Bunch of hooey," and Kenck bangs his knee with a fist once more.

Like many who spend their lives outdoors, Kenck has his share of disagreements with Montana's wildlife management practices. Because he's centered his life around predators and big game, it's reasonable to assume that his opinions have some value, carry some weight.

"I worked with Fish and Game [Montana Department of Fish, Wildlife and Parks] for several years and lived right there with the big game. The average years saw twenty calves to one hundred cows reach maturity. That's the game count over thirty years. Now the grizzly bears, the wolves, the eagles, the mountain lion, were all protected. A mountain lion will average a deer a week year round. That's fifty-two deer a year. If it's [the lion] got young, they'll kill up to three a week. Then we got the wolf. We got the eagle. We got the coyote. We got the black bear and the grizzly bear living on the calves. So where's our elk herd gone [on the Sun River Game Preserve]? From 2,500 head down to maybe 1,200 or less. They had a quota up here in hunting season. They haven't reached a quota in three years. Last year their quota was ten. What's happening? Where's our mule deer? They're way out somewhere on the prairie. Not here in the mountains or in the foothills where they used to be. Now whitetail are along the river here. Every creek is full of whitetail. Right here there's been six mountain lion killed within three miles of town this last winter.

"Mountain lions I track back in along the foothills. Nothing to see mountain lion tracks every day. One boy up here, he's fifteen years old. He lives right in the foothills. He's killed a deer, an elk, a bear, and a mountain lion with a bow and arrow. Now he's hunting mountain lion and guiding people and carrying a camcorder. He's shooting them with a camcorder. He's seen thirteen mountain lion within a couple miles of his house last winter.

"As I say, we've got the bear, black bear and grizzly, eagles, coyotes, mountain lions. Our big game's going down. It's going to keep going down. Our mountain [bighorn] sheep, our mountain goats, eagle is the worst enemy of the sheep and goat. It comes down and knocks them right off the cliffs. And then the sheep get a disease every so often and that pulls them down. I worked for the state trapping sheep and transplanting. A friend of mine did the same. He put sheep on Wild Horse Island [on Flathead Lake in western Montana]. He put antelope in Hawaii.

He put sheep all over the state down in the hills around Absaroka and Gates of the Mountains."

One of the issues Kenck is trying to get at with this is that much of the trapper's work involves capturing and relocating animals. Not just killing furbearers for their pelts. A common misconception these days. Earlier in the day he took pains to show me the lighter, quicker, more efficient traps he has stored on hooks in his garage and when asked about animal rights groups that oppose his way of earning a living, he looked long and hard at me, snorted a little, and handed me a wolverine skull to examine. I dropped the issue.

The best furs come in the winter when the animals have thick coats to protect themselves from the cold. When he was younger he covered vast distances up in the mountains in rugged, unforgiving country in extreme weather and he ran even longer lines on the plains along the Front out where the full force of the perpetual wind doesn't cut a break for anyone.

"I ran a trapline about sixty miles on snowshoes. I would cross the Continental Divide three times in that circuit. Had four cabins up there back then [in the thirties through the sixties]. The Forest Service burnt three of my cabins and built a trail to within fifty yards of the other. But they never touched that one. But now the hunters are tearing it apart, using it for wood. The last time I was up there, there was just two logs, you know."

Kenck shows me some old black-and-white photos of his cabins and of him up in the high country during the cold months. He looks lean, fit, and tough in the pictures. One shot shows him carrying a large pack nearly straight up a snow and ice trail and another shows the snow piled many feet deep around one of the cabins.

"That was up in the mountains, but when I got out here on the flats I had a Jeep station wagon and I ran about 150 to 200 miles. I trapped beaver clear up to Rogers Pass [about twenty

miles south of Augusta and where the lowest temperature in Montana was recorded, minus seventy degrees F].

"During the Depression I was married [his wife is alive
though in failing health] in '31 and I was working for the
county driving a Cat. Seasons got shorter and shorter. Got so
that three months and that was my employment for the year. I
could go out and work on a ranch for fifteen dollars a month
and board. To heck with that noise. I set trapline and had an
old Model T Ford and away I'd go. I trapped coyote and badger
and weasels. One morning I pulled fourteen skunks out of a
culvert. I come home and the missus said, 'Hooey.' There was
three kids staying with us going to school. [Years ago and to
some extent today students would board with family or friends
in town so they could get their education. Getting to and from
town out in the middle of nowhere was normally impossible on
a daily basis from fall through spring. Dirt roads turn into
muddy quagmires at the mere mention of moisture.] We had
groceries for practically two months off of those fourteen
skunks. I was making ninety to ninety-five dollars a month
trapping and these guys are working fifteen hours a day for fifteen dollars a month."

There is another long pause in the conversation and then Kenck
recounts an incident that is clearly painful to him, even though
it happened before he was born, something that occurred near the
end of the Indian Wars.

"My mother came to Montana on the steamboat *Rosebud* up the
Missouri. My grandfather came the same way. He was here first
and then my grandmother and mother came up. My grandfather
on my dad's side was born in Helena. My grandfather was killed
in Yellowstone Park in 1877 by Nez Perce Indians. Down in the
park there's a monument there.

"The Nez Perce were coming through see, trying to get to
Canada chased by the Army, and they were in Yellowstone Park

and this party from Helena had gone down. They went down to see the country on this kind of excursion. And these Indians, they saw these Indians the night before so they moved on out of there and moved away several miles. The Indians were across the river from them, right at the falls (Yellowstone River Falls, which are one of the most popular sites in the park today). They were all on one side and the Indians were on the other. So they moved and thought the Indians had gone on, but there were a bunch of renegades that came back and jumped the party. Shot 'em up and killed my grandfather. My dad talked to Chief Joseph sometime later and Joseph said it was a bunch of young braves that went against his orders. So I been in the country quite a while . . ."

Kenck's voice wavers and breaks. We get up and go out to his shop behind the house. The inside is filled with hundreds of traps of all sizes and shapes. Some so large, for grizzly, I could not open them. Kenck can, though, with the use of a bar and those strong hands of his. He brings out several boxes, removes a number of carefully wrapped items, which turn out to be skulls from weasels, black bear, grizzly, bighorn sheep, skunk, marten, and others. He lifts up a beaver skull and shows how the lower incisors retract into the jawbone several inches and explains that if the rodents do not constantly gnaw on bark and wood these teeth will grow to such a length that the animal will be unable to eat and eventually starve. Hence, the constant industry of the beaver. Gnaw or perish. Kenck also points out a number of hides he is tanning along with pairs of his snowshoes. We talk about this and that, the weather, fishing, and so on before Kenck concludes the visit with . . .

". . . Well, I got it all figured out. I figure when I get to be about one hundred I'm going to retire. Grizzly bear are protected so you can't take one of them. And I'm goin' to go shoot me a grizzly bear. I ain't goin' to pay no fine and they can put me in the Crowbar Hotel. I get my medical, my eats, my exercise, my library, my own place. How could you retire any better?"

And Kenck walks back to the house laughing out loud to himself.

An old "soddy" homestead a few miles south of central Montana's Bears Paw Mountains.

ఞ 16 క్ట

SOLID SEA ISLANDS

"These good times are like money in the bank
We were born lookin' for rainbows . . .
. . . Let's go fishin', Frank . . .
If anyone asks you what it's all about
wink and grin and tell 'em trout"

—FROM LET'S GO FISHIN', FRANK
BY DANNY O'KEEFE

THE SNAKE HELD ITS GROUND in the tall grass next to the stream, flickering tongue, sharp eyes, and even sharper fangs all aimed in our direction. The rattler was motionless, nearly invisible in his browns, grays, greens, and blacks. We waded out into the middle of the swift flow quietly and with as much respect as we could muster. Long emerald strands of aquatic plants swirled in the current and wound around our legs. Twenty feet upstream we cautiously turned and looked back at the rattlesnake. It was looking at us. No rattle or hiss. No need for that sort of garish display. The message was clear enough—"Leave me alone and I'll do the same."

"The hell with it, Ginny," and I launched a small streamer next to a brushy undercut. A smallmouth bass nailed the thing as it hit

259

the water and then made a run down toward the snake. I broke the
fish off. Don't like snakes. Not at all. Usually when I see a rattlesnake out here, the reptile takes me by surprise and I yell, lurch, and
weave doing the spastic ballet all the way back to the car. Quite a
sight I've been told by friends over drinks and cigars—a balding,
out-of-shape, six-three, derelict writer screaming bloody murder
while bouncing back and forth like a pinball off the invisible walls
of his visceral fears. But then that's part of the charm of this
country along with the wild, isolated mountains, the lakes and
streams hidden away, and, best of all, few if any people to fuck
things up. We don't bust and bounce for hours down a boulder-
studded, dusty two-track to shoot the shit with some big-monied
Wall-Streeter about how we just screwed our best friend out of
his last five mil. We like the loneliness of these island mountain
ranges that hold sway like surly yet dignified psychopaths out in
the vast, blown-away openness of central Montana. Keep the post-
card pretty snowcapped peaks now ski-resort-ravaged, the drift-
boat-clogged rivers, and, perhaps most of all, the stultifying
bed-and-breakfasts. Don't need 'em. Sure as hell don't want any
part of 'em . . .

No French wine, checkered tablecloth, crab salad, or other noi-
some ways to impress the hell out of each other. No Beemer
pretension. Only snakes, coyotes, spiders, cactus, antelope, vultures, mule deer, and, most generously, trout, smallmouth and
largemouth bass, pike, goldeye, sage, and sharp-tailed grouse and
turkeys and on and on . . .

  You don't read about them much and Hollywood doesn't make
those lovely movies about a dehumanized, serene Old West in
these hills, bluffs, ridges, and torn-up peaks. Some of us know
who they are—Big Snowy, Highwood, Bears Paw, Judith, Little
Belt. They don't have the name recognition or the drawing power

of the northern Rocky Mountains at chic national sacrifice zones such as Glacier, Jackson, and Yellowstone. These islands of intricate and elegant mystery thrust up into the sky with earned aloofness and arrogance, rising thousands of feet above the still-life sea that is the high plains. Countless square miles of native Bluebunch wheat grass, buffalo, and blue grama grass blow in the always-present, hard wind like waves on the ocean. Millions of acres of wheat shimmer in the intense sunlight, first deep green in late spring and early summer, then like white-gold feathers as the season grows hot and parched. Mammoth crops of canola blaze pure yellow in June. Sage-covered hills roll off east and west like even bigger waves. In the oil fields scattered about, pump jacks bob up and down like brain-dead dinosaurs, the rich, decayed smell of natural gas filling the air. These island mountain ranges are miles and miles from the sold-out, precious tourism centers of Bozeman, West Yellowstone (Hey, man, they got an Imax there now), Banff, and Whitefish. And star-quality rivers along the lines of the Madison, Beaverhead, or Flathead (Wow! There's Meryl Streep in an Avon raft. Is she looking at me?) don't flow through the dry, wind-blown country these mountains hang out in. The towns, if any, are places like Big Sandy, Garneill, Oilmont, or Geraldine. Way out-of-the-way enclaves offering an eight-room motel (with cable TV), a diner, and a bar called the Stockman or Mint or Pastime, a couple of service stations, a grocery store, a church or two (some of the people pray hard in this unforgiving country), a bank, and a Main Street that sometimes is paved. And the people are honest, tough, and friendly in a cautious way until they see whether you're playing it straight and just out in the middle of all this isolation because you love the land and can't hack the bullshit over in Hamilton or Missoula or Jackson Hole. Once they understand why you're here, they begin to open up and tell you things about their home, And the creeks, too little rain for rivers, that drift down out of the high country are the

likes of Peoples, Cow, Flat Willow, and Sweet Grass. Those are
the ones with water in them. Other stream courses rage with
lunatic floods in the spring when the snow melts or right after a
downpour. Otherwise they are dead-bone-dry, brush-clogged
ditches. Damn good bird cover, though. Some of these are called
Bullwhacker Creek, Brickyard Creek, Wildhorse Creek, and Shotgun Coulee.

The few casual visitors that drive through this country, usually
the result of a series of wrong turns, each one compounding the
errant nature of the superficial journey, take one look at all the
apparent nothingness including the island ranges, and say something along the lines of "What godforsaken land. Who'd ever
want to live here. The heat is awful and the winters, well I don't
even want to imagine those and what do they do here to amuse
themselves?" Not forsaken land at all, rather blessed. The best
stuff takes work, time, and a willingness to blow away preconceptions and ego. Submit to this country and it will come alive
for you. Maybe at sunset when the mountains and plains light up
like polished brass with shadings of orange, copper, purple, blue,
and other colors there aren't names for. Or when the wind stops
blowing like a crazed bitch and the whole world turns silent and
hums away inside you. Perhaps when the first stars come out and
the coyotes start riffing among the packs as Jupiter jumps up
above the eastern horizon goofing like an alien spaceship, growing
bigger and bigger and flickering red, green, blue, and white.
"Lord! Ginny. Your ethereal friend was right. There really are
aliens. Shit!" and then the planet reveals itself and we go back to
tossing a few twigs of sage or dried cactus on a small fire of
charcoal. We make some tea and grill a couple of trout over the
coals, a couple we nailed as they fed near a swampy spring. And
some rice with butter. Nothing fancy. Nothing gourmet. Later
we lay in our bags on the ground and let the stars put us away.
Owls boom and the packs of wild dogs talk among themselves,

sounding like jazz, canine style. The wind is back puffing, pushing, and racing up the slope of the grassy bench we're camped
on. Cool and very much alive with nighttime vibes. No fake lights
from cars or houses. We're far alone with all of this undisciplined
energy and our minds sail off with it conjuring all sorts of hideous
deaths and insane adventures. And there ain't no ghosts out here,
either. Just ask that tall shadowy guy without the hands, the one
floating above the juniper bushes over there . . .

. . . This trip started out in a cluster of mountains north of the
Yellowstone. Drove way back in on a dirt road that followed a
prairie creek that abruptly turned mountain cascade. Steep, timbered mountains slammed down on both sides and taller peaks
covered in new September snow moved in and out of fog and rain
up ahead. The creek was a just-found pleasure. We had no idea
the thing existed until about thirty minutes ago back where we
turned left on a gravel road that dipped and climbed through the
hilly ranch land. But here this water is. Pool after pool full of
rainbows that love gray elk-hair caddis. On a light rod the six-,
ten-, up to sixteen-inch fish slash at the pattern, then zip skyward
at the set of the hook. Leaping three, four feet above the water in
silvery sprays, the spectral colors of the trout fluoresce in the shafts
of sunlight that slice through holes in the clouds. The larger ones
run to the base of small waterfalls and use the hydraulics of the
flow to leap into the pool above, or they flee downstream and leap
out over the edge at the end of the watery hole and crash into a
swift, foamy run below.

On the way into this mountain valley I think, *God but the land
that rolls up to the edges of these mountains is dry and brown and faded
green, but once in the mountains things change.* The high country pulls
the water out of passing storm systems making the forests lush,
filled with thick undergrowth of huckleberry, alder, and a dense

carpeting of moss the greenest green I've ever seen. The creek runs wildly with melt from shrinking snowfields and perking spring water, cold and clear. The air smells of pine, icy water, and ferns. Whitetails bound off when we work upstream. Marmots whistle in the scree above. Jays, ravens, eagles, hawks, and chattering chickadees fill the airwaves. A tiger swallowtail butterfly, perhaps the last of a dying summer, floats by. Island ranges are oases. You could live here, forever, easily, at peace. The hell with what the see-it-through-the-windshield bozos think as they whiz by insanely on the interstate in overpriced motor homes (well made and designed, to be sure) far to the south. Boletus, chantrelle, and amanita mushrooms—sexy pink, glowing orange, bloody red with white scabs—push through the rich detritus and rusty brown pine needles. Pine trees tower well over a hundred feet and break any rainfall down into a soft mist. A strong wind moans through the tops of the trees. Another small fire, got to have a fire to keep away all our demons, and some of the rainbows cook golden brown in a crust of cornmeal seasoned only with salt and pepper and some lemon juice. Green peppers, a few chantrelles, and some cherry tomatoes coated with olive oil and cooked quickly. That's plenty. And a pot of black coffee and a few cigarettes (we really are going to quit and soon). A few days in this pocket of quiet and then on down the road . . .

. . . "No man is an island. He's a peninsula." So said Jefferson Airplane thirty years ago on "After Bathing at Baxter's." And what in the hell does this have to do with anything. Who knows? Merely moldering lyrics from a dead era stagger through the head as we wander through the Breaks on our way to a little something we've got going in another island range an hour or so south of the Canadian border. Dropping down a winding gravel road we cross the Missouri, flat and muddy here, and snake up the far side of the Breaks, up and out onto the plains. The view from here is everywhere rolling and bounding off in all directions. Pretty simple really. Deep blue sky. A few white, puffy clouds, native grasslands, and the mountains we're after standing silently well north of us. They look smooth, even gentle from miles away, but they aren't. They're rough, rocky, steep, secretive, and mostly dry. When we get into this country—isolated, subtly severe—the ranchers, trappers, malcontents, and benign sociopaths who live here don't know us, but they know we're around. Wherever they hole up—log cabins, soddys, ranch houses, trailers, rotted-out cottonwood tree trunks, rusting '49 Packards catching the rays in the middle of a fly-invested alkaline seep—they notice and drive by in a chaotic parade of old and brand-new pickups. They stare at us with hard, suspicious gazes, weathered, sweat-stained cowboy hats pulled down over wind-burned faces. We're sure they've never seen anyone rig up fly rods before, let alone seen anybody try to fish this few-acre cattail-shrouded, spring-fed pond sitting in the middle of these badlands. A game warden pulls up, no doubt alerted by the locals' CB chatter. Keith Jarrett playing Mozart booms from the CD player in the warden's truck. Busted again, but for what? Felonious possession of madness? Geez. Tough crowd they got goin' here.

The official is young and easily mollified. He buys our con about how we're only out here to fish, take pictures, and camp. We don't tell him that we're on the run—from crowds, bills, electronic jive, and, most of all, ourselves. Not outlaws, though. As O'Keefe says in another song, "You can't be an outlaw when you're not wanted anymore." The warden tells us about some other ponds and reservoirs in the region. Many of them are barren. Never planted or the fish all washed out when a dam burst after a rainstorm. Game fish in gay profusion flopping about among the prickly pear cactus and sagebrush. And there are other places that hold bass and pike and trout, and one creek where brook trout to several pounds swim. We take in the last information casually and with a polite smile, but the notion of a little creek filled with big, colorful fish fuels internal fires. The man gives the name of the rancher who owns the land where the streams flow.

We're out here casting woolly buggers to eager largemouths and the fishin' is easy. Lots of bass from a half pound to three pounds and while we're doing this three F16s crash the party, rocketing by at perhaps two hundred feet off the deck, the wash from the engines blasting the sage and grass, the noise deafening. The jets circle over us running a wide arc that takes them miles from the little pond and they disappear behind the high rise of the Bears Paw Mountains in the north up by where Chief Joseph surrendered to General Nelson A. Miles more than a century ago. The good general was forewarned by telegraph of the Nez Perce's approaching retreat toward Canada. The soldiers made the run up from Fort Keogh on the Yellowstone in one hell of a hurry. Big doings on the horizon. All Joseph had was feet, horses, and heart. He was doomed. After 1,600 miles of fighting, running, and hiding and finally a four-day battle in a place whose major distinguishing feature is a swampy, brushy, fly-invested creek (I know, I stood there reading the signs, staring at the gulch and hills, and swatting bugs two days ago in the heat beneath the sun), Joseph surrendered his warriors, women, children, and a large remuda of horses (that, as one story goes, numbered perhaps two hundred Appaloosas that following the surrender were used as target practice by the U.S. Cavalry or forced over cliffs to their deaths. Ain't extirpation grand?) on October 8, 1877. The reason the people were on the run in the first place was because they refused to be confined on a north Idaho reservation. The Nez Perce wanted to live where THEY wanted to live, not where the government wanted to plant them. The freedom trip once again. So they fled and fought running pitched battles and nearly made it over the sanctity of the Canadian border less than a hundred miles north.

And I'm thinking about this while playing a fat bass and listening as the roar of the three jets begins to grow ominously in the east once again and then the three aircraft blast by directly overhead dragging a hot, crackling, eardrum-rattling, crashing, mind-numbing sound behind them, a vibration that tears through me, makes the ground vibrate, and seems to ripple the still surface of the little pond, and I wonder what in the hell the largemouth is thinking about all of this nonsense—the hook in its jaw, the loss of freedom, the insane noise—and now the jets are gone again. I land and release the bass and think about the Nez Perce on the run from authority and how even far out here you can't get away from any of it. One way or another the bastards find a way to let you know who is running the show, who's in charge. The roar builds again, and if possible, the F16s are even lower.

Fuck this!

I drop the fly rod and stand my ground, both hands raised high in the air, middle fingers extended in timeless salute. The lead jet waggles its wings, shoots straight up into the sky, and vanishes in a wash of sound that makes my ears ring for hours afterward. The other two jets shoot off somewhere straight west. How could that guy have seen my flipping him the bird while traveling at Mach I or greater? Damn strangest bass fishing I've ever had right here in the good old U.S. of A., high plains style. After gathering myself and returning to the action at hand, catching largemouths that attack a woolly bugger like they've never been fed before, we head off in search of bigger things up in the sere foothills of the mountains. Brook trout are rumored to be swimming in a little creek a few miles from here, but I'm still with the jets.

"Damnit. F16s in the middle of this. Bastards."

Ginny notices all the muttering, turns away, and walks back to the Suburban.

"Bastards."

All of the good things in life seem to have, at the very least, overtones of sickness or addiction to them. The good things—booze, codeine, cigarettes, coffee, the Cubs. Running down trout in the middle of a high plains desert certainly appears to be symptomatic of what for the majority of people is nothing more than a sport or a way to kill off a summer afternoon. Try murdering any lame pretense of having a productive life. That night back at the bench as we lordly survey the ancient volcanic cones and the sweeping steppe country that reluctantly gives way to the mountains, we do nothing but talk about the little brook trout stream—where it might be, would the rancher give us access, and were there really trout in the sucker. The water didn't appear on any map we possess and we have a bunch of them. On an old, stained state map there is an intermittent blue line that starts below one of the peaks (these mountains are old and eroded; a peak in this country measures less than seven thousand feet) and seems to flow south toward the Missouri, but somewhere along the way the broken line stops and there aren't any roads marked near the thing. We'll trust in my cross-country navigational skills. Never been lost yet. Quite confused at times, but not lost.

At sunrise, one featuring the usual light suspects, golds, blues, reds, and so forth, we head off along the bench following a faint suggestion of a road, one that cuts between a pair of small bluffs before dropping down alongside a dry creekbed. For an hour or so we bounce along, passing decrepit log homesteads, the aforementioned decaying '49 Packard and a number of Angus steers who look at us with what I at first mistakenly believe to be abject idiocy. Later I realize the look was one of condescending comprehension. They know we are getting lost and up to very little good. After another hour we top a grassy, wind-ravaged rise and spot the creek. It really does exist. Roaring down the hill at perhaps eleven mph we come to a gate. It is padlocked and we are at once disappointed and pissed. So near yet a long way away.

Turning around we backtrack and pick up another "road" that leads up through a low pass in the mountains and then glides down through rich grazing land and eventually out to a smooth dirt road. The day is gorgeous. Clear sky, temperature in the mid-seventies. The sun sizzles. Sun dogs ring our star. Circular rainbows in shades of hard gold and soft silver. I walk behind a beat-down cabin and take a leak. A milk snake, bright red, white and black, looking for all the world like a venomous coral snake slithers under a rotted log. A good animal. One that eats other venomous snakes, like rattlers. The species takes its common name from the belief that it milks cows, taking gallons of the liquid in the process. Whatever.

Then we race along until we come to the creek. Another damn gate, heavy steel pipes, and a hefty padlock. Damn again. We find some men working on fence and they tell us where the gate's owner is except he isn't around. "Up north somewhere checking on his cows," one of the cheerful men mutters. What the hell. We follow the man's jerked-thumb-over-his-shoulder directions, which stagger down another dirt road far back in the mountains. Found the ranch. Found the barking ranch dogs. Didn't find the rancher.

"We know where he lives and we've got his number," offers my Ginny. "We'll get him next spring."

"You bet and I only wanted one or two shots of whiskey way back when, too. Screw this," I said in a patient, loving fashion.

Ginny takes the wheel. I take shotgun and lean out the window staring sadly at the locked gate and all of the promise flowing away clearly, beyond the barrier. I hang even farther out, grasshoppers and small rocks smacking the side of my head. I think of my old golden retriever, Zack. He used to do the same thing when I blew off what he knew in his heart was prime bird cover.

What goes around comes around. We pull up to an old, slumping wooden structure covered in vines. Neon signs flash "BUD LIGHT, COORS, MILLER." Has to be a burger in there somewhere. There is and we devour a couple. The bartender who is in love with Laurel, not a woman, a town near Billings, says a lake just up the road at the foot of the hills "is loaded with trout. Big ones. Guy brought in an eight-pounder the other day." All this while he wipes cracked highball glasses and smokes Camel straights. We finish eating, shoot the breeze for a bit, and drive up to the glory hole.

Windblown and the color of sick mud. Hundreds of cattle everywhere. On the banks. On the road. Standing shoulder deep in the water bellowing and shitting. That's what this lake was full of, shit. We look at each other and laugh. She did anyway. I'm still cursing about everything including the Cubs, book publishers, windshield wipers, cell phones, and foreign-made Converse All-Star tennis shoes. "Damn things don't last for a month. Hell, you can't even buy a good kitchen sponge anymore. As for the Internet . . ." and she plugs in Steely Dan's "Live in America." The song "Book of Liars" distracts me and within a couple of hours she pulls the Suburban up on a level rise overlooking the washed-out bass lake the warden told us about the other day. There's plenty of water down there now.

From this vantage point I can see small ponds and larger reservoirs scattered about the landscape. They sparkle and glint liquid silvers, puddled oranges, and deep purples as the sun drops down through building piles of clouds heralding the approach of thunderstorms. Lightning flashes and then thunder booms across the open distance. Nighthawks swoop and boom through the sky. Red-winged blackbirds trill in the cattails wrapping the edges of the still water. American coots laugh at us as they patrol the calm surface. A pair of hooded mergansers cruise the far shore. Ginny hands me a cup of tea, which I was just this moment thinking would be nice to have. The two of us are on the road and we're in sync. We get along and are truly of one mind. Back in town with the traffic and people (all 6,800 of them) we tend to quarrel a bit, argue about bills, what movie to rent, what to have for dinner. Important stuff. Not out here in open country away from the electronic, compressed madness of modern life. The brain scans for information thousands of times per second at a certain natural frequency. All of our electronics radiate at a different frequency, one that clouds, even cancels out, our natural radar. The end result is we perceive man-made crap and get somewhat confused and angry in the process. Drop into this wildness, away from phones, lights, and TVs, and life shifts back to a sensible and anciently familiar pace.

The storms build all around us, towering into the sky. Lightning flashing, thunder hammering across the grassy hills. But the weather stays away from camp and we watch the show, the sun sets first on the land, then moves its way up the base of the anvil-shaped storms toward the tops, shades of red, orange, and pink blending to form unnamed colors that set the stage for gold-dominated rainbows that arc across the exploding clouds and curve for miles from ridge to ridge. Thousands of tiny trout leap from the surface of the supposedly lifeless pond, their diminutive flights seemingly timed with the cracks of thunder. Coyotes bark at the weather while the nighthawks boom away as they gorge on mosquitoes and midges. Bats swoop above us and between us. The sky is full of life, stars shining through gaps in the weather and a new moon glows beneath the base of a thunderhead. On and on this spins and our fire dances and crackles with its own light and rhythm.

The next morning we walk up to an abandoned weather station replete with trailers, locked up instruments, corral, fire pit, picnic table, propane tank, wood pile, and most importantly an outhouse and running ice-cold water. A weathered cow skull is perched on a rusted spike hammered into a weathered fence post. A bright yellow government sign says "WARNING TO TRESPASSERS. PROPERTY OF THE UNITED STATES—DO NOT DESTROY THIS NOTICE." The sign is full of bullet holes. I go into the outhouse leaving the door open so that I can scan the terrain of ponderosa, sage flats, coulees, and hills that are radiant in the new day's sun. A couple of prairie dogs watch me from the perimeter of their underground compound a few yards away. They stand erect, chip and chirp at me, drop down, rise up again, stare at me, and then repeat the process. I nod in recognition of their efforts. The outhouse hasn't been used for years. No odor and the roll of toilet paper has been chewed, no doubt by the prairie dogs or perhaps field mice, into piles of confetti. I find a page from the May 19, 1996, *Great Falls Tribune* tucked between a beam. "Dole Kept Stunning Plans Secret For Weeks," says one headline about the then-presidential hopeful's retirement from the Senate. "Poisoning of Seagulls Underway in Boston," says another. "Two Plead Guilty to Yellowstone Antler Theft," and so on. I get up and head to the water spigot for the first bath-shower-whatever in days. It feels good to be clean again if only for a little while and so on . . .

. . . The narrow saddle we're standing on looks out over an expansive, verdant plain that wanders west toward the Rocky Mountain Front. A pair of isolated mountains-hills rise several thousand feet above the floor of the country. The protrusions are slightly lost in the haze of distance. A small stream curls through the land aiming for the Judith, then finally the Missouri River. This would be a great place to spend the night except for one thing. Late afternoon and already thunderheads are building in the northwest over the Breaks and to the south down by the Crazies and behind us. Dark,

angry bases support white clouds that billow tens of thousands of
feet into the sky, the thunderheads expanding in surges as we
watch. Lightning strikes are visible, lots of them, glowing rips of
current followed by pounding thunder. The air around this ridge
grows charged. Electrical storms scare the hell out of both of us.
Last summer we spent a night in the Little Rockies while lightning blasted the cliffs around us, chunks of rock clattering down
around camp, and still another pleasant evening lying in a shallow
coulee wrapped in a nylon tarp while bolts blasted the ground
above. The smell of ozone and flash-cooked sage (and cow?) was
thick. Black clouds billowed out of the onslaught only a few hundred feet above our terrified heads. The clouds thrust toward the
ground, exploding in sharp rain. Not fun. So we chicken out,
drive down below and out onto the plains. The showers let up
some. A brilliant rainbow curves down from the sky burying itself
in the mountains. Then it turns double and grows brighter, the
colors more intense. Up ahead a sign announces the Rainbow Bar.
Hard to argue with those signals. Serendipity of a sort. We pull
in for a drink and discover that the joint's owner is a fan of Danny
O'Keefe. Damn near spooky the way things run sometimes. We
talk some more, about the Allman Brothers, Mission Mountain
Wood Band, Missoula thirty years ago. Then we step out into a
clean, fresh late afternoon, hop in the rig, and eventually we turn
off the old, narrow highway and pull in next to some rarely used
railroad tracks. We make a relaxed camp by a designer brown
trout stream. Cobble streambed, millions of gallons of spring water perking up all over the place, thick aquatic vegetation, lush
bankside growth, caddis, mayflies, hoppers, sculpins, damselflies,
rainbow trout, and lots of browns, some of them large and ill-
tempered.

"Search and destroy," I say as I rig up a five-weight with a
brown woolly bugger and a couple of split shot. "Drag your camera along and let's go." Every tiny pocket or undercut and each

pool and run is flogged, the bugger banging off brush or slamming into the water. Smaller browns flee for shelter under the
onslaught. Eventually I make a cast that seems to snag on the
bottom. I pull back on the rod. Nothing. Bottom. A log. Then
the line rips upstream, downstream, under the bank, and back out
in the middle of the pool.

A brown and a nice one. The unruly creature holds on the
bottom and shakes his head. Several runs and head thrashings and
I drag the brown into the weeds growing in shallow water at my
feet. Eighteen inches, fat, deep brown, copper, and gold with large
black spots, and tiny gold flaking along the shoulders. A beautiful
trout. One of the best. Hell they all are. Lots of rapid photos, a
release, and the brown buries its head in the weeds at Ginny's
feet. He sulks for several minutes before she nudges its back and
the fish streaks for the dark shelter of the far bank.

"That's all I wanted. What I was after," I yell. "I know how
to bugger." One lousy brown and I'm the world's best. It always
turns out this way and I know better, but one wild fish destroys
any sense of reason or humility I may possess. We walk back to
camp happy and relaxed.

The embryonic beginnings of sunrise wake us. Thick mist ob-
scures the stream and heavy dew soaks our bags. We crawl out,
make coffee, bitching and moaning the whole time about our
aches and pains, the hard-earned wages of sinful lives. Semi-pro
whiners. All-pro road bums. As the sun climbs over the horizon
coyotes begin howling, chattering, and barking all around us.
Pheasants squawk in terror and beat their wings. A pair of hawks
works a ridge gliding easily on the cool morning air. Yesterday
I'd turned frantic with the lost brook trout and hunting the
browns. Time to slow down again. Lose that bullshit and enjoy
why I am here. I look over at Ginny and watch as she sips her
coffee. The stream and its trout flow behind her. In the distance
the small range of mountains shimmers in a silver aura cast by

the rising sun. Life's not always easy. Sometimes it is, like now. I could take some more of this kind of country away from the electronic, streaming hustle. Just hop from island to island, making the run along old highways in the deep of night with only the light of the moon and stars showing the way.

Montana's Yellowstone River with the Absaroka Mountains in the background.

17

LIVINGSTON, AGAIN

THE MIDDLE OF NOVEMBER OUT HERE and the temperature is almost seventy. Unreal. An appreciated reprieve from winter that always comes soon enough and stays until spring seems like a cruel dream. This time of year is usually gray and bitter with a hard-driving snow cutting across the dead landscape. I'm doing my best to take advantage of this late season stay of cold execution by driving out of town, fishing each of my favorite stretches of this river, one day at a time, one last time this year. The river is my favorite right now, has been for several years, ever since I moved here from Whitefish.

Flowing between the Bridger and Crazy Mountains the water, rarely perfectly clear or ice cold, holds large browns, Yellowstone cutthroat, brook trout, mountain whitefish, and some rainbows near where it merges with the Yellowstone. To the unpracticed eye looking at the water while driving down the highway, the river (actually more of a large creek in nature) doesn't look like much. Shallow, sometimes turbid, brushy banks making wading tough, unfloatable. I've caught my share of big fish here, a bunch of hefty browns on streamers, elk-hair caddis, and hoppers. Some days I take a half dozen or more fish. Some days only one. It's tough water, despite its small size and straightforward nature. The browns like to hold beneath the banks or underneath exposed tangles of cottonwood roots or behind rocks that are covered by overhanging willow limbs, and sometimes the fish, including the cutthroats, are just damn picky and refuse my presentations, but the good fishing is not why I love the Shields.

This valley is what the northern high plains are for me distilled to its essence. On a soft, sunny day like this one with a warm breeze drifting downstream, standing in the middle of the river, everywhere I look I can see rolling hills, bluffs, jagged rock cliffs, and steppes that roll away for miles to the Absaroka, Bridger, Beartooth, and Crazy Mountains. Geese fly overhead in strung-out V's. Mallards and mergansers jump up when I round a bend. Deer browse in the hay fields near the stream. Ravens, eagles, and hawks soar above. Sharp-tailed grouse burst out of cover in my face when I push through the tall, brown grass to cut an ox bow in the river short. Magpies screech and grumble at me from overhead limbs. The river is uncommonly clear today. When I cast my brown woolly bugger to a run along the far bank I can see it undulate up and down as I strip it back to me. I can see when an eighteen-inch brown comes out from cover and opens its jaws, that flash of toothy white, to attack the streamer. I can see the trout's colors intensify, even down through the few feet of water as it heats up with the struggle. All of this goes on around me and I am alone. I can't see any houses or ranch buildings or machinery. I'm far enough from the highway that the sounds of traffic are gone. Within minutes from Livingston I am out in perfect country doing what I love, enjoying a river and all that comes with it.

Ginny and I began this book in early April in the middle of a spring blizzard and we finished the research and photography a few days ago while walking along the Yellowstone where it runs only a few blocks from our home. Between those times we covered 26,000 miles wandering through Wyoming, Montana, parts of North and South Dakota, a piece of Saskatchewan, all over Alberta, and all the way up to the Northwest Territories, the geologic terminus of the northern high plains. I took many pages of notes, something I normally don't do. Ginny shot over six thousand exposures along the way—at dawn, the middle of hot days, near sunset in a blizzard, and at night beneath a full moon. We had our share of road-stress arguments, our tough times with the weather, bugs, highway buzz, tiredness, and anxiety about the book, bills, making a living. We dealt with rodeo officials who would not give us permission to shoot the events from the arena because they feared we were animal rights activists hell-bent on excoriating the sport; we drove blindly down bad roads that turned into no roads as we hopefully looked for new good country; we had flat tires and now sport a cracked and chipped windshield of truly back-road caliber; and we spent hours trying to find and talk to people who we believed were the real West, not the image-conscious phonies who have descended upon this land bringing their madness with them.

After thirty years of roaming the high plains, largely researching articles and books on the damage being done here by industry, developers, tourists, and myself; and also writing about the land and the fishing and the upland bird hunting I'd become a cynic. I thought the West was all gone or going, that it was done for. Ginny's lived here only a few years and through her fresh eyes I experienced the wonder, beauty, mystery, and freedom of places like eastern Montana, or northeastern Wyoming, as if I were seeing it all for the first time all over again. A lot of this country is gone or going, but so much of it remains largely as it's always been. You just have to look harder these days.

There are problems to be sure out here—oil and gas development, timber cutting, activists who want to inflict their sick form of control on the land and those who live here, greedy California and Colorado developers and their plastic, gated communities, strip mines, excessive irrigation, a fly-fishing industry that is more concerned with the bottom line than the resource it's exploiting, and the true bottom line issue, too many damn people. We're overbreeding like sewer rats and chewing the place down to the dirt.

But there are places like the Middle Fork of the Powder River, the open land around Broadus, the unimaginable power and immensity of the Territories. And there are the people that live on the ranches, here in town, out in the Missouri Breaks, or down in Kaycee. And there's the always-connected land with its constantly changing vistas and weather. Everywhere we went, if we looked hard enough, kept an open mind and just kept going, the country would eventually open up to us and reveal its splendor and magic. There's Livingston, our home. Typical of the West in its untypical nature—the friends we see at Sax & Fryer, Books Etc., the Livingston Bar and Grill, Ricci's Family Market, the video store, The Foreign Exchange, or walking along the Yellowstone River at Sacajawea Park, the honking of the resident and overfed Canada geese mixing with the sounds of flowing water. The sense of community here is like that in other towns on the plains—Plentywood, Pincher Creek, Hay River, Lovell. There is a sense of belonging out here, missing from other places. Once you commit to this country, people and the land begin to open up to you in a way not experienced before. Familiar, recognizable, but only vaguely recalled from somewhere.

Often I think we have it all backward. We think that we control and dominate the land and also are responsible for destroying it. To some extent we do and we are, but when our species has done its insignificant dance and is long gone, the land will still be here like it always was. Tectonic plates will shift, ice ages will come and retreat, weather will be weather, and the land will constantly reshape and naturally reinvent itself, wiping away all trace of our small, ego-driven existence. What Ginny and I learned this year, or rather are beginning to understand, is that country as spiritually powerful as the northern high plains is about nothing more than living and experiencing what takes place over the months, weeks, days, hours, minutes, seconds, that break down into infinitesimal fractions that eventually splinter linear time and expand into no time. The land flows if you know how to see without looking and all of us are here for but a moment. You know how it goes. Nobody gets out of this joint alive, well, not in the conventional sense anyway, but that's the silliness of another book.

Coyote Nowhere is our attempt to show the high plains through our eyes by examining small sections of this huge, varied place that when looked at together give a glimpse into the naturally mad scheme of things. My words and Ginny's photos moving to their own rhythms. A book within a book. Stories within stories. Our joys, sorrows, fears, angers, prejudices, dreams, illusions, and hates. Flawed human perceptions and feelings, but honest ones. That's all this book was or is. We aren't anthropologists, marginally adept philosophers, geologists, or highly trained reporters. We had no intent or interest in making our book a textual, perfectly accurate piece of reportage. That's not our style. We put down what we experienced, what we saw, felt, believed. Nothing less. Nothing more. I no longer worry about the fate of this land or the planet. I still care and raise hell whenever I can, but the outcome means nothing anymore. What damn difference does it make? Merely perceptions on our part. The land doesn't care, and, besides, our battlefield long ago left the physical realm and tumbled someplace else, light and dark, maybe.

I work my way up to the next deep run and make a cast. The woolly bugger sinks and then twists and turns in the hands of the current. The November light casts an ethereal silver glow over the dead brown leaves and ground, the tan fields and faded green undergrowth, bringing the land back to life one more time before winter. A brown slashes at my streamer, jerks the rod in my hand. I don't bother setting the hook. My head's too far gone flying over the sweeping hills, far down the river and along the edges of the mountains. The browns can wait. The northern high plains own me now.

About the Author

꙳

JOHN HOLT lives in Livingston, Montana, with Ginny Diers, his son Jack, and his daughter Rachel. He is the author of numerous books, including *Guide Wars, Kicking Up Trouble,* and *Knee Deep in Montana's Trout Streams.* His work has appeared in *Fly Fisherman,* the *Denver Post, Sports Afield, Men's Journal, Gray's Sporting Journal,* the *New York Times, Big Sky Journal, Fly Rod & Reel, Audubon, E,* and *Travel & Leisure.* He contributes regularly to numerous national and regional publications and is working on a series of novels about the West.